8.95
01

THE EVOLUTION OF
MODERN ECONOMIC THEORY

and Other Papers on the History of Economic Thought

The Evolution of
Modern Economic Theory
and Other Papers on
the History of Economic Thought

LORD ROBBINS,

Lionel Charles Robbins

ALDINE PUBLISHING COMPANY
CHICAGO

© Lord Robbins, 1970

MACMILLAN AND CO LTD, LONDON

First U.S. edition published 1970

ALDINE PUBLISHING COMPANY
529 South Wabash Avenue
Chicago, Illinois 60605

Library of Congress Catalog Card Number 70–94752

Printed in Great Britain

TO WILLIAM AND HILDA BAUMOL

who made glorious summer
of a winter of discontent

Contents

Contents

Preface

THE long paper which gives the title to this collection and which has never before been published was initially an attempt to promote international academic understanding. The Economics Department at the London School of Economics had arranged a colloquy between two groups of Russian and British economists; and I was asked to contribute a general survey of the present state of economic theory as taught in Western centres. For reasons which I explain in the opening section, I decided to adopt an historical approach; and the notes on which the present paper is based were the result. In working them up for publication I have added a certain amount of detail and amplified certain arguments. But I have not altered the general shape of the argument, nor have I attempted to carry the narrative or, save in one instance, the references beyond the date of delivery – the autumn of 1960. It has been a sad reflection when revising the final document to recollect the friendly camaraderie of our Russian guests then in contrast to the blackguardly barbarism of those responsible for the invasion of Czechoslovakia last summer.

The remainder of the papers have as their common denominator a continuing interest in the history of economic thought and the authors thereof which began when, as a student, I sat at the feet of Edwin Cannan, and will close, I fancy, only with expiring breath. Beginning with a lengthy critique of Schumpeter's magisterial *History of Economic Analysis*, they range from an appraisal of Bentham's continuing relevance to a review of Robertson's *Lectures on Economic Principles*, with some special attention to John Stuart Mill both as a human being and as an economist. They have been written at various times in the last thirty-five years; and minute scrutiny, if such were thought to be worth while – which of course it is not – might detect some

A 2

variations of emphasis, particularly perhaps in the implicit valuations of Marshall and his contribution, in the papers on Wicksteed and Schumpeter's *History* respectively. But in spite of a certain shift of perspective here, I have not thought it worth while to attempt substantial redrafting. If, as time has gone on, I have come to attach greater importance than I did in my salad days to certain aspects of Classical and neo-Classical analysis and to realise that some at least of the criticisms thereof were misplaced, that does not mean that I would wish in any way to depreciate or conceal the liberating stimulus, for me at any rate, which came earlier from the discovery of the works of other schools not so well known or taught in those times; and I still think Wicksteed deserves commemoration.

Apart from the correction of obvious inelegances or actual errors, the excision of some duplicating quotations and, in a few cases, the addition of supplementary material and references, the papers are reproduced as originally written. In each instance I have given footnote acknowledgements of the place of original publication. It remains for me here to express general gratitude to the proprietors and editors concerned whose permission has made re-publication possible.

ROBBINS

London School of Economics
  March 1969

I

The Evolution of Modern
Economic Theory[1]

I. INTRODUCTION

WHEN the organisers of this colloquy asked me to give a general
address on Western conceptions of the present state of economic
theory, I confess I felt daunted. I was daunted in the first place
by the nature of the subject: in any survey of so extensive a field,
the problems where to begin, what to include, what to leave out,
are indeed problems which should inspire apprehension, even in
the breast of the most self-confident. But I was daunted, too, by a
more delicate problem. Here we were to sit round this table, met
together in an attempt to create mutual understanding of positions
which certainly in the past have been assumed to be very far apart.
How could I present in short compass the general background of
thought of those of us on this side without introducing irrelevant
issues or appearing to be needlessly provocative? Yet how could I
avoid these dangers without running the risk of insufficient candour,
of all things least desirable in an exchange of this sort? I admit I
found this very perplexing.

Eventually, however, an idea occurred to me which I hope may
minimise these dangers. Why not start from Ricardo? Here, at
any rate, is a focus of common understanding, since for Marx,
equally as for Marshall, Ricardo was at once a stimulus to thought
and an object of admiration. If therefore I begin with Ricardo and
show how the development of economic theory in the West has
proceeded by way of reaction from, or extension to, his system, I
shall surely have a better chance of making our position intelligible

[1] An address at a colloquy between Russian and British economists on
30 Sep 1960 at the London School of Economics.

than if I attempted to say what that position is without explaining how it has come about. It is true that the elements of my story will be quite familiar material. But, used in this way, they may perhaps acquire a new perspective. At any rate, it is in that hope that I adopt this procedure.

My observations will fall into three main parts. In the first I shall set forth briefly the Ricardian contribution and the ways in which developments up to the outbreak of the First World War can be conceived as extensions or modifications of that contribution. In the second I shall try to give a short conspectus of what seem to me the most significant innovations of the period between 1914 and the publication of the *General Theory* of J. M. Keynes. Then finally, and even more superficially, I shall discuss some of the tendencies of the years since then. These divisions are not intended to be absolute. I shall not hesitate to postpone consideration of developments in one period where it seems that they are best brought into prominence in juxtaposition to developments of the next.

I should like to make it clear that in all this I shall be confining myself to the evolution of economic theory in its purely analytical aspect. I shall say nothing of the theory of policy. Nor shall I touch on the wider analysis of social tendency in which pure theory must eventually find its appropriate applications. My focus is entirely on the way in which economic theory, as an instrument for the understanding and explanation of observable economic events and relationships, has evolved among Western thinkers since the days of Ricardo, and on present developments in that respect.

II. RICARDO TO 1914

(a) The Ricardian System

(i) *Method*   I begin therefore with Ricardo; not with his various contributions on questions of practical policy, powerful though these be, but rather with his general economic analysis as it emerges in his conscious attempt at synthesis, the *Principles of Political Economy*. In this connection we have to notice both a method and a general picture of economic relationships.

As regards the method, there is comparatively little that need be said in the context of this survey. It would of course be quite wrong to suggest that it was completely new. The habit of sorting out in long chains of deductive reasoning the implications of hypothetical constructions, designed in some way or other to mirror possible realities, begins much earlier; it is to be found beautifully applied, for instance, in the works of Cantillon and of Hume, not to mention some Physiocratic contributions. But Ricardo pushed it so much further than it had ever been pushed before that it is no exaggeration to say that he gave it a new status. It is true that, without sufficient testing by reference back to facts, this method by itself may lead to false claims and misleading applications; and it is a valid criticism of Ricardo that, save in regard to the phenomena of money and the foreign exchanges, his own practice was often seriously defective in this respect. The strictures of the Historical School, although themselves founded on false conceptions of method, were not without considerable justification in this connection. Nevertheless, as experience shows – and as general logical considerations would lead us to expect – it is only by recourse to this type of reasoning that substantial progress has been made, or indeed can be made. The Marxian systems, equally with the systems of Marshall and Walras, not to mention more recent developments, all follow this procedure. In this respect at least it can be said that we are all Ricardians now.

(ii) *Analysis* As regards the picture of economic relationships emerging from Ricardo's analysis, matters are more complicated. There can be no doubt that if it were presented today as an explanation of the phenomena of a fully developed economy, we should regard it as very inadequate. We should not find the price relationships of such a system adequately explained by the relations of the quantities of labour expended in production of the commodities concerned, even if these were doctored to take account of differences in investment periods. We should not be prepared to exclude the influence of the use of varying quantities of land on relative costs of production. We should fight shy of explaining tendencies to declining profits solely in terms of diminishing returns in agriculture. We should find the assumptions about labour supply very much too simple. But against this, if we take into account the implicit assumptions of the system, it is hard to deny a certain compelling logic about the way in which it hangs together. If we are prepared to assume a more or less homogeneous labour supply, tending to multiply to some conventional sub-sistence level; if we regard land as having almost complete specificity in one agricultural use; and if variations in the invest-ment period are to be regarded as being of secondary importance; then it is not difficult to make out a case for many of the character-istic Ricardian propositions, if not on grounds of wide applicability, at least in terms of logical consistency. And I would certainly say that, whatever reservations we may have about the end-product of Ricardo's analysis, no one can work through it seriously without having to admit that in all sorts of ways his understanding of the ways in which an economic system can behave has been both deepened and enlarged. A taste for Ricardo has long been regarded as a fairly sure sign of a flair for economic analysis in general.

(b) Modifications and Extensions

Nevertheless, on any broad view of what is required of economics it should be clear that Ricardo is not enough; and it has been perception of the lacunae and imperfections of his system which has been responsible for much of the innovation and extension since his day. Certainly, the main developments of economic theory in the West up to 1914 are capable of being presented in such a context; and it is this that I now propose to try to do.

(i) *Demand and Utility*   We may begin with the theory of demand. This was an area in which the Ricardian system was obviously defective. It is, of course, untrue to assert, as Schumpeter and some lesser authorities have asserted, that Ricardo repudiated supply and demand as being any but short-term influences; in fact he assumed throughout that the longer-term influences worked through the forces of the market, and said as much in reply to Malthus.[1] And it is clear that his conception of the determination of price at the margin of agricultural production implied demand as a factor co-ordinate with costs; only where production could be conceived as taking place under conditions of constant cost could the supply side be highlighted as *the* 'determining' factor. But although from time to time there are hints of varying elasticities, we may search in vain for any clear-cut presentation of amount demanded as related to price.

It was therefore a definite step forward when this conception was clearly formulated and expressed both graphically and algebraically by Cournot in his path-breaking work on mathematical economics.[2] Nor should we fail to notice, within the narrow Ricardian tradition, a parallel recognition in John Stuart Mill's elucidation of the influence of 'reciprocal demand' in his famous essay 'Of the Laws of Interchange Between Nations', published seven years after Cournot but written some years before. Henceforward the idea of demand as a function of price was one of the most securely established conceptions in the whole range of analytical economics.

But developments on this side went far beyond this: they involved the linking up of demand and its influence with the idea of utility. This was a definite break with the Classical tradition. A long line of rather woolly thinkers, from some Scholastics

---

[1] See below, p. 62, for the relevant quotation.

[2] In any discussion of the evolution of the analysis of demand, the graphical treatment of the subject by von Mangoldt in the first edition of his *Grundriss der Volkswirtschaftslehre* (Stuttgart, 1863) bk III, chap. 3, pt 1, pp. 46–73, should not go unmentioned. Recognition of von Mangoldt's outstanding merits in this connection is due to Professor Schneider, to whose penetrating section on the subject in his *Einführung in die Wirtschaftstheorie* (Tübingen, 1962) IV. Teil, pp. 127–43, the reader is hereby warmly recommended. The relevant section of von Mangoldt's book appears in a translation by Elizabeth Henderson in *International Economic Papers*, no. 11 (1962) 32–59.

onwards, had maintained that there was *some* positive connection between utility and price, although they never made it precise. But this had been definitely repudiated by the Classical writers who, while conceding that in order to have value an article must have some utility, went on definitely to deny that there was any 'quantitative' connection. For them, Adam Smith's famous comparison of the value of water and diamonds – the so-called paradox of value – was the last word on this subject.

The introduction of the idea of the margin changed all this. Once it was realized that, in the majority of cases, what was significant for individual action was not the utility of a whole stock but rather the utility of small increments, it was also perceived that there must be an intimate connection between the marginal valuations of individuals and their influence on aggregate demand. This perception occurred independently to several economists – in the first generation, and without much influence, to W. F. Lloyd, Dupuit and Gossen, and later, with very much greater success, to Jevons, Menger and Walras. It became so influential that its consequences are sometimes referred to as the Marginal Revolution; and although, as we shall see, it has undergone much transformation since, it became the starting point and the stimulus for much of the theoretical development since their day. I think it is clear now that, in the excitement of new discovery, some of the innovators went much too far in regarding it as a substitute for Classical theory rather than as a valuable extension. You may feel, as I do sometimes, that some developments of this theory in the higher flights of welfare economics run the risk of unreality and sometimes at least of false constructions. But basically one can surely claim two outstanding achievements for the discovery. First, it resolves the so-called paradox of value: once it is realised that the relevant contrast is not between the utility of *all* the water and *all* the diamonds, but rather between the utility of *a drop* of water and *a single* diamond, the paradox disappears. And secondly, with its formulation of equi-marginal return in each line of expenditure as a condition of equilibrium, it throws important light on the fundamental conception of rational action, a light which I would claim is as relevant to the deliberations of collective action as it is to the actions of the individual.

(ii) *Costs*   I turn next to the theory of costs. As we know, in the Ricardian model all, or nearly all, the relevant costs of production were resolved into quantities of labour, direct or indirect. There were certain adjustments for variations in the investment period which made the theory – to use Stigler's happy phrase – not a 100 but a $93\frac{1}{2}$ per cent labour theory of value. But, in the uses to which the theory was put, these were of minor significance, no matter what eventual weaknesses they disclosed in any 100 per cent formulation. The main focus was on quantity of labour. Any influence of the use of varying qualities of land or other resources whose fundamental scarcity did not derive from the labour time necessary for their production, seems to have been thought to have been rendered irrelevant by the concentration of the analysis of cost at the *rentless* margin. The doctrine that rent does not enter into cost of production was, so to speak, the *pons asinorum* of Ricardian theory.

Now, of course, this was perfectly legitimate so long as the land in the model was completely specific to one use and the costs of production elsewhere involved only quantities of labour. But as soon as there was more than one use for scarce land and the different uses involved different proportionate combinations with scarce labour, then to ignore the influence of relative quantities of land was bound to lead to error. If there were two types of vegetable each requiring equal quantities of labour per unit for planting and tending, but one requiring twice the land area per unit of the other, we should not expect them to exchange on equal terms. Such complications were recognised by John Stuart Mill, emphasised by Jevons and grudgingly conceded even by Marshall, who disliked intensely abandoning the Ricardian way of putting things. Indeed, it is now clear that it was only Ricardo's focus on the composite agricultural commodity 'corn', the by-product of his preoccupations with agrarian protectionism, which rendered at all plausible the colossal simplifications of the rentless margin.

Otherwise we are confronted with Petty's problem, never yet solved in the terms in which he propounded it, of discovering the appropriate 'par' between land and labour. Once it is perceived that productive operations may involve the use in varying proportions of more than one type of scarce productive agent, then the idea that relative costs can be measured in terms of quantities of any one, be it homogeneous labour or homogeneous land, proves invalid.

Recognition of this surely incontrovertible fact has gradually led to a different conception of the ultimate influences determining costs – namely, the conception of costs as the value of forgone opportunities. This begins to appear in the writings of the Austrian School, particularly von Weiser, as the value of forgone *products*, the supply of ultimate services being taken as fixed. But in the works of later writers – Davenport, Wicksteed and Knight, for instance – the conception is rather the value of forgone *opportunities*, the distinction between opportunities and products being that the former includes alternative uses of time for purposes of leisure, thus allowing for elasticity in the supply of ultimate services. Even here, however, there are complications only to be resolved in the next approximation by the recognition, as joint products, of various pleasures, positive or negative, associated with the process of production; and this blurs the simplicity of the picture. But viewing the conception in the large, it is surely permissible to claim that it throws a vivid light on some at least of the ultimate influences on the cost side of the market and incidentally provides a most powerful instrument for the establishment of priorities in any type of economic planning, collectivist or otherwise. It is a solution of Petty's problem on a new plane.

(iii) *Marginal Productivity and the Demand for Factor Services*
Passing from the problem of the ultimate nature of costs, it is natural to consider the problems which arise in regard to the use of productive agents when more than one scarce type is involved jointly in each process of production. What are the influences determining the different proportions in which the different agents are combined, and what are the reciprocal relations between these

influences and the prices prevailing for the services of these agents?

These clearly were not problems which were faced directly by Ricardo, with his models of productive processes resolvable chiefly into the use of the single agent labour, with scarce land only involved in the production of 'corn'. Yet, strangely enough, it is the Ricardian analysis which contains the germ of what has come to be regarded as the general solution. The so-called Law of Diminishing Returns in Agriculture involved the conception of the incremental change of the return to the varying factor, labour, applied to the fixed factor, land. It was only a matter of time before it was realised that this form of analysis was universally applicable where proportionate combinations were anywhere variable; that, as Edgeworth said of the original conception of 'dosing' land with labour, the relation between dose and patient could be reversed; and that here was an instrument whereby in conception at least the incremental contribution of any factor could be identified. Marginal productivity analysis, both in regard to the problem of factor service combination and to the derivation of demand for productive service, is the lineal descendant of Ricardian rent theory, generalised, so to speak, in reverse. I need only mention the names of von Thünen, Wicksteed and Wicksell to put this part of the evolution in perspective.[1]

In this connection, I would like to go out of my way, here and now, to repudiate certain uses to which this analysis has been put. It has sometimes been argued – J. B. Clark is perhaps the chief culprit – that a proof that, under competitive conditions, productive agents are paid according to the value of their marginal physical product is a proof that such a system is just. This of course is a complete *non sequitur*, and one which is a temptation to tendentious usage. Before we can begin to discuss distributive justice in this connection, we must investigate the arrangements – the distribution of property, the accessibility to appropriate training, the availability of appropriate information and so on – which bring

[1] For further detail of the emergence of this solution in modern times, see the paper on Wicksteed below, especially pp. 194–7.

it about that a man's marginal product is what it is and not otherwise; and that involves many considerations quite outside the
range of the kind of analysis I am discussing. It is to be noted,
however, that the leading exponents of this idea, with the exception
of von Thünen, have made no such claims. If we take Marshall as
providing the *locus classicus* of its prudent application, we find that
he definitely goes out of his way to deny that it affords a complete
theory of distribution, even in the narrow sense, and throughout
puts it in its proper place as a partial explanation of derived demand
and as an essential ingredient of the idea of substitution.

(iv) *Capital and Interest* From the pricing of productive
services it is a natural step to the value of the agents which render
them. This involves the theory of interest and the influence thereon
of saving and investment.

Here the move towards greater generality is very conspicuous.
It will be remembered that, with the insight of genius, Ricardo had
perceived the importance of variations in the investment period
for the explanation of relative prices. His demonstration that, in
his particular model, a rise in wages might actually, via a fall in
profits, lead to a fall in the relative prices of products involving
a more than average proportionate combination of capital with
labour, is one of the intellectual triumphs of his system, however
fragile may be its relevance to most areas of reality. But all this was
limited to the theory of value. The treatment of the rate of profit
as determined mainly by the agricultural production function was,
to put it mildly, very restricted in application, and clearly left
unexplained many of the factors which we should regard as important; and the treatment of the influences on accumulation was
almost perfunctory.

The great step forward comes with the still unduly neglected
New Principles of Political Economy of John Rae, published in 1834.
In this extraordinary work, Rae first shows how investment
opportunities may be ranged in a descending order of profitability
according to the time taken for them to pay off. He then turns to
variations of the willingness to undertake investment, which he

describes as the effective desire of accumulation; and he shows
how the extent to which investment opportunities will be exploited
will depend upon the strength of this influence – regimes of low
effective desire being marked by high interest rates and capital
instruments of great simplicity and poor durability, regimes of
high effective desire having the reverse accompaniments. He even
anticipates modern discussion of the influence of the desire for
liquidity.

Rae died completely obscure, though his work was known to
Senior and John Stuart Mill,[1] the latter of whom said indeed that
he had done for the theory of accumulation what Malthus had
done for population. But the deep insights of his conjunction of
the conceptions of what we should now call the marginal rate of
return over cost – or in Keynesian language the marginal efficiency
of investment – and of varying rates of time preference had all to be
rediscovered later, partly by Jevons in a path-breaking chapter of
his *Theory of Political Economy*, partly by Böhm-Bawerk in his
masterly, yet tortuous and sometimes wrong-headed, *Positive
Theory of Capital*, and eventually synthesised by Irving Fisher in
his *Rate of Interest*, which is so complete a statement of the so-
called 'real' influences on the determination of interest rates that,
in spite of the fact that it is more than half a century old, it still
holds the field as the best statement extant even at the present day.[2]

You will not have failed to notice that all this development took
place within the context of the analysis of a competitive exchange
economy; and for that reason you, as members of a collectivist
community, might be disposed to regard it as having at best a
local and temporal relevance. But I question whether in fact that
would be an adequate appraisal? It is true that the ultimate focus
of explanation here is the phenomena of capital markets, peculiar
hitherto to certain phases of history. But the fundamental conceptions involved of a hierarchy of investment opportunities on the

[1] And, interestingly enough, to Buckle. See his *History of Civilisation
in England*, new ed. (1885) p. 334.
[2] A revised edition was issued in 1930 under the title *The Theory of
Interest*. But the essential solution remains the same.

one side and of degrees of evaluation of future benefits in terms of present sacrifices on the other, are these not ideas of a far wider significance, as applicable to the decisions of collectivist economic planning as to the explanation of saving and investment in a free or mixed system?

(v) *The Supply of Labourers*   Finally in this connection we must take account of changes in assumptions regarding the supply of labour.

In dealing with the theory of costs I have already shown how variations in the supply of labour from a given labour force can, if desirable, be subsumed under the analysis of variations in the demand for leisure. But I have said nothing of variations in the labour force itself, which were of cardinal importance in the general Ricardian system.

Here developments since Ricardo have tended to move towards restriction, rather than extension, of the functional relationships assumed. Ricardo operated on the assumption of a labour supply which responded directly to variations of wages and in the long run tended to a figure which, in the given conditions of production, involved a rate of wages affording some sort of conventional subsistence for the worker and a family of appropriate size. There can be no question that this assumption lent to his analysis an appearance of virtually quantitative precision which would otherwise have been lacking. Only in the short run, when capital was increasing faster than population, were other elements needed to explain the determination of the wage level.

Now there can be no doubt of the relevance of the idea of wages tending to subsistence for the explanation of conditions at some times and in some places. Even the most infatuated opponents of Malthus must admit that. But to assume so simple a connection as a general rule does not seem so sensible. By the time of Ricardo, the conception of subsistence as a *physiologically* determined quantity, varying only with climate and suchlike external conditions had given way to a conception of a level in part *psychologically* and conventionally determined; and Ricardo himself proceeded to complicate matters still further with his famous aspiration, on behalf of the 'friends of humanity', that wages might remain above this level long enough for the workers to acquire habits themselves sufficiently expensive to involve a change in its height. If this were possible, then the size of the population would depend, not merely on any predetermined subsistence level, conventional or otherwise, but also on the length of time that wages were above this level and the rapidity with which the workers changed what they demanded as the price of multiplication. Moreover, once it is recognised that changes in the size of the population are determined over comparatively long periods, not only by whatever is responsible for the number of births but also by whatever is responsible for the number of deaths, the idea of any very simple functional connection between the size of the working population and the level of wages becomes less and less plausible.

For this reason, since the time of Ricardo, even among economists who in other connections attach great importance to the Malthusian warnings, it has become the habit, at any rate for the purpose of the central analysis of value and distribution, to regard the size of the working population as an exogenous rather than an endogenous variable – something which, at least in part, is determined *outside* the system to be examined, rather than something which, in any simple way, can be assumed to be determined by other variables within the system. The amount of labour which members of a given labour force may be willing to offer on the market may be assumed, for some purposes, to be functionally related to its price and other elements in the system. But the size and variations of the labour force itself, while of great economic interest, are factors which are taken as data for this kind of analysis.

(c) *Walras and Marshall*

Up to this point I have been reviewing developments in regard to particular aspects of the original Ricardian system. Before completing this part of my survey, however, it is necessary to glance at what had taken place by 1914 in regard to the look of the system as a whole. What happened when all these modifications and extensions were fitted together as a self-contained model? For this purpose we may consider the systems of Walras and Marshall as representative in this respect.

At first sight few constructions could appear more different. Walras, a radical by temperament, who conceived himself to have few intellectual antecedents save his father, inspired chiefly by the formal constructions of Classical mechanics, sets out the elements of his economic universe and their interconnectedness with the unadorned rigour of elementary differential equations – equilibrium in the product market, equilibrium in the market for factor services, equilibrium in the capital market and equilibrium in the value of money. The exposition is prolix and repetitive. But its width and logical inevitability is highly impressive; and, on the surface at any rate, there is little compromise or continuity with the constructions of the past.

With Marshall everything appears to be different. A far more elegant and accomplished mathematician than Walras, he sought at every stage to relegate the more rigorous constructions to footnotes or appendices; as a Wrangler in the Cambridge tripos, he would have regarded the algebra involved as trivial. Having the greatest respect for his Classical predecessors – he probably taught himself economic analysis by putting Ricardo and John Stuart Mill into algebra or geometry[1] – he introduced even his most pathbreaking innovations as elucidations of the implications of their theories, so much so indeed that the unlearned, even in his own profession, have tended to classify him as chiefly an eclectic. Moreover, he deeply distrusted what he felt to be the facile rigour of closed statical systems which, he felt, often emphasised the elements which were easily put into mathematics at the expense of less tangible influences which were in fact more important;[2] and he wished to forge instruments of analysis which would be of

[1] See the authoritative article by G. F. Shove, 'The Place of Marshall's *Principles* in the Development of Economic Theory', *Economic Journal*, LII (Dec 1942).

[2] See an explicit statement to this effect quoted below, p. 67–8.

greater practical value in interpreting growth and change. It would be difficult to exaggerate the difference between the appearance of Books V and VI of his *Principles* and that of any part of Walras's *Éléments*.

Nevertheless, if one looks deep enough, the differences tend to disappear. Or perhaps it would be better said that the fundamental analytical techniques will be seen to be essentially the same in both systems. Demand for ultimate products as a function of price based upon comparisons of marginal utilities; cost functions involving the use of more than one scarce type of productive service; demand for services as a function of estimates of marginal contributions to the value of the final product; accumulation governed by investment opportunities and ability and willingness to sacrifice present enjoyments for future; the interconnectedness of all elements in the universe of discourse: all these architectonic conceptions are fundamental to both systems. In Walras they dominate all constructions to the virtual exclusion of other considerations. In Marshall their overt and rigorous statement is relegated to the celebrated Note XIV in the Mathematical Appendix. But since Marshall himself said once that most of his work on principles was devoted to working out the implications of that self-same note, it would be failing in analytical insight not to recognise its ubiquitous significance. It is true that, having solved these problems, the centre of gravity of Marshall's interest moved on to other areas which Walras did not begin to tackle. But this should not blind us to the fact that, in regard to what Sir John Hicks has described as the statical foundations, the systems were to all intents and purposes the same. The differences were a matter of the shop-window.

Thus it is fair to say that, by the end of our period, there had evolved a system of analysis covering a range of possibilities much wider than that of Ricardo. This is not to say that the original Ricardian analysis was *wrong* in the sense of logical inconsistency; it is only to argue that its implicit assumptions failed to include many of the elements which, given the complexity of an advanced economic system, most require explanation. It is not difficult to put Ricardo into mathematical terms comparable to those of Walras and Marshall; Victor Edelberg's well-known article on 'The Ricardian Theory of Profits'[1] showed how, with a certain degree of sophistication, it can be done. But if it is done, it will speedily be realised that, formulated in this way, it is simply a limiting case of the much wider modern synthesis – a case in which many of the more complicated parameters are left out and one, the simple functional connection between the size of the labour force and the wage level, superadded. Doubtless a description in these terms fails badly to do justice to Ricardo's historical position or the profundity of his analytical powers. But in a perspective which is avowedly concerned only with the development of logical systems, it surely is the way to put it.

III. 1914 – 1936

It is now time to pass to the second section of this survey, the section which covers the main developments of the period between the two wars. These fall into two groups; first, refinements and extensions of the synthesis we have already examined, and secondly, innovations in the sphere of aggregate theory culminating in the publication of the epoch-making *General Theory* of Keynes. My observations will follow this order.

(a) *Extensions and Refinements of the Neo-Classical Synthesis*

(i) *Revision of Demand Theory* Beginning therefore with extensions and refinements of the neo-Classical synthesis, the first to be noticed is the restatement and extension of demand theory.

The analysis of the influences behind demand which had developed in the earlier period had often seemed to depend over-

[1] *Economica*, no. 39 (Feb 1933).

much upon the validity of psychological hedonism. This was not true of Menger and his followers, who elaborated their theory on the assumption simply of the possibility of an ordering of marginal uses. But elsewhere the appearance was general. The constructions of Gossen, Dupuit and Jevons all looked as if they were direct corollaries of an hedonistic calculus. Jevons, for instance, began the argument of his *Theory of Political Economy* with a chapter on 'The Theory of Pleasure and Pain'; and his main exposition was illustrated by diagrams in which final degrees of utility or disutility were measured on a vertical axis. In this fashion he had many followers.

All this led to much misunderstanding. As the Austrians had perceived, what was ultimately in question was the relation between the private valuations of the individuals concerned and the valuations emerging in the market; to explain this in terms of nice calculations of anticipated pleasure and pain was to invite disagreement from all who did not happen to subscribe to this view of the springs of action. Moreover, the way it was set forth seemed to involve assumptions concerning the crude measurability of subjective processes which were bound to be a stumbling block to the philosophically fastidious.

It was only to be expected that there would be attempts to escape from this embarrassment; there is an inner compelling logic about the formal analysis involved which clearly transcends the limitation of particular psychological theories and calls for statement in terms which beg no extraneous questions. Thus from a very early stage we find explanations that utility is not utility in the sense of psychological hedonism, but rather a neutral quality of being the object of desire, whether hedonistic or otherwise – Pareto's ophélimeté – a point of view which later on, with Wicksteed, led to the substitution of the term 'marginal significance' for 'marginal utility'. Even with Edgeworth, the high priest of mathematical utilitarianism, we find assurances that the estimates concerned involve *ordering* rather than *counting*; and Pareto loudly proclaimed his own originality and virtue in going over to this assumption. And in Irving Fisher's *Mathematical Investigations of the Theory of Value and Price,* first published in 1892 – that greatly neglected masterpiece, the most astonishing doctoral thesis in the history of our subject – the analysis is developed in a way which the most severe critic of the earlier theories would find unexceptionable.

All these tendencies were beginning to make their appearance before 1914. Their consolidation, however, had to wait till the thirties, when the important article 'A Reconsideration of the Theory of Value' by Allen and Hicks[1] and the subsequent elaboration of its propositions by Hicks in his classic *Value and Capital* restated the theory of demand in such a way as to escape the strictures applicable to earlier theories and to extend the analysis to further and important insights.

The achievement of Allen and Hicks has a twofold aspect. In the first place it rests its constructions solely upon the assumption of direct comparison of the valuation or substitutability of one commodity in terms of another and the possibility of arranging such combinations in terms of equivalence or higher or lower positions on a scale of order. It thus dispenses with all appeal to comparison of utilities, however conceived, and eliminates all necessity for the introduction of cardinal measurements.

All this may perhaps be regarded as a matter merely of superior elegance. The ultimate form of the description of equilibrium in terms of equivalence of the subjective marginal rate of substitution with the objective relative price is not *formally* much different from the equivalence of marginal utility and price of earlier formulations; perhaps its main advantage is that it no longer furnishes a target for irrelevant criticism. But the second aspect of this achievement goes far beyond that. For, by means of their distinction between the income and substitution effects of price changes, the authors were enabled to formulate with precision the conditions necessary for the assumption of demand as a diminishing function of price – one of the most essential assumptions of practical analysis. It is true that anticipations of such an explanation are to be found in the earlier literature; the distinction appears in papers by Johnson

[1] *Economica,* new series, no. 1 (Feb and May 1934).

and Slutsky,[1] published as early as 1913 and 1915, which had completely escaped notice. But the main credit for the systematic development of the analysis and its establishment as a central feature of the modern theory of value rests essentially with the authors under discussion.

(ii) *The Theory of the Firm and the Market* We must next take note of developments in this period relating to the theory of the firm and its relations to various kinds of market. These fall conveniently into two groups, according as they are concerned with the relation between costs and supply or with decisions of market strategy.

As regards the first group, the situation is fairly straightforward. As we have seen already, the idea of variations of product with variations in the proportionate combination of productive agents was already established at the time of Ricardo and was incorporated on a large scale in the various systems emerging from the so-called Marginal Revolution. Developments in the inter-war period involved, first, more explicit recognition of the distinctions between the concepts of marginal and average returns, secondly, better understanding of the role played by indivisibility of productive agents in the phenomena and range of increasing returns combinations, and thirdly, elucidation of the difference between variations of returns due to variations of proportionate combinations and variations in the absolute scale of productive operations as such. All these were so much a by-product of intensive work in various parts of the field that it would be difficult to pick out single names as having prior claims to originality in this connection. But Professor Schneider's *Theorie der Produktion* may be cited as affording a fair conspectus of the state of thought by the middle of the thirties.

Clarification of the returns concepts naturally led to corresponding developments in related conceptions of costs. Here again much of the spadework had been done in the earlier period; in

[1] Johnson, 'The Pure Theory of Utility Curves', *Economic Journal*, XXIII (Dec 1913); Slutsky, 'Sulla teoria del bilancio del consumatore', *Giornale degli Economisti*, LI (1915).

particular, Marshall's conception of variations in the cost functions according to the length of the planning period in contemplation being especially fruitful. But, as usual, the attempt to give formal precision to the ideas concerned brought to light many important implications. In this connection, Professor Viner's well-known article on 'Cost Curves and Supply Curves'[1] deserves special notice as exercising a widespread influence both in its own right and as evoking further elucidations.

The second group of developments, those relating to the policies of firms in relation to different market forms, is more difficult to evaluate.

Much has been made of the alleged discovery round about the end of the twenties of the general formula for profit maximisation – marginal revenue equal to marginal cost. But this is historically untrue. The formula is implicit in Cournot's treatment of monopoly. A solution in terms of parallel tangents to the aggregate curves, which of course is exactly the same thing, is given in Auspitz and Lieben's famous *Untersuchungen über die Theorie des Preises*.[2] Alfred Marshall states it quite explicitly in the Appendix to the *Principles*,[3] although he goes on to say – not without justification in his universe of discourse – that, for some purposes, it may be neglected in favour of the simple formula for competition in which, marginal revenue and price being coincident, the equivalence of price and marginal cost may be regarded as the condition of equilibrium. And it is not as though this had escaped notice – though obviously the more recent 'discoveries' had not heard of it: it is reproduced in one of the most widely used pre-1914 textbooks, Chapman's *Outlines of Political Economy*.[4]

---

[1] Originally published in the *Zeitschrift für Nationalökonomie*, III (1932). Reprinted with a supplement in J. Viner, *The Long View and the Short* (Glencoe, Ill., 1958).

[2] (Leipzig, 1889) p. 263. It also appears earlier in Dionysius Lardner's *Railway Economy* (1850) pp. 287–92.

[3] 8th ed. (1920) pp. 847–50.

[4] Since this may surprise some people even at the present day, it is perhaps worth quoting Chapman's exact words: 'One way of defining a position of monopoly equilibrium is to say that it is a position which is

What can be said, however, is not that this conception was invented in this later period, but rather that in this period it came into general use. Clearly it has sometimes been badly used. There are some who seem to think that it is a suitable description of day-to-day price policy by business rather than a rough indication of a criterion of long-term policy. There are others who, when they make the not very remarkable discovery that businessmen do not act continually so as to maximise short-period gains, conclude that there is no counterpart to the idea of profit maximisation in real life. But in spite of such naïveties, when employed with a minimum of common sense – much harder to teach than pure analysis – the conception has proved a powerful means of analysing conditions not easily dealt with by other methods. To realise this it is only necessary to compare Mrs Robinson's beautiful treatment of discriminating monopoly with earlier attempts at solutions of this problem.

Much the most important development in this field was the discussion and the bringing into due prominence of the problem of oligopoly. The problem, of course, was not new. As the special case of duopoly, it had been discussed at length by Cournot as an intermediate step between his treatment respectively of pure monopoly and pure competition. Later on the Cournot solution came under criticism, first by Bertrand, then by Edgeworth. But it remained something of a *curiosum* – a fancy problem on which an ingenious fellow might try his wits in spare moments – rather than an abstraction seeking to mirror large areas of the field of production. The actual problems of oligopolistic industry tended to be dealt with on a more descriptive, less abstract plane. It was not until the inter-war period, largely as a result of the publication of Edward Chamberlin's *Theory of Monopolistic Competition*, that it

---

such (*a*) that *the addition made to aggregate receipts by an incremental addition to the monopoly's output equals the addition made to aggregate costs . . . by an incremental addition to the monopoly's output*, and (*b*) that departures from it in either direction mean that the loss involved exceeds the gain involved' (p. 177). A similar solution in algebra and geometry is given in the other chief textbook embodying the Cambridge thought of the period: Sir Alfred Flux, *Economic Principles* (1904), p. 293.

attracted its due share of analytical attention. It is true that the solution, first propounded by A. L. Bowley, which gradually came to be accepted, is still very formalistic and leaves most of the application to reality still to be provided from *ad hoc* empirical sources. But at any rate, it is general in character and covers, as special cases, the apparently contradictory solutions of Cournot, Bertrand and Edgeworth. It is also notable for a new technical device, the introduction into the determinants of the supply function of any one oligopolistic unit, of assumptions regarding changes in the prices and quantities produced by others in response to such changes by the unit concerned – the famous 'conjectural variations' – thus emphasising what in fact must be recognised as the special analytical characteristic of the oligopoly problem.

(iii) *International Trade Theory* Finally, still under the general heading of developments of the earlier synthesis, we may note clarifications of the theory of international trade.

In this connection there is less to report by way of radical change. There is substantial continuity since Ricardian days, and the general appearance of theory has changed less than elsewhere. Nevertheless, cumulatively a series of small changes have led to considerable extension.

You will remember that it was realised by Ricardo that his main theory of value was not applicable to conditions where there was no effective mobility of capital and labour – a state of affairs which, rightly or wrongly, he assumed to prevail between the different national areas of his time. In such conditions, he argued, specialisation and the possibility of mutually satisfactory exchange would be determined, not by comparisons of absolute costs *between* the areas concerned, but rather by comparison of the relations between costs *within* each area. This was the famous theory of comparative costs which, as it gradually came to be realised, was applicable, not only to the analysis of specialisation and exchange between national areas, but also wherever mobility between productive groups was not effective. It was realised too, although comparatively recently, that it is capable of providing, so to speak, an analytical stiffening of the traditional doctrine of the advantages of division of labour in general. Indeed, in our own time it has been represented with great cogency by von Mises as nothing less than the fundamental explanation of the spontaneous forces making for social co-operation in general – the *Ricardo'sche Vergesellschaftungs-gesetz* or Law of Association, as he calls it.[1]

The exposition of this important generalisation by the Classical writers, however, was open to criticism on grounds of the terms in which it was expressed. The comparative costs which it involved were comparative *labour* costs; the costs of using other scarce productive agents did not enter the formula; and this has led some people to believe that, with the recognition of the very limited applicability of a pure labour theory, the theory of comparative costs should also suffer a similar eclipse. But this is not so. It is not at all difficult to substitute for the comparative labour costs of the original theory the comparative opportunity costs of more recent conceptions. In the period under discussion, this was done with great force and lucidity by Gottfried Haberler in his authoritative *Theory of International Trade*; and now that it has been done, it is clear that the fundamental implication of the original theory, that it is differences of cost ratios which give scope for specialisation and advantageous exchange, remains completely unimpaired.

Powerful as it is in affording an ultimate rationale for the division of labour, whether territorial or otherwise, by itself the theory of comparative costs does not actually do what Ricardo set out to do. It does not provide an adequate explanation of the determination of international values. Even in a two-good world, it indicates only the limits within which mutually advantageous rates may be found; and in a many-good world, while it provides the means of ordering the alternatives, it does not by itself determine where the line of division will take place. To do this, to explain the actual determination of relative prices and the division of labour, it is necessary to take account of the forces underlying demand.

---

[1] L. von Mises, *Nationalökonomie* (Geneva, 1940) pp. 126–33; and *Human Action* (New Haven, 1949) pp. 158–63.

B

As is well known, this side of the problem received due attention even within the Classical period narrowly defined. There are hints of a solution in Ricardo. The influence of demand is recognised both by Longfield in discussion of Irish absenteeism and by Torrens in his discussions of commercial policy; and in the essay 'Of the Laws of Interchange Between Nations' in his *Unsettled Questions*, to which I have already alluded, and again at greater length in his *Principles*, John Stuart Mill provides a thoroughly systematic treatment of the problem. It only remained for Mangoldt to treat the many-good case in his *Grundriss der Volkswirtschaftslehre* (1863) and for Marshall to translate Mill's arithmetic into geometry in his famous paper on 'The Pure Theory of Foreign Trade' for the main outlines of the theory as it still holds the field to be firmly established. Even the theory of optimal tariffs, which has been treated in some quarters as a recent discovery, appears during this period, with all the paraphernalia of price vectors and indifference curves, in so conspicuous a place as Edgeworth's famous paper in 'International Values'.[1]

There is, however, one analytical development of the inter-war period which involves a useful addition to the conceptual apparatus of this part of the theory, namely the distinction between the terms of trade as measured in commodities and as measured in units of factor services. This distinction, which, so far as I know, was first explicitly introduced by Jacob Viner,[2] is of quite fundamental importance in any examination of the gains from trade. For it is clearly quite possible for the commodity terms of trade to move against the inhabitants of a certain area while the movement of the factorial terms is favourable. Indeed, this might well be a quite normal accompaniment of a certain kind of economic progress: a lowering of price in an elastic market could easily result in higher aggregate revenue to a constant volume of factor services. Incidentally, the use of the concept of factorial terms of trade serves to make it clear that, from this point of view, the theory of

[1] See his 'Pure Theory of International Values', in *Papers Relating to Political Economy* (1925) II, 39.
[2] See his *Studies in the Theory of International Trade* (1937) pp. 558 ff.

international trade is simply a special case of a general theory of distribution.

All this part of the theory was developed by Ricardo and his followers in 'real' terms. But, as is well known, they also developed theories of how the fundamental forces involved worked out through the medium of money. The Ricardian theory of the distribution of the precious metals, Senior's *Lectures on the Cost of Obtaining Money* and Taussig's further elucidations of this mode of approach, partly before 1914, partly in the magisterial work of his old age, *International Trade*, published in the middle of the period under discussion, all showed how, other things being equal, there would develop a distribution of power to purchase bringing it about that trade between non-competing groups would conform to the general expectations based on a barter theory. There is a diagram in Barone's *Principi*,[1] one of the most beautiful in the whole range of geometrical economics, which illustrates the core of this theory with incomparable elegance.

All this, however, depended on the assumption of the existence, not perhaps of a completely unified world money, but at least of what Jacob Viner has called simple specie currencies which in their functioning could be assumed to work much as a single monetary system would do. Once this assumption is waived, however, that is to say, once there are allowed in the model independent sources of supply of different national monies, the picture becomes much more complicated. If the monies concerned are independent inconvertible paper and no attempt is made to keep them in step, the exchange rate must be assumed to vary if there is to be any possibility of a tendency to equilibrium in the flow of trade, although in practice there are likely to be so many disturbing factors that it would be unwise to assume this as a model for universal adoption. But even if there is common adoption of gold as an ultimate reserve, functioning, however, through the medium of banking systems with the power of independent initiative, there are all sorts of possibilities of disharmony through

[1] (Rome, 1925) p. 98.

the creation or destruction of local purchasing power having no countervailing counterpart elsewhere.

This was fully perceived by the Classical writers. At an early stage, during the Bullion controversy, the influence of fluctuations of supply of inconvertible paper was clearly set forth. But even as regards convertible money on a so-called common standard, it gradually came to be realised that there were parallel possibilities of disharmony, at least in the short run of the different supplies of money getting, so to speak, out of step. This was indeed pointed out in Hume's famous essay 'On the Balance of Trade'. It was perception of the same potentialities which underlay Ricardo's, at first puzzling, insistence that disequilibrium in the exchange market *always* arose from excess issue. And it was the same possibilities which in the end were what the celebrated debates between the Currency and Banking Schools were about.[1]

In the inter-war period all this was especially relevant to current affairs; and the progress of theory in this connection consisted essentially in a refinement and a reformulation of earlier views occasioned by the direct needs of current understanding. In some respects at first this was a case of *reculer pour mieux sauter*. Cassel's famous purchasing-power parity theory of the exchanges was a degraded version of Classical doctrine in this respect, tending to assume that only positive movements in the relative price levels affected rates of exchange, which may have been a fair approximation to the explanation of the phenomena of hyper-inflation but obviously left potentially important 'real' influences out of the picture. And in regard to the problem of capital transfer, which had become of immediate practical interest in connection with German reparations, the original contentions of Keynes, who argued as if the possibilities of transfer and the effects on the terms of trade could be judged independently of shifts of purchasing power, served only to confuse the issue. But, in the end, further

[1] In 'A Note on the Formal Content of the Theory of International Trade', in *Contribuições a analise do desenvolvimento economico* (Rio de Janeiro, 1957). I have tried to show that the assumption of independent sources of money supply is one of the two distinguishing characteristics of international trade theory.

discussion of both these problems resulted in a clearer and better formulation of the relevant theories. Where the transfer problem was involved, the theory of the multiplier, originated by Kahn and exploited on a large scale by Keynes himself, resulted in a better explanation of what can actually happen when there is any slack in the economies concerned, than was afforded by earlier theories which tended to depend too much in this connection on assumptions rigidly appropriate only to high levels of employment.

(b) *The Kenyesian Revolution*

This brings me to the so-called Keynesian Revolution. So far, the developments of the inter-war period, with which I have been dealing, can be regarded as orderly refinements and extensions of a system of thought which had already been established. But although, as we shall see, the Keynesian innovations were not without antecedents, and although the extent of the divergence of their conclusions from the then accepted theory was capable of considerable exaggeration, their impact on thought was not of this nature. I personally think that, in the verdict of history, their ultimate influence will be found to reside much more in the realm of the theory of policy than in pure analysis. But even in this latter sphere the influence has been conspicuous.

To get this into proper focus it is desirable to return once more to Ricardo. In his system there is an underlying assumption throughout that the economy functions at full capacity. It is not denied that changes may take place in the demand for particular products. But it is assumed that aggregate demand must equal aggregate supply and therefore that, if demand in one sector falls away, there must be a compensating increase elsewhere, so that any disturbance to employment must be transitory. As against Malthus and Lauderdale, he denied that accumulation could be excessive, proceeding always – as indeed did Malthus – on the assumption that savings were not likely to be hoarded and that consequently there was no danger that abstention from consumption would not be matched by a corresponding increase in investment. The rate of profit was determined by 'real' factors; and although it was possible for policy to fix interest rates below the levels which harmonised with this, this was an artificial development, not something demanding special investigation in a general view of natural interconnections.

Now it would be a great mistake – often, however, committed – to suppose that between Ricardo and Keynes nothing was ever said to dispute the adequacy of this analysis. There were subtler views of money and credit in the works of many writers even before Ricardo, notably in Thornton's *Paper Credit*, probably the best treatment of the subject before the twentieth century. And after him, still in the Classical literature, John Stuart Mill's paper 'Of the Influence of Consumption on Production' disposes of the crudities of the so-called Law of Markets in a way which has not been bettered even in our own time. Later on, the evidence of Marshall before the Gold and Silver Commission and the Committee on Indian Currency deploys, albeit in unsystematic fashion, a theory of money and the capital market into which most, if not all, modern developments can very easily be fitted, a theory which was further developed and refined by subsequent Cambridge economists, particularly Pigou, Lavington and Robertson. And elsewhere, especially in the works of Wicksell and his followers, notably Lindahl and Myrdal, there were elaborated systems of analysis which even at the present day are thought by some to present a more balanced view of the subject than the *General Theory* itself. Thus by the beginning of the thirties there existed in solution, as it were, in monetary theory proper and in the closely allied field of the theory of business cycles, most of the elements which appear in the Keynesian and later syntheses.

There is therefore at least some substance in the complaints of those who object to the term 'revolution' in this connection. And there can be no doubt that Keynes himself and some of his followers were apt to overstate the element of discontinuity in their contribution, Keynes partly because of his very bad memory for anything in which he had not become intensely interested, the followers in question, I am afraid, because they often had so little to remember.

Nevertheless, it would be to fall into the opposite error of arguing that nothing is new to deny the appearance of important novel elements or of a significant quickening of the pace and nature of change. In the history of most revolutions, it is often possible to trace antecedents such that, in the final analysis, there appears to be more continuity than there seemed to be at the time. But that is no ground for denying that something revolutionary occurred.

What were the leading features of this development? Let me try to state them with the crude emphasis with which they appeared at first reading of the *General Theory* without the qualifications which were to be found tucked away on closer inspection. They are as follows:

First, an insistence on the pivotal importance of aggregate demand in the determination of the volume of employment and output at given rates of wages.

Hence, secondly, an exhibition of the dominating role of consumption, expressed as a simple function of income, and of investment, expressed as a function of what the author called the marginal efficiency of capital, which in effect was Fisher's marginal rate of return over cost, disguised in different terms in the determination of aggregate demand.

Thirdly, a repudiation of the adequacy, or indeed of the logical consistency, of a non-monetary theory of interest, and the substitution of an explanation running in terms of the quantity of money and a schedule of liquidity preference.

Fourthly, an assertion of the possibility, sometimes it almost seems the probability, of underemployment equilibrium. The old quantity theory, of course, would have given the same result, with the assumption of rigid wage rates. The element of novelty consisted in the attempt to show the same possibility with flexible wage rates.

Now I am not arguing that all this was entirely new – at any rate in its more refined manifestations. I am not arguing that it was necessarily correct – I shall be showing later on how subsequent elucidation has put a good many of its apparently more startling divergences into a considerably more sedate perspective. But I do argue that no one who has read it with anything like an open mind can ever think of things in quite the same way again.

IV. SINCE KEYNES

I must now say a word or two about what has happened since that day. In this connection my remarks must be even more superficial than they have been in dealing with earlier periods. Economics is now a widely established university subject, with widespread intellectual division of labour; and to keep in touch with, let alone survey in any comprehensive manner, the whole field of pure theory is beyond the scope of most of us. I can only touch on what seem to me the developments which are most interesting from the point of view of this colloquy.

I will not spend time on the influence on pure theory of the techniques of activity analysis, in particular of linear programming. As has been urged with great force by Professor Baumol, fundamentally linear programming is simply a novel and very powerful mathematical technique; and as such it adds nothing to economic theory. But I think it is clear that the availability of this technique has enabled a clearer grasp of some essentially economic problems, not only in the theory of the firm but also in general equilibrium theory. It would be difficult to argue that either Professor Baumol's own splendid article[1] or the comprehensive treatise of Dorfman, Samuelson and Solow[2] have not deepened our insights in many directions. And I am inclined to agree with the verdict of Sir John Hicks that, in the last analysis, from the point of view of pure theory, its most valuable service is the way in which it brings into bold relief, in ways which have not been available before, the *raison d'être* of the price mechanism as some-

[1] 'Activity Analysis in One Lesson', *American Economic Review* (1958).
[2] R. Dorfman, P. A. Samuelson and R. W. Solow, *Linear Programming and Economic Analysis* (New York, 1958).

thing inherent in any maximisation process within the restraints of different degrees of scarcity.[1]

Much more profitable for purposes of this survey is to concentrate on developments in the field of macro-economics. Here there are two groups which especially invite attention, the aftermath of the *General Theory* and the development of economic dynamics. I will take them in that order.

(a) *The Aftermath of the* General Theory

As might have been expected – and as its author clearly did expect – the impact of the *General Theory*, with its simplified highlights and its apparent repudiation of everything which had preceded it, save the works of Malthus and a few obscure heretics, provoked instant adverse reaction. Much of this need not concern us here since it rested upon indignation or misunderstanding. But even on a view of the subject as superficial as this talk, it would be an error of perspective to omit the critiques of Dennis Robertson. Robertson, who came from the same intellectual stable as Keynes and had indeed worked closely with him in that renaissance of monetary and fluctuation theory which marked the earlier part of the inter-war period, was deeply shocked by the tone and by many of the more dogmatic assertions of the *General Theory*. But, unlike the critiques to whom I have already referred, whose response was mainly emotional, he set himself to learn the new language and to do battle on the grounds of Keynes's own choosing; and, as a result, in a series of exchanges, painful to both parties, he succeeded in forcing admissions that, even in a Keynesian model, both productivity and thrift played direct parts in determining the level of interest rates, rather than the indirect roles assigned to them when Keynes was not insisting over-simply that liquidity preference and the quantity of money were the *only* influences. With the extortion of these admissions and the focussing of the discussion on the more sophisticated formulations tucked away

[1] In his masterly survey, 'Linear Theory', *Economic Journal*, LXX (Dec 1960).

in qualifications of the stronger assertions of the *General Theory*, an important step was taken towards the establishment of a perspective in which what was novel and what was traditional in this explosive publication were more clearly revealed.[1]

A more definite clarification, however, was accomplished by its translation into algebra and geometry. This has been done many times in recent years. But the *locus classicus* is still Sir John Hicks's 'Mr Keynes and the Classics'.[2] In this important article, Sir John first put the main propositions of the *General Theory* into simple macro-economic equations, amplifying certain functional relationships omitted by Keynes, but not out of harmony with the spirit of his analysis. He then translated the purport of these into a diagram in which the ultimately significant variables were exhibited by the intersection of two curves – the famous *IS* and *LL* curves – reflecting, as do the hands of a clock, the outcome of a more complicated mechanism in the background. From this it followed that, over a large range of possibilities, the differences between the Keynesian approach and a neo-Classical approach explicitly taking account of the dependence of the demand for money on the level of interest rates, was very largely a matter of alternative formulations leading to substantially the same conclusions. On the assumption of rigid wage rates, both yielded a picture in which underemployment equilibrium was possible. The Keynesian model, however, showed a region in which underemployment equilibrium was possible, even with flexible wages. But, this possibility apart, the difference between the two approaches lay more in the sphere of conception of the strategic variables of policy than in ultimate differences of analysis.

As regards the exceptions, however, it has been urged by some that the Keynesian analysis is incomplete in that it fails to take account of the reactions of changes in the real value of cash balances due to changes in prices and costs on the disposition to

[1] The main substance of the criticism is to be found in the first paper in Robertson's *Essays in Monetary Theory* (1940), where there will be found appropriate references to the antecedent controversial exchanges.

[2] *Econometrica*, v 2 (Apr 1937), now reprinted in the author's *Critical Essays in Monetary Theory* (1967).

spend and invest. This conception of what is osmetimes called the real balance effect has been made by Patinkin the basis for a complete reassessment of the Keynesian universe of discourse. His *Money, Interest and Prices*, one of the most thought-provoking works of recent years, reaches the conclusion that, to quote his own summary:

> The propositions of the quantity theory of money hold under conditions much less restrictive than those usually considered necessary by its advocates and, *a fortiori*, its critics. Conversely the propositions of Keynesian monetary theory are much less general than the *General Theory* and later expositions would lead us to believe. But this in no way diminishes the relevance of Keynesian unemployment theory for the formulation of a practicable full employment policy.[1]

With the pure theory of the subject in such a state that, over a greater part of the field at least, either of two apparently contrasting approaches seems equally applicable, the role of empirical testing becomes of pivotal importance. Thus although it is beyond my terms of reference, I cannot leave this part of the subject without referring to developments in this connection in the United States, where Professor Friedman and his associates at Chicago claim to be able to show by the analysis of time series that a reformulated quantity theory gives a closer fit to facts than the Keynesian apparatus. It would be quite wrong to leave the impression that this contention is generally accepted. I mention it partly for its intrinsic interest, partly as showing the plane on which work in this context is now tending more and more to move.

(b) Dynamic Theory

I come now to the last matter which I need to discuss in this survey, the recent development of theories of economic dynamics.

An interest in economic change and its causes is of course no new appearance in the literature of our subject. Indeed, it could

[1] Op. cit. (New York, 1956) p. 3. A second edition published in 1965 greatly amplifies the treatment.

be argued that concern with economic development has provided one of the main stimuli to economic speculation from the times of mercantilism onward. This is certainly true of the Classical period. Adam Smith's *Wealth of Nations* at one end and John Stuart Mill's *Principles* at the other were chiefly focussed on explanation of the causes of economic growth, in the sense of income per head; the analysis of value and distribution, although it eventually developed a semi-independent status, was originally instrumental to an explanation of the organisation of production. With the so-called Marginal Revolution, there was indeed some shift of interest to problems of allocation and imputation. But there is still the towering figure of Marshall to remind us of the overriding implicit concern with change, particularly change in what might be judged to be a favourable direction.[1]

The centre of gravity of all such speculations was the ultimate causes of improvement or deterioration. It was concerned with the underlying reasons why progress, or decline, takes place, not how exactly it happens. Doubtless there was a good deal of mixture in the looser treatments of the subject. But the more formal analysis was essentially comparative statics rather than a truly dynamic theory. It might be argued that trade-cycle theory was an exception to this generalisation; and there is some substance in this objection. But it is still true that although this branch of theory was indeed concerned with movement, and movement which was only likely in a state of change, yet the focus was different; it was on fluctuation rather than on growth or decline as such.

This is true even of the Keynesian analysis. Needless to say, with Keynes, as with the great Classical writers, there is much which has an incidental bearing on the problem, especially in his discussions of the behaviour of speculative markets. But viewed as pure analysis, the propositions of the *General Theory*, equally with the propositions of Ricardo's *Principles*, are fundamentally static in nature. The central Keynesian approach is essentially the Marshallian statical method applied to the macro-economic sphere.

[1] On the history of theories of development, see my *Theory of Economic Development in the History of Economic Thought* (1968).

The beginnings of a truly dynamic theory are to be found, not in the theory of development but rather in the theory of markets. The analysis by Walras and Edgeworth of the conditions of determinateness of price indicate at least a problem of the path. The so-called cobweb theorems, first elaborated, I believe, by Rosenstein-Rodan, are an explicit exercise in this field. The gradual spread in the inter-war period of the explicit introduction of assumptions regarding expectations of price and quantity changes also pointed in the same direction.

But the main impetus to recent developments came in the field of aggregate analysis. I think it could be claimed for Dennis Robertson that in some respects he was, to use Sir John Hicks's words, the forerunner of the theory of growth. One of the few claims he ever made for himself was to have anticipated the Domar equations, and there must be many more such anticipations in the literature of the theory of the trade cycle. But for an explicit formulation of the requirement and the first tentatives of a solution, full credit must go to Sir Roy Harrod, whose article in the *Economic Journal* of 1939 must be regarded as the origin of the vast volume of work on the subject which has appeared since that day.

The form which this speculation has taken has a twofold aspect. On the one hand, effort has been devoted to describing equilibrium paths of movement given various changes in the data. On the other, attempts have been made to ascertain how a given system will actually move when changes of this sort take place. As typical of the first, I think of the pioneering work of Harrod already mentioned; of the second, the equally original and suggestive researches of Phillips into lags and responses.[1] But the literature of the subject is vast; and much of it is beyond my competence. Not to mention it here, however, would certainly be to omit some of the most significant developments of recent times.[2]

[1] See his 'Some Notes on the Estimation of Time Forms of Reaction in Interdependent Dynamic Systems', *Economica*, XXIII (May 1956).

[2] If this paper had been written a few years later, clearly a conspicuous place would have to have been given in this section to Sir John Hicks's *Capital and Growth* (Oxford, 1965), the most powerful work of synthesis which has yet appeared in this field.

V. CONCLUSION

It is high time I brought this survey to a conclusion. How much of importance I have left out, even on the plane of positive theory, must be very apparent; and as I said at the beginning, I have left the whole field of the theory of policy deliberately untouched.

But what I should hope to have suggested to our Russian friends is this: that although perhaps we shall have to talk much longer about policy and institutions before we find completely common ground, here, in the sphere of pure theory, there has developed a series of propositions which, while in form more concerned with the exchange economy than with others, yet do represent an effort to find intellectual solutions to intellectual problems and may well form the basis in years to come for scientific exchanges between us without necessarily treading on each other's ideological toes.

2

Schumpeter on the History
of Economic Analysis[1]

I

THE contents of this large and (physically) very heavy volume are correctly indicated by its title. It is not a history of theories of policy; nor is it a history of economic systems; these matters are discussed only in so far as they throw light on the central subject – the evolution of those techniques of thought which enable us to describe and explain the economic aspects of reality. The plan falls into five parts. Part I (pp. 3–50) is devoted to a vindication of the autonomy of the subject and a discussion of its relations with other branches of knowledge. Part II (pp. 51–378) traces developments from the beginnings in Graeco-Roman times to the promulgation in the last half of the eighteenth century of the Physiocratic and Smithian systems. Part III (pp. 379–752) deals with the period 1780 to 1870, so covering the English Classical School in its full development. Part IV (pp. 753–1138) takes us down to 1914 'and later', and ranges far and wide over the evolution of analysis since the Jevonian Revolution. Part V (pp. 1139–84) is a fragment and deals in a sketchy way with certain very recent developments.

The genesis of this most ambitious enterprise lies a long way back. The monograph, *Epochen der Methoden- und Dogmengeschichte*, which as a young man Schumpeter contributed to the Tübingen *Grundriss der Sozialökonomik*, had at once taken its place as

[1] A review of Joseph A. Schumpeter, *History of Economic Analysis*, ed. from manuscript by Elizabeth Boody Schumpeter (New York: Oxford University Press, 1954), *Quarterly Journal of Economics*, LXIX 1 (Feb 1955). Reproduced by courtesy of the *Quarterly Journal of Economics* and Harvard University Press.

incontestably the best short introduction to its subject; and several attempts had been made to induce its author to consent to an English translation. But he always held these at arm's length, declaring himself to be desirous of making some revision before allowing such a version to appear. Eventually, in 1941, when he had finished his *Capitalism, Socialism and Democracy*, he embarked upon this task, apparently conceiving it as a convenient side line to his main concern of preparing a major work on theory. Gradually, however, his interest developed; and thus for the last nine years of his life, so Mrs Schumpeter tells us, it became a dominating preoccupation.

At the time of his death, his labours had resulted in the work which is embodied in the present volume. But the materials were far from their present form: they were scattered in many manuscripts in many places, some typed and corrected, some only typed, some merely in longhand. We owe it to Mrs Schumpeter, devoted to this task through a prolonged illness even to the last weeks of her life, that the manuscripts have been assembled in their present form – a coherent, if not finally completed, book. The story of this reconstruction is itself almost a minor epic. The annals of our profession abound with the examples of wives whose unselfishness has made possible their husbands' books; and more than one wife has successfully supervised the publication of posthumous works. But it is doubtful whether there is any parallel to such a labour as this – a shining example of what comradely devotion can achieve. It is quite true that the book is not finished in the sense in which the author would have finished it had he lived to see it through the press. A few chapters are unwritten; several are unfinished. Occasionally even sentences tail off without a conclusion – the editor conceived her 'editorial task to be the simple one of presenting as complete and accurate a version of what J.A.S. actually wrote as possible but not attempting to complete what he had not written'. But, as with the Leonardo 'Adoration' in the Uffizi, the grand proportions are there: and if some details are unfinished and others lacking, if here the perspective is only indicated by a sketch and there alternative versions blur the outlines, yet it is essentially an integral creation, to be judged and enjoyed as a whole.

II

There were many reasons why Schumpeter should have been peculiarly well fitted for an enterprise of this sort. He was born and brought up in one of the most brilliant and cultivated societies of Europe before the decline, at that time one of the chief centres of speculation in theoretical economics. As a young man he had travelled widely and studied in many other places; he had personal contact with many of the founders of modern economic analysis elsewhere. He had thus exceptional opportunities for appreciating the unity in apparent diversity of different traditions and different schools of thought. His experience, moreover, was not wholly academic. He had some knowledge of the world of affairs, both of politics and of business – although, if common report is to be believed, his achievements in these fields were not of any conspicuous excellence. He thus approached his subject with that modicum of practical experience without which, although it is no integral part of the subject, so much economic analysis is apt to be sterile. Then, in his middle age, when still at the height of his powers, a great American university had called him to a position, remote from these temptations, with exactly the right combination of academic duty and leisure, in which, all passion spent – or nearly spent – these powers could express themselves without distraction.

There were gifts, too, of intellect and temperament reinforcing these environmental advantages. He had a first-rate mind. He had himself made contributions of distinction to the corpus of modern analysis. Unlike many who have written on the history of this subject, he knew what it was about from the inside; he spoke with the authority of a high practitioner. He was, moreover, an excellent expositor and showman; in our profession, with the single exception of Keynes, he was probably the best talker of his generation. Then, although he was not incapable of the slightly feline dig,

he was essentially fair and good-tempered. Himself the product of
many streams of influence, his whole intellectual bent was eclectic
– an excellent thing in an historian of thought. Indeed, it is arguable that at times this quality was present almost to excess; there
are places in this book where the distribution of praise is on so
lavish a scale that it is hard to suppress a feeling of being present
at some very high-grade get-together at which the exceptionally
knowledgeable chairman is almost too meticulously careful not to
leave unmentioned any guest, however humble. Finally, with all
his erudition, he was no pedant. He felt none of that compulsion
often felt by men of high ability to see good only in one line, no
matter what else is excluded. He knew enough of the world to know
why some men of sense are irritated by economics; but he knew so
much of economics that he knew too at what stage this irritation
ceased to be justified. All of which, it must be agreed, constituted
quite exceptional qualifications for writing the history of analysis.

Let it be said at once that the result, slightly unfinished as it is,
is something which is without serious rival. The history of economic
analysis has attracted some very first-class talent: some of the
contributions – such works, for instance, as Professor Viner's
Studies or Mr Sraffa's *Ricardo* – are outstanding in the scholarship
of historical studies in general. But for the most part the work of
high excellence here has taken the form of special studies rather
than general history. There is very little that is absolutely first
class in this latter sphere and nothing that will stand comparison,
either in respect of scale or insight, with this work of Schumpeter's.
This is a really serious and mature treatment of the subject. And,
although every expert reader will probably find something to
grumble about in the parts which deal with the periods or authors
he knows best, yet taking things in the large, it is safe to say that it
will be a long time before it is displaced as the leading work in its
field. Whether at the same time it is a good introduction is a
matter of greater dubiety. If one has some familiarity with the
material discussed, it is not easy to decide whether all the copious
references and allusions are necessarily well suited to convey a
clear picture to the beginner. My own guess would be that very

frequently they are not. But this is no criticism of the book on the plane on which it elects to move. The right way to begin to acquire a knowledge of the subject is to read the original texts themselves. Reading about them, pondering comments on their significance, comes later; and it is at this stage that Schumpeter comes into his own. And if any beginner, not knowing his way about, is in need of a compendious guide, he can always read the *Epochen* – now at last fortunately available in translation.

If this verdict is correct, if here at last we have something which can be regarded as a standard work on its subject, it follows that criticism must be concerned chiefly with matters of particular perspective and detail. That, indeed, in the main is the substance of what follows. But before thus closing up to the canvas, it is perhaps worth asking whether there are no critical comments to be made of its general appearance and execution.

In my judgement there are two – not, I think, of such importance as seriously to detract from the total achievement, but still perhaps deserving to be put on record.

First, I must confess that I find it hard to resist a certain impression of undue length. By this, I hasten to say, I mean no derogation of its aim or its merit as a treatise on the grand scale – despite the canons of a somewhat short-winded age, there *is* a certain virtue in bigness, provided that it is proportionate to its object. I refer rather to a certain tendency to discursiveness, a certain lack of control of the impulse to elaborate, which at times at least seems to be excessive. I suspect that this book could have been a couple of hundred pages shorter with advantage. This is perhaps partly due to the unfinished state of the manuscript: a final revision would almost certainly have involved a slimming process here and there – it would be unfair not to take this into account. But partly it is probably due to a more fundamental cause; I suspect that Schumpeter's literary habits did tend to over-elaboration – think, for instance, of the *Wesen und Hauptinhalt* – or even, dare I say it, of *Business Cycles*. I ought perhaps to add that I do not think that the result is boring; the many long summer days that I have devoted to reading these 1184 pages have been most agreeable. It was always pleasant to hear Schumpeter hold forth, even if now and then his points were a little otiose. But prolixity is a fault, even though it may sometimes be a fault on the good side; and I think that this book is a little prolix.

Secondly, I suspect that now and then there is a tendency to overemphasis and even to paradox in connection with certain reputations. This is not an easy point to make, since, taking the book as a whole, one of its chief merits is its excellent perspective. Moreover, it may well be that some differences with Schumpeter here are irreducible differences of temperament and local affiliation. Nevertheless, I do think that from time to time there are errors of this sort, so that, so to speak, certain figures suddenly pop out of the canvas and lose relation with their surroundings. Thus, for instance, on p. 465 in the course of a well-merited eulogy of von Thünen we are surprised to read that 'If we judge both men exclusively *by the amount of ability of the purely theoretical kind* that went into their work, then I think Thünen should be placed above Ricardo or indeed above any economist of the period with the possible exception of Cournot.' Now, of course, arguing about class lists at this level is not a particularly profitable occupation; and arguing about von Thünen in particular is highly esoteric. But surely there is something wrong about a judgement which, leaving aside von Thünen, even on Schumpeter's somewhat specialised criterion, would place Cournot above Ricardo. Cournot was certainly a highly talented man whose formulations of the demand function and the theory of monopoly were contributions of absolutely first-class importance. But let us apply the good Austrian test of the so-called loss principle. Suppose the theoretical contributions of Ricardo and Cournot to be alternately withdrawn – which would involve the greater impoverishment? Can there really be any hesitation about the answer? Certainly the relative amounts of space given to the work of these two authors by Schumpeter himself would seem to leave no doubt about it. Similarly, later on in the book, we find pre-eminence in his period assigned to Walras rather than to Marshall (p. 827) – although it must be said at once that Schumpeter has many fine things to say about the latter. Again, I cannot but feel a certain artificiality of emphasis. Undoubtedly Walras was a great economist, perhaps among the greatest. But is it really to be argued that the loss of his contribution, outstanding though it was, could outweigh the loss of Marshall's? We may agree that Walras had a raw deal during his life and is probably not sufficiently appreciated even in our own day. But I submit it is to get our perspective wrong if, in the laudable effort to rehabilitate him, we rate him as high as all that. But more of this later.

III

Part II, where the history really begins, runs from Plato and Aristotle to the Physiocrats and Adam Smith. It is easy to see the advantages of this arrangement. The vision of streams of fragmentary pieces of economic analysis springing from the treatises of moral philosophers and the *ad hoc* utterances of administrators and pamphleteers and culminating in the eighteenth century in the discovery of the system in economic life, is a fine one and opens up grand perspectives. But to exhibit it without a break in time has two disadvantages: it tends to minimise the degree of achievement in the eighteenth-century discovery of system: Quesnay and Adam Smith (and Cantillon before them) were not just two more moral philosophers or pamphleteers. And to have a break after Adam Smith but not before tends to suggest a certain divorce between the *Wealth of Nations* and the Classical writings of the nineteenth century which may foster misunderstanding; the unity of the English Classical School, either as regards analysis or as regards policy, is not to be understood save in the light of a common acceptance of the general outlook of Adam Smith. In the *Epochen* there were two parts covering this period: Part I, *Die Entwicklung der Sozialökonomik zur Wissenschaft* which dealt with the philosophers and pamphleteers, and Part II, *Die Entdeckung des wirtschaftlichen Kreislaufs*, which, as its name implies, dealt with the discovery of the economic system. I am inclined to think that for the main purpose of the book, although perhaps not for

the treatment of such subjects as money and interest, this arrangement was superior.

So far as the philosophers and pamphleteers are concerned, the
treatment seems to me to be in the main well proportioned and
just. I say this with some reserve, since so far as the Scholastic
writings are concerned, I have never lived with the original texts
long enough to form more than the broadest impressions; and there
are a great many aspects of the Mercantilist literature about which
I still find it very hard to make up my mind. It is quite clear that
the rejection of most of this literature as worthless was a gross
error: if the Classical economists have suffered from over-crude
interpretations of their point of view, it must be admitted that they
themselves were guilty of the same kind of unfairness in regard
to their predecessors. But I am fairly sure that more recent interpretations, either by members of the Historical School or by Keynes,
tend to err in the opposite direction: the theory of the barrenness
of money did not rest upon a liquidity preference theory of interest,
nor did emphasis, in a regime of advancing prices, upon the
accumulation of treasure necessarily rest upon dread of deflation.
In spite of a certain love of paradox and of the *recherché*, Schumpeter treads very delicately here. I suspect that some of those who
know best these branches of the literature would tend to the view
that his interpretations were still too charitable; and there is
doubtless much scope for dispute about particular interpretations.
But in general his treatment must command respect: if it is not a
final verdict, it provides at least agenda for grown-up talk.

On the eighteenth-century developments I find him less impressive. He has none of Hume's feelings about the Physiocrats – very
much the contrary indeed[1] – and he provides an account of
Quesnay's position which I venture to say is much more impressive and very much more intelligible than anything that that very
gnomic expositor ever wrote himself. But he still leaves one reader

[1] 'They are, indeed, the set of men the most chimerical and arrogant
that now exist, since the annihilation of the Sorbonne . . . I wonder what
could engage our friend, M. Turgot, to herd among them': *Letters of
David Hume*, ed. J. Y. T. Greig (1932) II 205.

at least with the feeling that, individually and as a group, they have sometimes been overpraised and are indeed overpraised by him. Doubtless the *Tableau économique* can be construed to stand for an idea of great power and importance – though I fancy that there is more jobbing backwards in this interpretation than we are often prepared to admit. But it is surely a significant circumstance that among the rest of the group, with the exception presumably of Mirabeau, the scientific aspect of the *Tableau* had hardly any influence; it was an object of worship, the symbol of a cult rather than a stimulus to further development. If profundity of thought and scientific detachment are the qualities to be valued, the work of Petty and of Cantillon seems to me to be on a much higher level.

As for the treatment of Adam Smith, I am inclined to regard it as one of the few real lapses in the book. There can be little doubt that Adam Smith was one of Schumpeter's blind spots. In an earlier, though not so much earlier, essay, he describes Smith's achievement as a ' "burst into publicity" – the *Wealth of Nations* was not more than this'.[1] And in the present volume he actually says that nobody who had not read them would credit the author of the *Wealth of Nations* with the power to write the posthumously published essays (p. 182). It would be possible, of course, to quote sentences which in themselves convey high praise. But I do not think that it is open to question that the general impression which is left by the treatment of Adam Smith is one of slightly patronising, slightly derogatory debunking – the man was a good systematiser of other people's ideas, an excellent expositor, lucky in his period, whose 'very limitations made for success' (p. 185). Why this was so, whether it was because of Smith's coolness about Political Arithmetic – he 'took the safe side that was so congenial to him' (p. 212) – or whether it was because of some chemical disaffinity of temperament – 'a fact which I cannot help considering relevant, not for his mere economics, of course, but all the more for his understanding of human nature – that no

[1] 'Professor Taussig on Wages and Capital', in *Explorations in Economics* (New York, 1930) p. 213.

woman, excepting his mother, ever played a role in his existence' (p. 182) – it is difficult to say. But the existence of some non-rational inhibition is incontestable. It is not the first time that a scholar with Schumpeter's background has been baffled and irritated by the unpretentious clarity and restraint of eighteenth-century English moral philosophy.

IV

Part III, which occupies nearly four hundred pages, contains the fullest and most systematic account to be found anywhere of the Classical system in its full development. For this much gratitude is due. But I have some reservations about matters which are not altogether unimportant.

First a matter of background influence – the role of Utilitarian moral philosophy. I am inclined to think that Schumpeter got this all wrong. I am not thinking here of his description of this outlook as 'the shallowest of all conceivable philosophies of life' (pp. 133, 407); that can conceivably be overlooked as a lapse into neo-Hegelian cliché which might perhaps have been expunged in a final revision. I am thinking rather of his suggestion that the Utilitarian background was to be conceived as confined to Bentham and the two Mills (p. 408).

This seems to me very questionable. I would have said rather that the background of the entire school, from its beginnings in Hume's *Essays* right through to Cairnes and Sidgwick, was through and through Utilitarian – and this stands even for Adam Smith whose explicit moral philosophy had a somewhat different complexion. In my judgement it is a mistake to regard Bentham and the Mills as *the* characteristic English Utilitarians. They represent – or at least Bentham and James Mill represent – a peculiarly severe and idiosyncratic version of a general outlook which, from a philosophical point of view, has had much more persuasive advocates both before and since.[1] And the habit of judging actions

---

[1] Schumpeter's footnote (p. 408) in which he tries to rescue Sidgwick from this classification is not one of his happier efforts.

and policies by their consequences rather than by reference to some intuitive norm, which is the salient characteristic of this outlook in contrast to that of the Continental metaphysicals, was common to almost all the English-speaking economists of the age. The contrast is well exemplified in Nassau Senior's conversation with the de Broglies:

> This led us to talk of Bowood and from Bowood we went to Bentham. The Duke had never seen his Bowood correspondence: indeed he seemed to be little acquainted with his works. The Prince knew more of them but admitted that he had not studied them accurately.
>
> *Prince de Broglie* — There are valuable hints in them as there must be in the works of a man of diligence and originality, but they scarcely repay the labour of mastering a system based on error.
>
> *Senior* — Do you reject then utility as the foundation of morals?
>
> *Prince de Broglie* — Certainly I do. It is generally rejected in France.
>
> *Senior* — And what do you substitute?
>
> *Prince de Broglie* — Our innate feelings of right and wrong.[1]

It might be argued, of course, that Senior was just the neutral interrogator, as he so frequently was in his conversations. But I am pretty sure that in this instance this interpretation would be wrong. The question, what is to be done if we reject considerations of utility, is typical of the attitude of the main tradition of English political economy. I hasten to add that I fully agree with Schumpeter that the logical coherence of their analytical propositions does not stand or fall with this background.[2]

Next comes a matter of position and influence. It is Schumpeter's contention – or at least, so it appears at a certain stage of his

---

[1] Nassau Senior, *Conversations with M. Thiers, M. Guizot and other Distinguished Persons* (1878) II 176.

[2] Painful experience compels me to register the hope that the above piece of historical diagnosis will not be taken as a manifesto of personal affiliation. Personally, I am content to be something of a pluralist in moral philosophy. I think a Utilitarian calculus is quite a good first approximation to many of the workaday problems of social policy. For the ultimate problems of personal conduct I am much less disposed to regard it as helpful. See the paragraphs on the Utilitarian norm in the paper on Bentham below, pp. 80–2.

argument – that Ricardo's influence has been overstressed, that there were no conspicuous Ricardians save James Mill, McCulloch, and De Quincey, and that, by the beginning of the thirties, the school had spent itself and was no longer a living force. There were the Ricardian socialists, of course, there were Marx and Rodbertus – and Rossi! But the main stream of English Classical analysis had emancipated itself from this influence. This is a point of view which recently has had some support in other quarters. It is, therefore, perhaps deserving of more thorough examination.

A great deal of the paradox in this position begins to vanish if we are prepared sufficiently to narrow our concept of what the Ricardian position was. Of course, if we interpret this position as chiefly involving a simple assumption of an absolute standard of value, on the lines attacked by Bailey,[1] and the peculiar doctrine regarding the relation between 'wages' and 'profits' (i.e. proportionate wages and proportionate profits) which from that day to this have been such a stumbling block to correct interpretation, it is perhaps just to say that it died with James Mill – with De Quincey's *Logic* as a very belated posthumous progeny – and we can even bring ourselves to stomach the astonishing proposition that J. S. Mill was not really Ricardian (p. 529).

But this surely is an intolerable restriction. A juster definition, I suggest, would leave the influence of Ricardo over a very wide field quite dominant throughout the whole of the Classical period. It was a stroke of expository genius, on Schumpeter's part, to make Senior's fundamental propositions the peg on which to hang his central analysis of the Classical position. But how much of Senior's work would have seen the light in the form in which it did, were it not for the influence and example of Ricardo? It is true that at many points Senior is critical of Ricardo. But where else in his book does Schumpeter restrict the significance of the term 'influence' to slavish reproduction? What is relevant in this connection is not whether the analysis of value and distribution of Senior and J. S. Mill – not to mention money and international

[1] It is more than doubtful whether Ricardo would have pleaded guilty to this indictment.

trade – followed Ricardo in all respects, but whether it conformed to the type of analysis of which his works are the archetype. I cannot help thinking that, once he had released his paradox, Schumpeter would not really have disputed this position. At any rate, by p. 677 we find him arguing, apropos of the theory of rent, that 'so great was Ricardo's success that even some writers who adopted Say's scheme in other respects, inserted into it a Ricardian treatment of rent without betraying any symptom of logical discomfort'.[1]

In this connection I am inclined to suggest that much too much can be made of some of the things said at the celebrated evenings of 13 January and 15 April 1831 at the Political Economy Club, at which the question was debated 'What improvements have been effected in the Science of Political Economy since the publication of Mr Ricardo's great work: and are any of the principles first advanced in that work now acknowledged to be correct?' A recent writer[2] in *Economica* has made the account of the proceedings given in Mallet's diary a reinforcement for a diagnosis of rapid decline of Ricardian economics. In fact, however, Mallet's account is by no means decisive on this point. The general conclusion, at the end of the second meeting, seems to have been that 'Ricardo is a bad and obscure writer, using the same terms in different senses: but that his principles are in the main right'.[3] What is perhaps, however, even more significant and what has apparently escaped Dr Meek's attention is that Torrens, who on this occasion was the ringleader of the anti-Ricardians, subsequently repented of this attitude and published one of the most candid retractions in the history of economic discussion. I do not think that this covered his critique of the Ricardian search for a measure of value: he continued to give praise to Bailey. But it certainly covered the rest. The Introduction to *The Budget* is largely an attempted vindication

---

[1] The writers were Roscher and J. S. Mill.

[2] R. L. Meek, 'The Decline of Ricardian Economics in England', *Economica* (Feb 1950). I should be sorry if this mild disagreement were thought to imply disparagement of Dr Meek's many splendid contributions to the history of economic thought. [Note added in 1969.]

[3] *Centenary Volume of the Political Economy Club* (1921) p. 225.

of Ricardo on profits and a disavowal of earlier strictures on this doctrine and on the theory of rent. 'Some of the commentators on the doctrines of Ricardo appear to have fallen into the misconception that, in altering his nomenclature, and in modifying his principles as varying circumstances required, they refuted his theory of profits. In this censure I include myself.'[1]

I now come to a number of more detailed points. In his discussion of population theory, Schumpeter gives the impression that the law of Diminishing Returns had nothing to do with the original formulation of Malthusian doctrine. This view, of course, has very formidable supporters. No less an authority than Edwin Cannan, who was so seldom wrong on his texts, gave it a classic form in his dictum that 'to imagine that the *Essay on the Principle of Population* was ever based on the law of diminishing returns is to confuse Malthusianism as expounded by J. S. Mill with Malthusianism as expounded by Malthus'.[2] Nevertheless, I do not think that he was right. Admittedly, the mere comparison of geometrical and arithmetical potentialities of increase does not itself necessarily involve this relationship. But the idea underlying the comparison is of the same order of conceptions; and it is surely no mere coincidence that in another connection Malthus was one of the first to formulate the so-called law. This, of course, has been perceived before and, indeed, is clearly the basis of the view which is attacked by Cannan; up to this point, perhaps, the issue might be regarded as undecided. But the textual evidence seems to indicate otherwise. It is true that there is no overt mention of diminishing returns in the *first* edition of the *Essay*. I am not so clear, however, that this can be asserted of the second edition, where, on p. 7, we are told that 'in proportion as cultivation extended, the addition that could yearly be made to the former average produce must be gradually and regularly diminishing'. What, however, seems to me decisive is the language of the *Summary View of the Principle*

[1] *The Budget*, p. xxxvi.
[2] *Theories of Production and Distribution*, 3rd ed. (1917) p. 144. In my youth, in a *Festschrift* for Cannan, I echoed this view very strongly. The curious may consult *London Essays in Economics*, ed. T. E. Gregory and H. Dalton (1927) pp. 104–5.

of Population, the extract from his article in the Supplement to the *Encyclopaedia Britannica* which Malthus issued in 1830:

> It has already been stated, that while land of good quality is in great abundance, the rate at which food might be made to increase would far exceed what is necessary to keep pace with the most rapid increase of population which the laws of nature in relation to human kind permit. But if society were so constituted as to give the fullest scope possible to the progress of cultivation and population, all such lands, and all lands of moderate quality, would soon be occupied; and when the future increase of the supply of food came to depend upon the taking of very poor land into cultivation, and the gradual and laborious improvement of the land already cultivated, the rate of the increase of food would certainly have a greater resemblance to a decreasing geometrical ratio than to an increasing one. The yearly movement of food would, at any rate, have a constant tendency to diminish, and the amount of the increase of each succeeding ten years would probably be less than that of the preceding.[1]

Clearly this is not a very strict formulation. But at least it makes it very difficult to maintain that there was no connection in Malthus's mind between his ratios and diminishing returns to labour applied to land. The good sense of the matter seems to be admirably expressed by Dr McCleary when he says that 'although Malthus did not explicitly base his arithmetical ratio on the law of Diminishing Returns, the concept of diminishing returns was present and influential in his mind'.[2]

I find myself equally unable to agree with Schumpeter upon an important aspect of the Ricardian theory of value. On pp. 600 and 601 he has a long disquisition on Ricardo's perversity in opposing the supply and demand theory for the explanation of long-run values, contending that he was 'completely blind to the nature and the logical place in economic theory of the supply and demand apparatus . . . had he but stopped to ask *why* exchange values of

---

[1] Op. cit., reprinted in D. V. Glass *et al.*, *Introduction to Malthus* (1953) p. 139.

[2] *The Malthusian Population Theory* (1953) p. 111. This excellent essay may be strongly recommended as the sanest study of this highly controversial subject. It is worth observing that Dr McCleary's view has the support of the high authority of Marshall.

commodities would be proportional to the quantities of standard labour embodied in them, he would, in answering this question, have found himself using the supply and demand apparatus by which alone (under appropriate assumptions) that law of value can be established'.

Now there can be no doubt that Ricardo had himself to thank for a great deal of the misunderstanding which has arisen in this connection. To have written a whole chapter *against* the supply and demand theory, without defining more clearly exactly wherein lay the nature of his opposition, was simply asking for trouble. Moreover, it is clear that once we get away from the very peculiar basis of the Ricardian theory, there is a wide sense in which the cost of production which may be opposed to supply and demand as an explanation of normal value, is itself determined by the forces underlying supply and demand for factors and their products; the special theory which side-tracks all this proves to be based on intolerably restrictive assumptions. Nevertheless, the idea that while he accepted supply and demand as determining market values he ignored their operation in the determination of natural values, is a complete mare's nest, despite the very high authority, from Senior onwards, by which it has been supported. This is conclusively shown by the very *Notes on Malthus* to which Schumpeter refers us; the relevant note stands out half a mile:

> Mr Malthus mistakes the question – I do not say that the value of a commodity will always conform to its natural value without an additional supply, but I say that the cost of production regulates the supply and therefore regulates the price.[1]

V

Part IV, 1870–1914 (and later), is in effect a review of modern economic theory since Jevons and, in my judgement, is the best thing in the whole book. These were the developments which were most congenial to Schumpeter's own temperament, and it was

[1] *Notes on Malthus*, in *The Works and Correspondence of David Ricardo*, ed. P. Sraffa, II (Cambridge, 1951) 48–9.

here that his roving eclecticism and the conciliatory side of his character showed themselves to their best advantage. The story is told both in terms of persons and of theorems. The leading personalities are reviewed; some of the sketches here are astonishingly felicitous: for instance, I do not think that Böhm-Bawerk and his contribution have ever been more persuasively depicted. The general character of theoretical developments in different fields is set forth. A special chapter is devoted to elucidating the contents of equilibrium analysis, with the *Éléments* of Walras playing the part here which, in the section on the Classical theorems, was allotted to Senior's four propositions. There are special studies of the evolution of the idea of the production function and the vicissitudes of the theory of utility, and a separate chapter on money and cycle theory. If any enquirer wishes for a unified account of what modern theory (not merely to 1914 but, as the title says in brackets, 'and later') has been about, it is here for him to read.

Perhaps the most admirable feature of all this is its cumulative demonstration of the underlying unity, amid apparent diversity, of all this speculative activity. Schumpeter excelled at this. It was his real conviction, as I think he once said, that there are fundamentally no schools nowadays, but only good economists and bad economists, and he brings this out with extraordinary sympathy and force in regard to the work of this period. Perhaps from time to time this is overdone. There was, for instance, more at issue in the controversy about real costs than Schumpeter is willing to concede – though I should be perfectly prepared to agree, and indeed to argue, that it can chiefly be resolved into a question of appropriate approximation.[1] Again, the undeniable hostility of the Lausanne School to any form of partial equilibrium analysis, however safeguarded and qualified, was a very real barrier between members of that group and their colleagues elsewhere; and their intransigence in that respect, I should say, quite as much as the blameworthy indifference of the outside world, was one of the

[1] See section II (*b*) (ii) of the paper on 'The Evolution of Modern Economic Theory' above, pp. 17–18.

chief reasons why the good side of their work had to wait so long for recognition. But in the main the assertion of a common subject matter and common methods is sound and it is no small service thus so definitely to have distinguished the wood from the trees.

In this general perspective, perhaps the least satisfactory feature is the treatment of Marshall. This is a delicate and difficult matter to elucidate: delicate, since I am fully aware that the main criticisms in this notice may be represented as defences of a local tradition, difficult, since in many respects Schumpeter writes so well about Marshall – how refreshing, for instance, it is to see it clearly recognised that markets peculiar to individual firms are one of the important features of Marshall's analysis.[1] Nevertheless, there are misconceptions and criticisms on which some comment seems to be called for.

Perhaps the best method of approaching the core of discomfort here is by way of examining Schumpeter's contention that Marshall was ungenerous, that he did not pay sufficient tribute to the originators of some of his most fundamental ideas (pp. 838 ff.). It seems to me that there is very little in this. I should not be prepared to contend that Marshall was always an altogether agreeable character; he was obviously a bit of a Turk at home, and his behaviour to Sidgwick on one occasion certainly calls for explanation.[2] But there is really no evidence at all that he did not handsomely acknowledge the debts of which he was conscious. His references to Cournot and von Thünen probably did more than anything else to revive and spread the reputation of these authors, and his solicitude for the position of Ricardo even comes under rebuke from Schumpeter. It is true that he wrote a severe review of Jevons. But there is no reason to doubt his own explanation that he was angered by the treatment of Ricardo and disappointed by the fragmentary nature of the *Theory*. Elsewhere he paid ample tribute to the lively and powerful intelligence of its author.

In this connection it is perhaps worth quoting from a manuscript note of Marshall's which is reproduced in the *Memorials*; it gives

[1] See the detailed references quoted above, p. 30.
[2] See A. S. and E. M. S., *Henry Sidgwick: A Memoir* (1906) pp. 394–6.

a more vivid account of a state of mind than any amount of second-hand conjecture:

> I looked with great excitement for Jevons' Theory, but he gave me no help in my difficulties and I was vexed. I have since learned to estimate him better. His many-sidedness, his power of combining statistical with mathematical investigations, his ever fresh honest sparkling individuality and suggestiveness impressed me gradually and I reverence him now as among the greatest of economists. But even now I think that the central argument of his theory stands on a lower plane than the work of Cournot and von Thünen. . . . My youthful loyalty to him [Ricardo] boiled over when I read Jevons' *Theory*. . . . I have a vivid memory of the angry phrases which would force themselves into my draft, only to be cut out and then reappear in another form a little later on, and then to be cut out again.[1]

This is not the utterance of an ungenerous spirit.

A similar quotation may serve to indicate his position regarding Dupuit, another victim of neglect according to Schumpeter:

> The notion of an exact measurement of Consumer's Rent was published by Dupuit in 1844. But his work was forgotten; and the first to publish a clear analysis of the relation of total to marginal (or final) utility was Jevons in 1871, when he had not read Dupuit. The notion of Consumer's Rent was suggested to the present writer by a study of the mathematical aspects of demand and utility under the influence of Cournot, von Thünen and Bentham.[2]

This surely is complete enough recognition. Schumpeter speaks of 'footnotes in the wrong place' (p. 840). But this footnote is just where it should be – after the exposition of the doctrine of Consumer's Surplus in the text. He might have asked with greater cogency why it was omitted in later editions. But the charitable solution here would rest upon Marshall's conceptions of the exigencies of a textbook in popular use; and when one thinks of the way in which Marshall consistently underplayed his own originality, seeking to present the most path-breaking constructions as notions assumed implicitly by the masters of the past, it is reasonable to assume that he did not attach overwhelming importance to the

[1] *Memorials of Alfred Marshall*, ed. A. C. Pigou (1925) p. 99.
[2] *Principles*, 2nd ed. (1891) p. 184.

C

acknowledgement on all possible occasions of all possible patents.

There remains the question of his attitude to Walras, to whom reference in the text of the *Principles* is very sparse and that not at all on the main Walrasian contributions. Here we reach considerations much more important than scientific etiquette and the presence or absence of a magnanimous disposition. We have to consider the nature of the respective contributions of the men concerned and Marshall's probable attitude towards that of Walras.

Now there can be no doubt whatever, as Schumpeter himself acknowledges, that Marshall was fully seized of the conceptions of general equilibrium. The attempt, sometimes made by members of the Lausanne School, to oppose a suppositous Marshallian partial equilibrium system to a Walras-cum-Pareto general equilibrium system just will not bear examination. The opening chapters of Book VI 'Preliminary Survey of Distribution' together with the famous Note XIV in the Mathematical Appendix are essentially the presentation of an approach as ambitious in its scope and vision as anything presented by Walras, although much more concise in expression. The idea that there can have been anything particularly novel to Marshall in the Walrasian equations is not at all plausible. He certainly knew about utility theory and, as we have seen, he had acknowledged his sources – which were not Walrasian. The influence of demand on the pricing of productive services, explained in terms of the net product and marginal product principles, was a central feature of his own system. Explanation of interest, and hence capitalisation, in terms of the productiveness of permanent capital instruments and the discount on the future restraining their supply, was equally prominent in his thought; and the filling out of this statical theory by a cash-balance approach to the theory of money had figured prominently in his evidence to the Gold and Silver Commission – some time before Walras had fitted it into his own system. Charged with neglect of the Walrasian contributions, I am sure that Marshall would have defended himself in this manner.

But if asked why nevertheless he did not make more specific reference to their treatment by Walras, I am inclined to think that he would have moved to the offensive. He did not make more specific reference to the Walrasian treatment of these problems, he would have said, because that treatment was on lines with which he was very much out of sympathy. This lack of sympathy arose for a variety of reasons.

First, there was no obvious practical use in this way of setting things forth. 'Professor Edgeworth's plan of representing U and V as general functions of x and y', he said in relation to a different but not dissimilar problem, 'has great attractions to the mathematician; but it seems less adapted to express the every-day facts of economic life than that of regarding, as Jevons did, the marginal utilities of apples as functions of x simply.'[1] Marshall, who wanted to use his theory of demand for statistical applications, would tend to be impatient with the complications of the Walrasian functions, and probably felt that, in the first approximation at least, for suitably chosen commodities, they could be neglected.

But, secondly, there was a deeper reason which he himself has set forth very explicitly. On his view the important problems of theory were not problems of describing stationary equilibrium – which was altogether too easy – but rather problems of describing change and development. And while, doubtless, here the statical method was appropriate enough, nay, even indispensable, mathematical methods of presentation tended to become intolerably complex and – what is more to the point – to emphasise the wrong factors. 'It would be possible', he said – obviously with Walras and others of that school in mind, but, with characteristic reticence, omitting derogatory explicitness –

> to extend the scope of such systems of equation . . . and to increase their detail, until they embraced within themselves the whole of the demand side of distribution. But while a mathematical illustration of the mode of action of a definite set of causes may be complete in itself, and strictly accurate within its clearly defined limits, it is otherwise with any attempt to grasp the whole of a complex problem of real life, or even any considerable part of it, in a series of equations. For many important influences, *especially those connected with the manifold influences of the element of time* [my italics], do not lend themselves easily

[1] *Principles*, 8th ed. (1920) p. 845.

to mathematical expression: they must either be omitted altogether, or clipped and pruned till they resemble the conventional birds and animals of decorative art. And hence arises a tendency towards assigning wrong proportions to economic forces: those elements being most emphasised which lend themselves most easily to analytical methods.[1]

He goes on to say that nevertheless 'in discussions written specially for mathematical readers it is no doubt right to be very bold in the search for wide generalisations'. But the general disinclination is writ large – and with Marshall it cannot be ascribed to any lack of aptitude for this kind of analysis.

I am not here concerned to defend this attitude. I am concerned only to explain it. I think myself that it was a great handicap for those of us who had to learn our economics from Marshall's *Principles* that he left so much unstated in the way of statical foundations. We have had laboriously to rediscover for ourselves theorems and implications with which he was completely familiar all the time; and this has taken up too large a part of our lives. In this respect at least his passion always to be intelligible to businessmen and practically helpful to the world at large has been a hindrance rather than a help. But I do think that, whether he was right or wrong in this respect, the underlying attitude which I have tried to make explicit provides quite a sufficient explanation for the absence of much reference to the Walrasian system. He felt no personal debt in respect of those propositions of Walras with which he was in harmony; and for the rest I suspect that he definitely felt that the emphasis was either superfluous or in the wrong direction. The hypothesis of lack of generosity or of a desire – Schumpeter actually goes out of his way to suggest this – to 'uphold the national tradition' against the wretched foreigners (p. 840), seems quite uncalled for.

What I think is perhaps even more surprising is Schumpeter's failure here to perceive more clearly the true nature of Marshall's contribution. In estimating the relative merits of Walras and Marshall – it was he who started this hare, not the reviewer – it is

---

[1] *Principles*, 8th ed. (1920) p. 850.

not enough to compare their achievements and priorities in the analysis of stationary systems. On this plane, perhaps, there is not much between them; as we have seen there is no doubt that Marshall had all the main theorems and some of the priorities. The point is rather that Marshall did so much more. The characteristic features of the Marshallian system, the analysis of the time element, the doctrine of short and long period normal price, quasi-rents, the dynamic theory of money and credit, the study of growth and decline, are all in a sphere which begins, so to speak, where the Walrasian system tends to leave off. Marshall himself protested against the notion that the central idea of the *Principles* was statical;[1] his claim was that it was 'concerned throughout with the forces that cause movement', and that 'its keynote' was 'that of dynamics, rather than statics'; and this claim was surely justified.

It might have been thought that this was a feature which would have made special appeal to Schumpeter, whose own central contribution had been so much in the theory of development; and there are passages, notably where he deals with Marshall's theory of monopoly, where such an attitude emerges. But on more fundamental conceptions there was, of course, a very deep cleavage. It is not true, as Schumpeter seems at one place to suggest, that Marshall attached no significance to the innovating function of entrepreneurship (pp. 892–3): quite the contrary indeed. Book VI and the historical sections, both of the *Principles* and of *Industry and Trade*, pay great attention to such factors. But viewing things in the large and not abstracting from the facts of fluctuation, he was inclined to emphasise the continuity of things – *Natura non facit saltum* was the motto of the *Principles* – whereas we know that Schumpeter's conception of the world involved much more of discontinuity and seismic convulsions.

VI

Part V, which is supposed to deal with the most recent developments, is a mere fragment – a series of first drafts which doubtless

[1] *Ibid.*, p. xix.

would have been completely remodelled had their author lived to finish them. Indeed, if the aesthetic unity of the book were the criterion, I should say that their inclusion was a mistake; though as a series of indications of the trends of Schumpeter's thought they were possibly worth preserving. The Introduction consists largely of the syllabus of a rather elementary course delivered at Mexico City. Chapter 2, 'Developments Stemming from the Marshall–Wicksell Apparatus', breaks off almost before it has begun. Chapter 3 on 'Economics in the "Totalitarian" Countries' seems almost pointless for the little it manages to scrape together; and Chapter 4, if it were intended to make very high claims for the progress of dynamics and business-cycle research, falls considerably short of achieving its object. This is especially true of the short section on econometrics; after all that has been said earlier in the book about the prospect of placing economics on a more exact basis by research of this type, this jejune report has a distinct effect of anticlimax.

The only chapter which has any pretensions to move on the same level as the rest of the book is Chapter 5 on 'Keynes and Modern Macroeconomics'. This chapter is as interesting for its overtones as for its explicit content. It is clear that the spectacle of much contemporary Keynesianism inspired in Schumpeter a distaste that must have been almost physical. It is clear too that he was profoundly shocked by Keynes's occasional indifference to scholarly considerations, his eccentric and frequently unjust judgements of his predecessors, and his obvious ignorance – or forgetfulness – of much earlier work that was very relevant to his subject – deficiencies which, indeed, are inexcusable in smaller fry but which somehow or other do not seem to matter so much with him. His reaction to the man himself, too, was very ambivalent; there seems to have been something in Keynes that alternately attracted and repelled him. But in this chapter he has made a great effort to be fair. The influence of Keynes is acknowledged, his stimulating effect on thought, especially the thought of the young, is conscientiously emphasised. A handsome tribute is paid to his qualities as economic adviser. And while the assumptions of his theory are set out in a form in which an obvious light is thrown on its limitations, I do not think that any point that is made in this connection is unfair or invalid. Certainly the conclusion that the Keynesian paradoxes hold chiefly in a state of deep underemployment, and that when the appropriate corrections are made for conditions of fuller employment, the theory becomes much more 'Classical' in general content and implication, is one which would almost certainly have been accepted by Keynes himself – at least in his latest period.

None the less, I doubt if this is a chapter which will satisfy many. It certainly will not satisfy those who hold extreme views on either side: the extreme Keynesians will be content with nothing less than 100 per cent idolatry, the extreme anti-Keynesians with nothing less than excommunication with bell, book and candle. But the satisfaction of more middle views is very doubtful. The thing does not really come to life. There is little to which exception can be taken.[1] The general perspective is not seriously wrong. But it is as though the effort to be fair, the desperate resolution to say nothing that was not just and right, has used up all the author's vitality and penetration. The portrait is not incorrect. But the life has gone. This judgement may be too severe – after all, the chapter is an uncorrected fragment. Nevertheless, I cannot suppress the feeling that however extensive and finished the treatment, it would still have shown the same characteristics.

[1] There is one very bad error of detail on p. 1171, where the outlook of the earlier pages of the *Economic Consequences of the Peace* (1920) is represented as anticipating, at least in regard to England, the author's views on saving – 'the arteriosclerotic economy whose opportunities for rejuvenating venture decline while the old habits formed in times of plentiful opportunity persist'. This is just not true. The outlook here is exactly the contrary – the war has shaken the institutions which fostered a high rate of saving, it has 'disclosed the possibility of consumption to all and the vanity of abstinence to many' (p. 22), the consequences for the future of capitalism may be disastrous. If anyone doubts this version, he may be referred to the following pronouncement from a *Manchester Guardian Reconstruction Supplement* (17 Aug 1922), written only shortly after: 'In order to keep our heads above water, the national capital must grow as fast as the national labour supply which means new savings at the rate of £400,000,000 to £500,000,000 per annum.'

VII

But I must not end on a note which might suggest any subtraction from the high praise of this book as a general performance which I gave at the beginning of this review.

The last time I met Schumpeter was on a river picnic in the middle thirties. He had turned up unexpectedly from the United States on the day of our annual seminar outing at the School; and he was immediately co-opted as an honorary member, so to speak, and pressed into joining the excursion. It was a lovely day in June; and, as we glided down the Thames between Twickenham and Datchet, I can still see him, cheerfully ensconced in the prow of our ship, surrounded by the eager spirits of the day, Nicky Kaldor, Abba Lerner, Victor Edelberg, Ursula Hicks – Webb, as she then was, the master-organiser of the party – the four fingers and thumb of each hand pressed against those of the other, discoursing with urbanity and wit on theorems and personalities. So I conceive of this book, a splendid excursion down the river of time, with good talk and magnificent vistas.

3

Bentham in the Twentieth Century[1]

I

MAY I begin by saying with what a sense of honour and pleasure I received your invitation to speak at this assembly. It is just forty-nine years since my father, anxious to give me the taste of a university education before being engulfed in the First World War, brought me to be interviewed – and admitted, age sixteen – by Gregory Foster, then Provost of this college; and although my stay here was a very short one, I never walk into this building without a feeling of nostalgia for the lectures where I first heard the great scholars of those days discoursing on the problems of history and literature at a grown-up level.

In recent years, perhaps, my most intimate relation with the work of this college has been in connection with the fine project, initiated by some of your number, at last to publish a proper edition of the works of Jeremy Bentham, that great thinker, who, if not actually a founder of this college, was the inspiration of many who were, whose manuscripts are deposited in your library and whose skeleton is still preserved in a cabinet in one of your main arcades. It was, therefore, natural that, searching for a suitable subject for my address, it should occur to me to take Bentham for a theme; and this I have decided to do. I do not propose, however, to expatiate at any length on his life and his influence, for that was the subject years ago here of an unforgettable oration by my old teacher, Graham Wallas.[2] Nor do I propose to discuss systematically the content of his works and their editions, for that is a

---

[1] An Address to the Assembly of Faculties, University College, London, 16 June 1964. Reproduced by courtesy of University College, London.

[2] Delivered 1923, reprinted in Wallas, *Men and Ideas* (1940) pp. 19–32.

specialised and somewhat esoteric topic, unsuitable for such an occasion as this. My intention rather is to discuss him in relation to the problems of this century. There can be no doubt that the edition which is projected will be one of the outstanding scholarly monuments of the century. The question I should like to ask is to what extent it will be only that, to what extent have Bentham and Benthamism still a bearing on problems of the present day.

II

But first of all let me make plain the conception from which I start of Bentham's actual role and achievement in history. In many academic circles, even at the present day, Bentham is mainly conceived as a moral philosopher: refutations of his particular version of Utilitarian ethics have long been the stock in trade of the sterile and pretentious. Now I shall have a good deal to say about the greatest happiness principle later on. But, for the moment, let me say that to regard the first few chapters of the *Principles of Morals and Legislation* as Bentham's chief legacy is to get the perspective all wrong. From my point of view, Bentham's position in history – his unassailable position – is that of a great law reformer and a great inventor of constitutional and administrative devices.[1] If you like to use the term in the loose way in which it has established itself in the academic terminology of the Anglo-Saxon world, he was a political scientist – and if we have regard to the way in which he spent his life and the magnitude of his achievements, he may well be regarded as the first and the greatest of the full-time practitioners of that discipline. Many famous philosophers, many lesser pamphleteers and essayists, have discussed the great questions of the law and its sanctions and the desirable forms and practices of government. But who has discussed them with such system and comprehensive range or with

[1] A comprehensive survey of Bentham's achievements in this respect is to be found in W. S. Holdsworth, *History of English Law*, XIII (1952) 41-134.

such a professional attention to detail? I do not know any – either before or since.

We can form some idea of the extent of this achievement if we list some of the main changes and innovations in the law and the political and administrative structure which can be traced to his influence. Thus, in the sphere of law, he is to be given the main credit for those reforms which in the course of the nineteenth century transformed the whole apparatus of judical procedure. It was to him and Romilly that we owe the mitigation of the horrors of the criminal law; and it was largely due to his influence that imprisonment for debt was abolished. He was one of the leaders of the movement which led to the reform of Parliamentary representation in the successive Reform Acts of the nineteenth century; and the institution of a Civil Service, recruited by examination and not by influence, was definitely his invention. If you will look at the contents table of the *Constitutional Code* – I do not ask you to read the text until it has been clarified by the labours of Professor Everett and Dr Burns – you will find indicated in a work written, please note, in the twenties of the last century, plans and suggestions for all sorts of institutions and practices only realised in our own times – a health ministry, a ministry for interior communications, an education minister, a register of births and deaths, a central statistical office, a meteorological office ... if I were to name them all I should use up too much of my time. If Bentham's views on moral philosophy were completely wrong – which, as you will see, I am not at all suggesting – still, who could doubt, in the face of such a record, his eminence as a reformer and an inventor?

III

But, as I said at the beginning, my object this afternoon is not to praise his past achievement, but rather to ask to what extent in our own speculations on contemporary and future problems there is guidance or stimulus in his works. For this purpose I propose to examine briefly first his views on certain issues which are still outstanding and then his general position in regard to political and legislative action.

To begin then with particular issues: let me take first the question of individualism versus collectivism. Now I hope the day is past when Bentham can be pilloried – as Keynes pilloried him – as standing for extreme individualism in the shape of a purely *laissez-faire* conception,[1] in the mode of Bastiat or Herbert Spencer, of the economic functions of the state. You have only to think of the contents table of the *Constitutional Code*, which I have already cited, to see the absurdity of that. But equally, I suggest, to represent Bentham, as some have tended to do, as actually or incipiently a complete collectivist in, shall we say, the Fabian sense of the term, with the ideal of the state owning all productive capital and regulating all economic activity, would be a travesty of the truth. The fact is that Bentham's conception of the division of function between state and private activity in the economic sphere was essentially one of leaving to the individual and groups of individuals all that area in which individual or group initiative can be made to harmonise with the public good, and assigning to the state all those functions where individual or group action is plainly insufficient and where only central regulation or initiative can be effective. In this respect, therefore, his general attitude is very similar to that of more recent representatives of the Classical liberal position, such as Marshall and Keynes himself. But in regard to the more specific question as to what, in present circumstances, this implies for the specific functions of the state, it is not possible to be at all confident. I can conceive him as acquiescing in, or even positively recommending, state control, or even perhaps ownership, of the so-called public utility undertakings – undertakings involving in some way or another extensive use of long continuous strips of land, electricity, gas, telephones, and so on: I do not conceive him as being in anything but strong opposition to such an organisation of the typical manufacturing or extractive industry. But all this is pure conjecture. Similarly, since he was

[1] See p. 21 of *The End of Laissez-Faire* (1926) – not, in my judgement, one of the author's more enlightening or historically accurate productions.

always distinctly heterodox in matters of money and finance, I should not find it difficult to think of him entering with relish into the devising of instruments for the control of the aggregate system of income and expenditure. But in all this I should be moving chiefly in the rather unprofitable sphere of imaginative projection. On individualism and collectivism, therefore, I think it may be said that his general mode of approach is still sympathetic, but that on more specific issues it has ceased to provide new inspiration.

If we now turn to the ultimate problems of government, I confess that I find little that is either helpful or relevant to the more urgent problems of the day. It is true that, on the whole, the Western world has evolved in the directions which Bentham recommended. He would not have approved of the extension of the suffrage to illiterates, but, unlike James Mill, he would have had no objection to the inclusion of women – rather the contrary indeed. And the tendency, outside the United States, for legislatures to become, in effect if not in form, unicameral conforms, of course, to his most emphatic recommendations. Now, needless to say, I do not oppose this general trend of evolution: one may find it difficult to be very enthusiastic about democracy up to date, but the practicable alternatives are even less attractive. Yet I find little that is stimulating or perceptive in the arguments by which Bentham recommends it. Caught up in the ardours and endurances of the movement for Parliamentary reform with which one can fully sympathise, he seems to have regarded his recommendations as final solutions rather than remedies for specific abuses. There is nothing that I can find in the writings of Bentham or his contemporaries which shows the least awareness of what we should regard as the dominant problems of democracy, its indifference to the position of minorities, its dependence on party organisation and the frequent tendency of party government to lead to deadlock and its own overthrow. Some of these dangers were indeed perceived by John Stuart Mill, who feared them and strove to find ways of defeating them. But for Bentham and James Mill they hardly existed; and for that reason we must find their somewhat cock-sure pronouncements in this field not only mostly irrelevant to present problems but also a trifle antipathetic.

The position is different again if we turn to the great questions of the relations between states and international peace. Here we must surely find highly sympathetic Bentham's passionate arguments against aggressive war and against false notions of the benefits of colonial possessions. We must also give him full credit for his insistence on the importance of international law – incidentally, the term is of his invention – and his plea for an international court for the decision of differences between nations. There is something which touches close to the heartstrings of 1964 when we read his question, written, according to Bowring, somewhere between 1786 and 1789, 'Why should not the European fraternity subsist as well as the German Diet or the Swiss League?' He has even a hint of an international force to enforce the decrees of his court.

But it would be going too far to claim much more insight for Bentham in this respect than such as was dictated by the general humanitarian principles of his moral code and of his age. His plea for the emancipation of colonies strikes a sympathetic chord. But the detailed argument, although abounding in good sense, scarcely rises to the complexities of the subject: if there were absolutely nothing intellectually valid in the desire for large areas within which there is no fear of separatist restriction, the problems of the last three centuries would have been much simpler.[1] Moreover, although he may rightly be claimed as one of the foremost of those who have seen the need for international government, and even, as we have just seen, a European Diet, there is little in his work which recognises the fissiparous influences of democratic nationalism and the extraordinary difficulties of maintaining peace in a world of communities and races at vastly different stages of education, wealth and social habit. The reader of Bentham's *Plan for an Universal and Perpetual Peace* may thrill to its vision and applaud its contemptuous dismissal of superstition and prejudice. But he will not find here the solution to many modern difficulties.

[1] See my *Economic Causes of War* (1939) pp. 88–98.

I have now touched on Benthamism in relation to three sets of problems which are still actual; and the conclusion which emerges, I suggest, is that although he is nearly always stimulating, as is usually true of the great minds of the past, and although in many respects – though not all – his vision brings him nearer to our times than that of most of his contemporaries, yet, if it is a matter of precise recommendation of the kind which was so fertile and influential in regard to the reforms with which his name is historically connected, there is comparatively little that he has to contribute to the solution of present-day problems. But is that all? I answer no. For although, by reason of the lapse of time and the change of circumstance, many of his specific recommendations, even if they have not actually been adopted, have lost their edge or their appropriateness, there remain what I would claim to be Bentham's chief contributions – a method and a working rule which are still supremely relevant and which in my judgement are likely to retain a lasting value, however much circumstances change. It is to the examination of these contributions – the method and the working rule – that I wish to devote the second part of these observations.

IV

I cannot better describe the method than by using the words of John Stuart Mill in the famous essay on Bentham. 'Bentham's method', he said, 'may shortly be described as the method of detail; of treating wholes by separating them into their parts, abstractions by resolving them into Things – classes and generalities by distinguishing them into the individuals of which they are made up; and breaking every question into pieces before attempting to solve it.'[1] Now doubtless this is one of the main ways in which all knowledge has been advanced and in that sense it cannot be said to have been original. But Bentham was the first to apply it on a large scale to problems of law and administration and in that context it was therefore a revolution; and if you think of the terms in which political discussion is normally carried on, even at

[1] *Dissertations and Discussions*, 3rd ed. (1875) 1 339–40.

the present day – the clichés, the catchwords, the empty generalities – it must be admitted that it was a revolution which has not yet fully informed our habits. It is perhaps worth adding that, with this method in view, it was no accident that Bentham was one of the first to insist on the importance of what he called the statistical function, the collection of information making it possible to put the objects of discussion into some sort of quantitative perspective. We have gone a long way with this method since Bentham's time. But we are still a long way from exhausting the use that can be made of it, which may be well exemplified by reference to Professor Moser's path-breaking investigations of the so-called pool of ability problem – investigations which, if I may say so, have placed the discussion of the whole problem of higher education on a completely new footing.

Such was the Benthamite method – a relatively non-contentious business – but what of the working rule, the greatest happiness principle? Here we touch on something which is still acutely controversial. We have all heard *ad nauseam* of the deficiencies of this principle: its failure to distinguish between qualities of happiness; the difficulties of aggregating the happiness of different individuals; the fact that, as Sidgwick perceived and brought out with such clarity, the alleged obligation to seek the happiness of the greatest number rather than of oneself, or of a restricted group, itself rests upon just that kind of moral intuition which in other contexts Bentham did so much to bring into disrepute. And so on. How many second-rate persons and psychopathological major prophets have established reputations for superior sensibility by dwelling on these difficulties?

Nevertheless, if we consider it, not as the ultimate solution to all problems of ethics and valuation, as Bentham in the ardour of his invention was sometimes apt to claim, but rather as a working rule by which to judge legislative and administrative projects affecting large masses of people, it still seems to me to be better, more sensible, more humane, more agreeable to the moral conscience if you like, than any other I can think of. I am sceptical of attempts at quantification. I do not believe that the Utilitarian rules are necessarily the most useful or practical guides on matters of private conduct. But I submit that there is no more salutary thing for a legislator or an administrator to do than continually to be submitting his possible actions to the test they pose: how will this affect the happiness, positive or negative, of the different members of the present and future community; where, on balance, does it stand on this criterion?

And that, on my reading, is what Bentham actually did. In spite of certain memorable, but not very convincing, passages at the beginning of the *Principles of Morals and Legislation* and some very peculiar passages, whose exact place in his *œuvre* has yet to be identified, in the *Deontology*, the actual use made of the greatest happiness principle in the main body of his work is precisely this, a working rule by which to judge generally applicable laws and procedures. Bentham knew perfectly well the logical limits of his procedure – in one of his manuscripts he goes out of his way to describe inter-personal aggregation as an essentially necessary *convention*[1] – it is only later in the century, in the works of some of the mathematical economists, that the Utilitarian calculus seems to be making claims which are repugnant to good sense. And in spite of an occasional resort to fanciful phrases suggesting quantification, it will be found that, in the main, in his work, the greatest happiness principle is used simply as an instrument to make sure that, in making recommendation for action, *all* the effects on *all* the different sets of people liable to be affected are given due consideration. It is as a working rule rather than as an ultimate moral norm that the greatest happiness principle finds its justification. And to me, at any rate, it carries at least this degree of final authority, that, if it is rejected, the onus of proof must rest always on the other side.

Now conceived in this way, we can regard the Benthamite outlook as something which definitely transcends its historical origin and achievement. To ask of any contemplated law or administrative order, will it, on balance, achieve more happiness

[1] Quoted by E. Halévy, *The Growth of Philosophical Radicalism* (1934) p. 495.

or less pain than the other possibilities, is a habit which, in my
judgement at least, is just as incumbent today as it was at the time
of the publication of the *Principles of Morals and Legislation*; and
it is difficult to conceive of a state of affairs in which it would not
be so. It is in this spirit, therefore, that I will conclude these remarks by attempting, by way of illustration, to depict a Benthamite attitude to certain outstanding problems of the modern age.
I choose my examples in areas where it is possible to be reasonably
certain about the attitude of Bentham himself.

V

Let me take first the problems of penal law. We may be quite sure
that there are still plenty of elements in the laws of this country
in this respect which Bentham would have found defective. He
would have viewed with horror the state of affairs which until the
other day made attempted suicide a crime carrying with it severe
penalties;[1] he would regard certain aspects of the law relating to
sexual abnormalities as smacking of pure barbarism;[2] and, in spite
of his belief in democracy, I am sure that he would have viewed
with some contempt the attitude of ministers who, for fear of
popular criticism, refrain from repealing provisions whose chief
effect is to perpetuate conditions leading to blackmail and often to
self-destruction. But, beyond details of this sort, he would have
preserved a very lively concern with all matters relating to punish-
ment – something which, in itself, as tending to pain, he regarded
as a positive evil. He would have thrown himself with zest into the
developing subject of criminology and the application of statistical
and psychological methods to the study of crime and the deterrents
to crime; and he would have shown deep interest in the develop-

[1] 'They talk against suicide. And yet there is not a text in which it is
prohibited. But how little do Christians care about the commands of
Christianity': *Works*, ed. J. Bowring (1843) x 582.

[2] On this subject, see the paper on 'Offences against Taste', printed
from the original manuscripts as an appendix to C. K. Ogden's edition of
The Theory of Legislation (1931) pp. 476 ff.

ment of therapeutic methods for dealing with young criminals. But he would, I fancy, have shown considerable difference from some who busy themselves with such matters nowadays, in that, *because of his working rule,* he would have been concerned, not only with the welfare of the criminal, but also with the protection of society other than the criminal. 'To prevent an offence,' he said in an important passage,

> it is necessary that the repressive motive must be stronger than the seductive motive. The punishment must be more an object of dread than the offence is an object of desire. An insufficient punishment is a greater evil than an excess of vigour: for an insufficient punishment is an evil wholly thrown away. No good results from it, either to the public, who are exposed to like offences, nor to the offender whom it makes no better. What would be said of a surgeon who, to spare a sick man a degree of pain should leave the cure unfinished? Would it be a piece of enlightened humanity to add to the pains of the disorder the torments of a useless operation?[1]

I take as my second illustration the problems created by the population explosion. As most of you are aware, in our own day, the advance of knowledge in the fields of medicine and civil hygiene has so reduced death rates, especially in the more backward parts of the world, that the population is advancing on a scale never before known in history. In India alone, every five years there is an addition to numbers equal to the entire population of Great Britain; and it is difficult to overestimate the difficulties which are already resulting. I say without any fear of reasonable contradiction that, next to the danger of nuclear warfare, it is the population explosion which is the chief menace to human happiness on this planet. Even if it does not provoke wars and mutual destruction, it bids fair to absorb, and more than to absorb, the full product of future accumulation and technical progress, and to frustrate for generations, if not for ever, the prospects of that deliverance from poverty which otherwise it is within man's ingenuity to achieve.

Confronted with such a menace, the reaction of anyone inspired

[1] J. Bentham, *The Theory of Legislation* (Hildreth's translation), ed. C. K. Ogden (1931) p. 325.

by Benthamite principles is unequivocally determined. As Professor Jacob Viner has pointed out,[1] there is strong evidence, in fact, that even before Francis Place and the Mills, Bentham himself had realised the relevance to human welfare of the possibility of the control of conception. Can there be any doubt that, with the probability, the virtual certainty, of the demographic catastrophes looming ahead, he would have lent all his argumentative and persuasive powers to hasten the widespread adoption of deliberate contraception? He would have regarded it as a moral duty to facilitate the knowledge of such methods; and he would have deemed it, as I do, a discredit to any religion or creed that there should be found among its priests and high dignitaries those who would withhold from suffering humanity the means of preventing the misery and disasters with which it is threatened.

Hence, when I pass the cabinet in your arcade in which Bentham's remains are preserved, or when, on festive occasions, he is wheeled into the company, I think of him, not only as a great historic figure to whom we owe so many of our liberties and better constitutional arrangements, but also as one whose methods and working rule still have the profoundest importance for human happiness – an inspiring example of the type invoked by the Pities in the great opening chorus of Thomas Hardy's *Dynasts*:

> those of kindlier build,
> In fair Compassions skilled,
> Men of deep art in life-development.

I hope that the men and women of this college may long be imbued by the humble, rational, humanitarian spirit of this great man and that they may never cease to regard the greatest happiness of the greatest number as a worth-while objective of social policy.

[1] Jacob Viner, *The Long View and the Short* (Glencoe, Ill., 1958) p. 308. Professor Viner's reference is to an early work by Bentham entitled *The Situation and Relief of the Poor*, first published in 1897 in Arthur Young's *Annals of Agriculture*, reprinted the same year as a pamphlet and reproduced in Bowring's edition of Bentham's *Works*, VIII 367.

4

Malthus in Perspective[1]

MAY I begin by congratulating our ex-President on the content and the manner of his address. As I sat listening to it, I could not help thinking of the pleasure it would have given to Malthus himself, whose bicentenary we meet to commemorate. I am sure that he would have heard it with both interest and gratification: with interest because, as we know, he had an endless curiosity to discover how the broad tendencies in population growth which he detected actually worked themselves out in practice – and Mauritius is a most piquant example; with gratification because he could not but feel that, whatever the failure of fact to conform to his gloomier predictions in the decades immediately following the publication of his essay, recent developments – the developments to which Professor Meade has been drawing our attention – were abundant justification for his diagnosis.

Our purpose this evening is to give public recognition to the bicentenary of Malthus's birth and to express our respect and admiration for one of the most distinguished figures in the earlier history of our subject. I am sure that this is the right thing to do. But it is not altogether easy. It is not so easy to get Malthus into proper perspective as, for instance, it would be with Adam Smith or Ricardo. There can be no doubt at all that he is a great figure in the general history of thought. From the moment of its publication, his famous essay had an immediate impact on public opinion; and from then to now it has never ceased to agitate the waters. It has provoked endless attempts at refutation. It has been a most powerful stimulus to thought in the whole field of demography.

[1] Remarks on opening the discussion of Professor Meade's Presidential Address to the Royal Economic Society, reprinted from the *Economic Journal* (June 1967). Reproduced by courtesy of the Royal Economic Society.

Nor has its stimulus been confined to speculation and research in this region. We should never forget that it was the perusal of the *Essay on Population* which set Darwin thinking on the lines which led eventually to the fundamental propositions of the *Origin of Species*.

But the problem today is not to emphasise Malthus's obvious eminence in this broad sense, but rather to pay tribute to him in his role as a Classical economist. And for that purpose we have to ask what were his specific contributions to the subject – not necessarily contributions in the shape of ultimate truth but contributions which were part of the process of building up the system of thought which has come down to us, evolving, as it has come down, since that time. And even today, the answer to this question is a matter likely to arouse much more controversy than the answer to a similar question in the case of the other great Classical economists. Yet I am sure that the contribution was outstanding; and I think that it should be possible to present it in broad outline in comparatively few words.

Let me begin with population theory. We must certainly agree that it was Malthus who really put this on the map. Of course, it is very easy to cite earlier writers, illustrious and obscure, who had perceived the tendency for population to be regulated in some way or other by the availability of subsistence. Some of the contributions to pre-Malthusian population theory are indeed both interesting and profound – it is difficult to think of a more vivid statement of the central core of the matter than Cantillon's dictum that 'men multiply like mice in a barn' when subsistence is available.[1] Nevertheless, it was Malthus who made the main impact on thought. It seems to me to be just silly to deny him the credit for that.

But what of the content of his theory? Surely it is very important. I can understand the case for the view that, in the hundred years after his book was published, events in the Western world at any rate to some extent belied his gloomiest apprehensions: the improvement of agricultural techniques and the opening up of the

[1] *Essai sur la nature du commerce,* ed. H. Higgs (1931) p. 83.

great open spaces of the world deferred the onset of diminishing returns in the historical sense and made it possible for population to advance with an improving standard of living. I can understand further the view that not all his policy recommendations were well conceived: his attitude to the Poor Laws was, to put it mildly, unsubtle; and, as we all know, he rejected the ultimate solution to the population problem, the restraint of numbers by the deliberate control of conception – he does not share the credit due to Bentham and Francis Place in this connection. What I cannot understand is the view that his main emphasis on the danger to human welfare of the unlimited powers of human multiplication was not of the utmost importance. But I will not argue this matter on this occasion. If there were any doubters in this audience, I should hope that the Chairman's address would be sufficient to convince them.

But what of the detail of his argument? At this juncture it is necessary to become a little more technical. It is often said that the famous contrast between the geometrical and arithmetical ratios of increase of population and food respectively was false and misleading and, furthermore, that this argument has nothing to do with the idea of diminishing returns. No less an authority than Edwin Cannan argued in an often quoted dictum that 'to imagine that the *Essay on the Principle of Population* was ever based on the law of diminishing returns is to confuse Malthusianism as expounded by J. S. Mill with Malthusianism as expounded by Malthus'.

Both these criticisms seem to me to be radically overdone. Of course, it is easy enough to pick holes in the ratio argument. It is hardly necessary to say that one can choose examples of geometrical rates of increase which proceed at such a snail's pace that the contrast with Malthus's particular arithmetical ratio would appear to be completely without the terrors which he wished to invoke. But this is niggling stuff. Malthus's figures were intended to be illustrative of what he conceived, rightly or wrongly, to be realistic tendencies. And, speaking for myself, I must say that the broad idea behind his contrast still seems to me to be good sense despite the looseness of its formulation.

Furthermore, I confess that I find it singularly difficult to accept the suggestion that there was no perception of the idea of diminishing returns underlying this main argument. After all, in his contribution to the controversy about the Corn Laws later on, Malthus was one of the main promulgators of this conception. Surely it is odd to contend that not the least suspicion of it had crossed his mind at the time when his main population theory was developed.

In fact, you can find traces of the idea, even in the second edition of his essay, where on p. 7 we are told that 'in proportion as cultivation extended, the addition that could yearly be made to the former average produce must be gradually and regularly diminishing'. And in the *Summary Review of the Principle of Population*, the reprint of his article in the supplement to the *Encyclopaedia Britannica*, which Malthus wrote comparatively late in his career, we find a passage in which the conjunction of the principle of population with the idea of diminishing returns, although not very strictly put, is, in my judgement, unmistakable.[1] It is true that it is not a very rigorous formulation. But at least it makes it very difficult to maintain that there was no connection in Malthus's mind between his ratios and diminishing returns to labour applied to land.

For all these reasons, therefore, I find implausible the view that there is little or no relation between the population theory as propounded by Malthus and the population theory which on contemporary analysis we ourselves should find broadly acceptable.

I find equally implausible the view that none of this had any relevance to the central core of the Classical theory of value and distribution. I know that this view has been expressed by no less an authority than Schumpeter.[2] But, in my judgement, it is quite erroneous. The idea of the tendency of wages to some sort of subsistence level which, although not new, derived enormous force

[1] For a full quotation of the passage in question, see section III of the paper on Schumpeter's *History*, p. 61.

[2] 'Das klassische System bleibe was es ist, wenn man das Bevölkerungsprinzip daraus streichen würde': 'Epochen der Methoden- und Dogmengeschichte', in *Grundriss der Sozialökonomik* (Tübingen, 1925) I. Abteilung, I. Teil, p. 77.

from the Malthusian propositions, was quite fundamental to much of the theory of value and distribution. It was fundamental also to many of the propositions of Ricardo's theory of taxation. I am not saying that this assumption was correct; I should be quite willing to admit that it introduced a false precision into some of the analysis. But, for good or for bad, it was certainly quite central; and to regard it as something quite apart from the main body of Classical analysis – a separate subject, so to speak, in which the Classical economists just happened also to be interested – seems to me to be almost perverse.

Again, still moving in the same context, I should be inclined to claim a fairly central role for Malthus in the development of the theory of rent. I should not be prepared to apologise for all the preliminary small talk: Ricardo certainly made his point when he contended that it was the niggardliness of nature, the scarcity of the more fertile lands, rather than the incidental circumstances which Malthus adduced, which was fundamentally responsible for the emergence of rent. But the explanation of rent as a differential surplus was well put by Malthus; and there is no reason to suppose that his thought in this respect was derivative. Furthermore, as regards the dynamic question of the effect of improvements on rent, there is good reason to argue that Malthus's contention that this need not necessarily be adverse had at least as much good sense in it as Ricardo's insistence that such changes must always be damaging to landlords. There is a well-known appendix by Marshall which makes this abundantly clear.[1]

So much for Malthus's contribution to the central traditions of the theory of value and distribution. It is much more difficult to propound an estimate which would be universally acceptable in regard to his contribution to the maroc-economic part of the subject. This is a matter on which opinion is still considerably divided.

I imagine that we should all agree in according praise to his contribution to the discussion of the Bullion Report and the theory of international monetary relations implied therein. His two articles

[1] *Principles of Economics*, 8th ed. (1920) pp. 833–7.

in the *Edinburgh Review*[1] on this subject seem to me to be exemplary, both in tone and analysis; and his eclecticism in the explanation of disturbing influences on the rate of exchange is surely to be preferred to Ricardo's attempt to reduce everything to a single 'cause' – a relative excess of circulating media. Of course, as we can now see, their differences on this score can easily be explained away in terms of a difference of focus. Malthus was concerned to indicate originating influences, among which a positive issue of excess of circulating media is clearly only one. Ricardo was concerned to show that disequilibrium could only persist if the circulating media were allowed to continue in excess – which, of course, allows the original causes of excess to be either real or monetary. But, of the two approaches, Malthus's surely carries more conviction as an historical narrative – even if Ricardo suggests profounder thoughts concerning the implication of the existence of independent national sources of money supply.

The main difficulties of appraisal arise in regard to his attitude to the problem of aggregate equilibrium. As is well known, Keynes hailed Malthus as a pre-Keynesian, both in the *General Theory* and in his memorable biographical essay.[2] He quotes telling extracts which seem to bear out this interpretation and expresses the view that if only Malthus and not Ricardo had been victor in the controversy, the subsequent evolution of economics would have been much more satisfactory.

The trouble is that, from the analytical point of view, this interpretation is hard to sustain. Malthus's fundamental theory of depression and under-employment is certainly *not* Keynesian. Over-saving for him means over-*investment* – using investment in the Keynesian sense. Depression arises because too much saving gets invested. He goes out of his way to deny the likelihood of hoarding.[3] The idea of savings running to waste in the modern sense does not figure in his central argument. On the basis, there-

[1] Feb and Aug 1811.

[2] See his *Essays in Biography* (1933) pp. 95–149.

[3] Malthus, *Principles of Political Economy* (1820) p. 32. On all this aspect of Malthus, see Dr Bernard Corry's *Money, Saving and Investment in English Economics, 1800–1850* (1962), especially pp. 125–33.

fore, Ricardo had no difficulty in refuting him. Malthus failed to win the theoretical argument because, on this plane, his logic was not convincing. If the will and ability to save are always matched by the will and ability to invest, then there is nothing much wrong with the general position of Say, James Mill and Ricardo.

But, of course, that is not all that there is to say in this connection. On the plane of practical judgement, I have no doubt that Malthus's position is preferable to Ricardo's. His instinct was against the rigidity – or assumed rigidity – of the Law of Markets. He could not believe that it was consonant with fact. He was against the repayment of debt at times of depression. He could not see the point in exhortations to save when the system was underemployed. On this plane, how greatly superior in good sense is his attitude to that of Ricardo, bombinating away in a stratosphere of abstract logic which led him to attribute the post-war depression in part at least to agricultural protection. On this plane therefore it is, perhaps, legitimate to claim him as an anticipator of Keynes, who, as we know, also rebelled against interpretations of economic difficulties in terms of theories which omitted ingredients essential to a reflection of contemporary reality.

I hope I have said enough to vindicate the claim that Malthus is one of the most illustrious of our predecessors. But perhaps I have not said enough to explain the feelings which some of us have for Malthus as a man. For that you must read his correspondence and his recently published *Travel Diary* – so beautifully edited by Mrs James. You must turn to contemporary accounts of his personality and the temper of his mind.[1] If you do that, then, whatever you think of his analysis, I am sure you will echo the sentiments of Ricardo in the last letter of the famous correspondence between the two friends: 'And now, my dear Malthus, I have done. Like other disputants, after much discussion we each retain our own opinion. These discussions, however, never influence our friendship. I should not like you more than I do if you agreed in opinion with me.'

[1] e.g. *A Memoir of Maria Edgeworth*, by the late Mrs Edgeworth (1867) II 151.

5

Torrens's *Letters on Commercial Policy*[1]

ROBERT TORRENS, the author of these letters, was in many ways the most eminent of the minor English Classical economists. He was born in 1780, eight years junior to Ricardo, and he died in 1864, the year also of the death of Senior and McCulloch. Thus he lived through two generations of thought; and he made significant contributions to each. As a young man he was a military officer, decorated for valour on active service. When the wars were over, he settled in London; and for more than forty years he was a leading figure in the journalistic and political life of his time. In the twenties he was a founder of the Political Economy Club, part proprietor of *The Traveller* and *Globe* newspapers, and for a short time a Member of Parliament. In the thirties, after another period of duty in the House of Commons, he became one of the leaders of the colonisation movement and for several years was Chairman of the South Australian Commissioners. In the forties, besides being involved in discussions of commercial policy, of which there will be more to say later, he was prominently associated with the movement for the reform of the charter of the Bank of England which culminated in the Bank Act of 1844. Thenceforward, until late in the fifties, his active pen was devoted to the defence of the Act and to the further propagation of his own particular brands of commercial policy and systematic colonisation. As we shall see, in one very important respect, he came to part company with his fellow economists. But there is no figure in the

[1] This is an Introduction to the 1958 London School of Economics reprint of the letters in question, reproduced by courtesy of the London School of Economics and Political Science. The matters mentioned are treated at much greater length in my *Robert Torrens and the Evolution of Classical Economics* (1958).

history of the first half of the nineteenth century whose work is a more significant reflection of the main movement of economic thought.

Torrens's chief contributions can be divided into two groups, according to the period in which they appeared.

In the first period, as the contemporary of Malthus and Ricardo, he is chiefly to be remembered for having formulated clearly the famous theory of comparative cost in international trade – this independently of Ricardo, and before him in time. But he also played some part in the discussion of the central theories of value and distribution. It was chiefly as a result of his strictures that Ricardo made substantial additions to the first chapter of the second edition of his *Principles of Economics*; and he had a rival solution to the general problem of value.

In the second period, as a senior contemporary of J. S. Mill, McCulloch and Senior, he made important contributions in no less than three distinct fields. In the field of money and banking, together with Overstone, he was leading protagonist of the theories of the so-called Currency School, according to whose doctrines the fundamental *desideratum* of credit control was to produce movements of the total circulation of a mixed system similar to what would have taken place had that circulation consisted wholly of metallic money. In the field of colonisation, together with Gibbon Wakefield, he was an active exponent of the so-called system of self-supporting colonisation, according to which an orderly and self-financing development of virgin territories was to be secured by charging a price for holdings sufficient at once to finance emigration and to prevent dispersion of the emigrants through unrestricted appropriation of free, or very cheap, lands. In the field of commercial policy, having abandoned the cause of unilateral free trade, he became the chief intellectual advocate of the alternative system of reciprocity and a colonial *Zollverein* – an advocacy which involved the development of a theory of the role of demand in international exchange with special reference to the effects of tariffs on the terms of trade.

It is in this last connection that the *Letters on Commercial Policy* here reprinted have their main historical significance. It is commonly believed that this development of Torrens's thought was first sprung on the world in the second and third letters of his famous *Budget* series, published in the autumn of 1841. But, as Torrens himself protested, this was not so. As far back as 1827, in the new section of the fourth edition of the *Essay on the External Corn Trade*, which dealt with 'the Effects of Free Trade on the Value of Money', there were clear hints of his eventual position; and these letters of 1832–3 contain a substantial outline of the main theory. Indeed, as most cursory inspection will show – though I am not aware that it has been noted until just recently – Letter III of *The Budget* consists very largely of extracts from Letters I to V of this earlier series.

The letters were first published at intervals in the *Bolton Chronicle*, Torrens being at the time a candidate for the Bolton constituency. They were subsequently reprinted and published as a booklet in 1833. (The dates of original publication are given at the foot of each letter as thus reprinted.) Half-way through their original publication they were the subject of a vehement attack in the *Westminster Review* from the pen of Perronet Thompson, one of the leaders of the free-trade movement, who was outraged by the tendencies of Torrens's analysis. Letter VII is a reply to these strictures. In Francis Place's copy of the tract[1] there appears this note in Place's handwriting: 'The argument is founded on Gross Fallacy, which having been exposed, the whole of the Edition was sent to *Bolton* and none were sold in *London*.' This is presumably a reference to Perronet Thompson's strictures. But while the extreme rarity of the work may suggest a predominantly local sale, there is no reason whatever to suppose that its author felt convicted of any fallacy, gross or otherwise. Indeed, why should he? Whatever the eventual practical relevance of Torrens's analysis, Perronet Thompson's attack was largely claptrap; and Letter VII is a very adequate rejoinder.

The core of the argument, which is to be found in Letters II and III, consists of a discussion as to whether it is a matter of

[1] Now in the Goldsmiths Library of the University of London.

indifference to buy goods from countries which admit our goods freely or from countries which limit their imports. An elaborate example is developed which purports to show that the switching of demand from Portugal (which is assumed to tax them heavily) means that we have to export more to obtain the means of payment, i.e. that the terms of trade are affected adversely. Duties on commodities other than food and raw materials are said to enable a country to maintain a higher comparative scale of prices than would otherwise be the case and thus to have higher incomes for the purchase of imports. Hence to repeal such duties, without obtaining reciprocal concessions from the other parties concerned, risks a loss of gold and inferior terms of trade. Torrens argues that some at least of the distress of the time was due to the pursuit of just such a policy of unilateral tariff reduction by the Government of the United Kingdom; and the latter part of the tract contains an impassioned plea for the abandonment of this policy and the substitution of a policy of reciprocity.

Here in outline is the characteristic position adopted throughout the better-known *Budget* series. In that series, Letter II to Lord John Russell develops the argument on a plane of greater generality; the effects on comparative prices and incomes of the specific introduction of a tariff are examined with the aid of a more or less abstract model – the famous Cuban example. Later on, in the Supplement to Letter IX to Peel, the demonstration is repeated with a model which involves no specie flows but relies exclusively on the assumption of barter trade. The *Budget* series, moreover, develops at much greater length thoughts which were only in their earlier stages in Torrens's mind at the time of the Bolton letters, the importance of colonisation and commercial arrangements founded thereon as a safeguard for imperial trade against a lack of reciprocity elsewhere: he eventually proposes a colonial *Zollverein*. But if the historian of economic thought is seeking the first systematic exposition of Torrens's beliefs in this connection, it is to these *Letters on Commercial Policy* that he must turn.

On the analytical importance of these propositions, it should be unnecessary to expatiate: the theory of demand thus foreshadowed is the cornerstone of the modern theory of international trade and much beside. Their practical and ideological significance is more difficult to focus. Like some others who have rediscovered this analysis in recent times, Torrens was perhaps apt to exaggerate its importance; the apocalyptic tone of his fulminations against the policy of unilateral free trade for the United Kingdom would be difficult to justify in the light of history. Marshall's discussion, in his classic *Memorandum on the Fiscal Policy of International Trade*,[1] shows a much better sense of perspective. But at least Torrens did two things: he made it intellectually indefensible to argue the case for free trade for particular national areas – as distinct from the world as a whole – as a matter of *a priori* principle rather than of practical expediency and good sense; and, although the general case for a colonial *Zollverein* had long ceased to be realisable before it became popular, he did provide an argument for federal or confederal arrangements precluding customs barriers over wide areas, the force of which still has considerable practical relevance. Indeed, in our own time, the main argument for economic integration can be conceived in terms which we owe to Torrens. It is partly an argument for a wider scope for the territorial division of labour – it is Torrens's term, introduced in an earlier tract – and partly an argument for arrangements under which neither local governments nor national states shall have the power to upset that division by restrictive practices each designed to turn the terms of trade in favour of the particular area imposing them.

The germs of these important conceptions are to be found in these letters.

[1] Reprinted in his *Official Papers* (1926) pp. 365–420.

6

The Life of John Stuart Mill[1]

I

I T is an interesting circumstance that, although he died more than seventy-five years ago, there has been no full-length biography of John Stuart Mill until just recently. Until then the leading works were still the *Autobiography*, published by Helen Taylor immediately after his death in 1873, and Alexander Bain's *John Stuart Mill: a Criticism*, which was published in 1882: the *Life of John Stuart Mill* by W. L. Courtney, published in 1888 in the 'Great Writers Series', is largely based on these and, although not negligible, is of very minor importance. Later on, in the nineties, two important series of letters were published – the letters to d'Eichthal[2] and Comte,[3] and in 1910 Hugh Elliot published a two-volume edition of other correspondence.[4] These added considerably to the volume of Mill's works available. None of them, however, threw much light on the more private side of his life; the papers bearing on this were closely guarded by the family, and although Elliot saw them, he was not permitted to use them. In 1922 and 1927, however, after the death of Mary Taylor, Mill's niece, they were put up to auction and acquired chiefly by Lord Keynes and the libraries of the London School of Economics and Yale. But it was not until much later that they were used extensively. Then, in 1951, Professor Hayek produced his important study of

[1] A review of *The Life of John Stuart Mill*, by Michael St John Packe, with a Preface by Professor F. A. Hayek (London: Secker & Warburg, 1954), *Economica*, XXIV (Aug 1957). Reproduced by courtesy of the London School of Economics and Political Science.

[2] *John Stuart Mill, Correspondance inédite avec Gustave d'Eichthal*, ed. Eugène d'Eichthal (Paris, 1898).

[3] *Lettres inédites de John Stuart Mill à Auguste Comte*, ed. L. Lévy-Bruhl (Paris, 1899).

[4] *The Letters of John Stuart Mill*, ed. Hugh Elliot (1910).

D

the relations between Mill and Harriet Taylor,[1] which was based directly on this material, at the same time marshalling in a masterly manner the relevant information which had accumulated incidentally in other biographical literature. At last, in 1954, Mr St John Packe published the full-length biography which is the subject of this notice.

In his Preface to this imposing volume Professor Hayek remarks 'there may be details to be filled in here and there: but on the whole I feel that Mr Packe has given us the definitive biography of Mill for which we have so long been waiting'.

Coming as they do from one who has done more for our knowledge of Mill's life than anyone else this century, these words are very high praise; and even if we are not willing to go all the way with Professor Hayek, we must certainly note the appearance of an important contribution. Mr Packe has put an enormous amount of work into the book. He has worked through all the extensive material now available. And, inspired by real sympathy for his subject and admiration for the ideals for which Mill stood, he has succeeded in painting a full-length portrait which, whatever our reserves about details and execution, undoubtedly conveys an impression of life and authenticity. As will appear from what follows, I find a good deal in the presentation which jars ever so slightly – it has been consciousness of this quality and difficulty in getting it into a fair perspective which have largely been responsible for the inordinate delay in bringing this review to birth. But it would be ungenerous and, indeed, unjust not to pay tribute to a very considerable achievement made possible only by great industry and devotion.

II

Yet, for me at least, the reserves are quite extensive, and if only because of the very favourable reception which has generally been

[1] F. A. Hayek, *John Stuart Mill and Harriet Taylor: Their Friendship and Subsequent Marriage* (1951).

accorded to this book, I think it is right that they should be made explicit. They fall into three groups.

In the first place, while Mr Packe has displayed towards his main figures a respect and a sympathetic understanding which are all that could be desired, it is to be noted that he has not shown the same attitude to important persons in the background. The general account of the Benthamite circle falls far below the level of the treatment of Mill and Harriet Taylor. It is true that in one place some tribute is rendered to Bentham's eminence as a legal reformer and that elsewhere, doubtless, phrases could be adduced which show some awareness of his importance. But for the most part the references are to quite a different sort of figure, a pseudo-Stracheyesque comic property giving light relief to the background of Mill's early days. Nor does James Mill fare very much better. It is probably true that he was intrinsically unsympathetic – although, as we can see from his correspondence with Ricardo, not nearly so grim outside the family circle as within. But he was one of the most important thinkers of the period and I doubt very much whether in his young days he made the impression of the somewhat circumspect go-getter of Mr Packe's early pages. Grote, the most eminent Greek historian in this country at that period, takes his place in the clowns' gallery, as being 'sentenced' as the 'conquered mate' of his wife 'to the plodding lifelong labour of compiling a history of Greece, a work which she felt was needed, and well suited to his patient talents' (p. 68). As for Ricardo, I am very sorry to say that Mr Packe has swallowed all the clever-clever mythology, hook, line and sinker. 'All in all, Ricardo's hero was the capitalist' (p. 38). Dear me!

Secondly, in retailing the various events with which he deals, Mr Packe all too frequently resorts to a method of presentation which makes it very difficult to distinguish fact from fiction. An easy example of what I have here in mind is furnished by the opening sentence of the chapter on the early relations between Mill and Carlyle:

'It is a work of genius, dear,' sighed Jane Carlyle one day in 1831: the Man of Destiny growled ungratefully, stuffed into his pocket the biography of his first thirty-five years of life, and stumped out of the house.

The reference quoted – there is a reference on this occasion – is to Froude, *Carlyle, the First Forty Years* (1882) II 161. Here indeed is the remark that *Sartor Resartus* was a work of genius. But of 'the ungrateful growl', the stuffing of the manuscript into the pocket and the stumping out of the house – not a word. One cannot but ask where did Mr Packe find out?

Such questions come thick and fast when we come to Mr Packe's details of Mill's personal history. In the *Autobiography* the account of the famous mental crisis runs as follows:

> It was in the autumn of 1826. I was in a dull state of nerves, such as everybody is occasionally liable to; unsusceptible to enjoyment or pleasurable excitement; one of those moods when what is pleasure at other times, becomes insipid or indifferent; the state, I should think, in which converts to Methodism usually are, when smitten by their first 'conviction of sin'. In this frame of mind it occurred to me to put the question directly to myself: 'Suppose that all your objects in life were realised; that all the changes in institutions and opinions which you are looking forward to could be completely effected at this very instant: would this be a great joy and happiness to you?' And an irrepressible self-consciousness distinctly answered, 'No!' At this my heart sank within me: the whole foundation on which my life was constructed fell down. All my happiness was to have been found in the continual pursuit of this end. The end had ceased to charm, and how could there ever again be any interest in the means? I seemed to have nothing left to live for.[1]

And now Mr Packe:

> One evening in 1826 just as the year was dying John Mill looked up restlessly from the magic circle of his lamplit books. He was depressed. Away in the country the south wind trumpeted, driving before it close swathes of low damp cloud: the leaves fell sodden and heavy from the sweating trees, and stuck together. He was twenty. He felt old: his mental age already had the timelessness of the Sphinx; but he still did not feel independent, he felt cramped and incomplete. He had been busy enough these last five years, since he first read Bentham, ranting away with brittle zeal about the means of the betterment of the race. He had even felt a faint relish that the betterment

[1] Op. cit., 1st ed. (1873) pp. 133–4.

of the race was not likely to be achieved in his lifetime, at any rate not in any final degree: for that gave him a guarantee of continued enthusiasm, a prospect of perpetual bridges to be forced, on a road bounded by a brightening but ever receding rainbow. He had been taught to seek his own happiness in the betterment of the race. The means of that betterment were never in doubt, they were before him all the time. So axiomatic had they seemed that he had gone on mechanically day by day pursuing them, without questioning that he was happy any more than he questioned that the aims were good. He had not had the time, nor yet, perhaps, the power, to stand outside himself and say, 'Exactly, now, what are you trying to do?'

But now, he was not happy, he was depressed. Some part of his system missed its beat. He got up, looked out of the window: in the London streets steam rose from the shining flanks of cart-horses towards the foggy roofs, and the muffled draymen blew on their chilly hands and shook the reins. The grey was giving way to black, and with the night came the long tunnel of the English winter, and endless darkness, oppressive, cheerless, raw. He drew the curtain.

. . . He was alone.

That did not matter. He was used to that. Loneliness was a necessary symptom of greatness for anyone dedicated to noble aspirations. He turned back to his chair. He pictured again the anodyne, mankind perfected, intelligent, strong and free, and heard in answer to his gull's cry invocation, the insensate roar of the turbulent ocean of humanity. He put the question to himself again, more formally: 'Suppose that all your objects in life were realised: that all the changes in institutions and opinions which you are looking forward to, could be completely effected at this very instant: would this be a great joy and happiness to you?' To this direct question the rebellious fiend inside him which he preferred to call 'an irrepressible self-consciousness', distinctly answered, 'No!'

He was dumbfounded. 'At this my heart sank within me: the whole foundation on which my life was constructed fell down. All my happiness was to have been found in the continual pursuit of this end. The end had ceased to charm, and how could there ever again be any interest in the means? I seemed to have nothing left to live for.' Soberly, he went to bed, to see what a good night's sleep would do (pp. 74, 77).

Now I have not Mr Packe's familiarity with all the documents. He gives no reference for the unfamiliar constructions. But it is conceivable, I suppose, that somewhere there is allusion to the 'shining flanks of cart-horses' and the 'long tunnel of the English winter', etc., just as there may be a passage which justifies the statement elsewhere that 'as the earth went thundering down upon [his wife's] coffin, it seemed to Mill as if he were being crushed' (p. 397). And I know that devices of this sort have been employed by authors who are deservedly respected. But for me the dilemma remains: *either* there is documentary evidence that, as Mill was drawing the curtain, 'steam rose from the shining flanks of the cart-horses' and that 'as he heard the earth thundering, etc., he felt as if he were being crushed – in which case it were better quoted than paraphrased – *or* there is not – in which case, however likely the reconstruction, it is not biography but fiction. Lytton Strachey may have done this sort of thing but Boswell did not. And, for serious biography, I submit, Boswell is the better model.

Thirdly, despite Professor Hayek's commendation, I think it is a deficiency, in any biography of Mill which aspires to be definitive, that there is so comparatively little said of the substance of his contribution to economics and philosophy. Mr Packe may perhaps justly plead that this was no part of his intention – and when we read of Mill's attitude at fifteen that '*within the graphs* (my italics) of Political Economy' (there were no graphs to speak of at that time) 'he saw swarthy, sweaty folk, laughing and loving, suffering and dying all to a tune of music unwritable and unknown' (p. 46) we may feel that this may have been just as well. But despite his love affair and his participation in journalism and politics, the interest of Mill's life is so pre-eminently the interest of an intellectual progress, that a narrative which deals only perfunctorily with the substance of his intellectual contribution, even if superficially it does not appear ill-proportioned, must lack definitive status. That is the ultimate ground for not going all the way with Professor Hayek. It may be agreed that it is most improbable that, in our day at least, anyone will be found who will think it worth while to re-read all the difficult material relating to biographical detail which Mr Packe has investigated. But it remains true that he who wishes to get Mill and his spiritual pilgrimage into full perspective will have to look elsewhere as well – to Bain's terse and manly sketch, to the interesting studies of Professors Anschutz[1] and Britten,[2] to Miss Iris Mueller's excellent recent monograph[3] – and even then the picture will lack completeness. Recollecting the fine scholarship, the deep understanding and the admirable literary restraint of Professor Hayek's own contribution, it is difficult to repress a regret that it was not he who attempted the definitive life as well.

But when all this has been taken into account, let there be no mistake, our debt to Mr Packe must still be very considerable. If he has not achieved a masterpiece without blemish, he has at least produced an interesting and valuable book. It is certainly safe to say that in future no one who wishes to write seriously about Mill can afford to neglect what he has done.

III

Mr Packe's book abounds in new information. The collections at Yale, King's College, Cambridge, and the London School of Economics have yielded a rich harvest, which together with gatherings from other biographies published since Mill's death, put us in possession of what may well be felt to be more or less continuous knowledge of the main events of his life. Only the details of his career as an administrator remain comparatively obscure. I suspect that a scholar with the right combination of Indian history and political economy at his disposal could write a very instructive monograph on the Mills at the East India Company. Apart from this there does not seem much left to be investigated.

Of all this new information much the most important is that

---

[1] R. P. Anschutz, *The Philosophy of J. S. Mill* (1953).

[2] Karl Britten, *John Stuart Mill* (1953).

[3] Iris Wessel Mueller, *John Stuart Mill and French Thought* (Urbana, Ill.: University of Illinois Press, 1956). Owing doubtless to its publication by an American university press whose books are not sold on a large scale in this country, this work does not seem to have attracted the notice it deserves. It is a most useful and scholarly elucidation of an aspect of Mill's thought which has great significance for the general history of ideas.

which relates to Mill's friendship and marriage with Harriet Taylor. There can be no doubt that the discovery of their correspondence was one of the great literary finds of the century – a revelation of a story of enduring human interest. What Mill and Harriet would have said of its publication scarcely bears thinking of. But this is no condemnation of those who published it. Time wipes out the entitlement to privacy; and although this may be a warning to the living to take every possible precaution to ensure that their really private letters are destroyed at death, it would be absurd to demand that scholars should not find out and publish as much as they can when a decent interval has elapsed. After a hundred years everything is fair game to the historian. We should all be thrilled to read Shakespeare's letters to the Dark Lady. Do not let us pretend that we do not find a similar, if diluted, interest in Mill's somewhat awkward and perhaps a little shy-making letters to Harriet Taylor.

On the actual progress of the relationship, I doubt if there is much which calls here for extensive comment. It is clear that John Taylor is the real hero of the triangle. But only a prig would pass judgement adversely on the behaviour of the other parties. Indeed, perhaps the main interest of the episode, which after all starts from a very normal situation – a sensitive and unworldly young man enamoured of a lively young woman not very happily married to a man many years her senior – is the degree of consideration which all concerned showed for each other's feelings and the degree of restraint practised by the infatuated couple. It is disillusioning to find Mill behaving with what seems to be downright unkindness to his mother and family. But we do not know his explanation: and, in any case, let him who, in periods of emotional stress, has never behaved badly to anyone, be the first to cast a stone.

Much more interesting is the light which is thrown upon the personality and intellectual status of Harriet Taylor. This has always seemed to me one of the most fascinating problems of literary history. There is Mill's own tribute in the *Autobiography* and elsewhere. There is Carlyle's denigration – and Carlyle was not always so bad a judge of character as he was of general morality.

There is the scepticism of more neutral observers such as Grote, who thought that only a man of Mill's outstanding stature could survive such displays as the incredible memorial inscription at Avignon. How resolve such striking differences? How often have I sat gazing at the portrait of Harriet,[1] wondering what really lay behind those extraordinary Matisse eyes.

Here the correspondence does clear up at least some perplexities. After reading Harriet's letters, no one can deny that she had a mind of her own; and after reading Mill's, no one can deny the very considerable influence she exerted. I think it may be possible to exaggerate the part which she played in the general transition of Mill's mind towards what he called 'socialism'.[2] It is clear from the much earlier correspondence with d'Eichthal that some predisposition in that direction was latent already; and there is no reason to suppose that his negative reaction to the approval in certain quarters of the allegedly 'anti-socialist' tendency of the argument of the first edition of the *Principles* would have been very different if Harriet had been dead. But there is no doubt of very considerable influence in the formulation of particular arguments – as evidenced, for instance, in the letter of 16 February 1849.[3] Similarly, I would not doubt for a moment the exercise of considerable influence in the planning of *On Liberty* and *The Subjection of Women* – though here the evidence is less direct. And, speaking generally, the correspondence testifies to a continuing marriage

[1] It belongs to Professor Hayek and is reproduced facing p. 128 of his book, cited above, p. 98, note 1.

[2] It is perhaps not unimportant to stress how unlike the modern article Mill's mild stirrings towards what he called 'socialism' actually were. In spite of the attempts which have sometimes been made to claim him as the spiritual ancestor of *Labour and the New Social Order*, it must be clear from any unprejudiced reading that, even at the point of maximum inclination in that direction, his approval was given only to a society based upon co-operative organisations of producers – duodecimo syndicalism rather than socialism in the modern sense. Any doubt concerning what he would have felt about far-reaching nationalisation is surely resolved by the famous passage in the *Liberty* declaring that the greater the extent of centralised state ownership, the greater the danger to freedom. See the quotation of this passage below, pp. 161–2.

[3] Hayek, *John Stuart Mill and Harriet Taylor*, pp. 136–7.

D 2

of minds in which Harriet's part can certainly never again be regarded as negligible.

But just how significant it was still seems to me to be something of a problem. Mr Packe seems almost inclined to accept it at Mill's valuation without any reservation. 'Except for the *Logic* the principles underlying the more important works of John Stuart Mill were defined, although not actually composed, by Harriet Taylor. And whatever in them cannot be ascribed to his lucid reasoning must be attributed to the sheer force of her personality' (p. 317).

I confess that this seems to me to go much too far. Mr Packe says that 'it is difficult to see why Mill who was so soberly and carefully exact in every other matter should be discredited in this'. Discredited is a strong word. But personally I do not find it at all difficult to see why Mill should not have been capable of exaggeration here. We know that his experience of women was not at all extensive. We know that he derived an emotional stimulus, which it was probably impossible to exaggerate, from his association with Harriet. We know, too, that he applied terms almost as strong to the eulogy of Helen Taylor; yet it is inherently improbable that there should have been two women in his life whose intellect and conscience were more considerable and more original, to use his own standard of comparison, than his own.

The fact is that there is little in what we know to be Harriet's unaided work which would really justify claims so far-reaching as these. The early essay on Tolerance, reprinted by Professor Hayek, is good but not so very good; plenty of essays as good as this must have been written by people who have never been claimed to be the intellectual equals of so outstanding a figure as Mill. The essay 'On the Enfranchisement of Women', in Vol. II of *Dissertations and Discussions*, which Mill goes out of his way to attribute mainly to her, is certainly not so distinguished as *The Subjection of Women* which we know she did not write. Nor do her intimate letters show that distinction of thought and style which would justify a rating anything like co-equal with her partner's; and one of them at least seems to show that she would not have disagreed with this verdict:

About the Essays, dear, [she writes] would not religion, the Utility of Religion, be one of the subjects you would have most to say on – there is to account for the existence nearly universal of some religion (superstition) by the instincts of fear, hope and mystery, etc., and throwing over all doctrines and theories, called religion, and devices for power, to show how religion and poetry fill the same want, the craving after higher objects, the consolation of suffering, the hope of heaven for the selfish, love of God for the tender and grateful – how all this must be superseded by morality deriving its power from sympathies and benevolence and its reward from the approbation of those we respect.

There, what a long-winded sentence, which you could say ten times as well in words half the length (p. 369).

On this very difficult matter, it seems to me that Alexander Bain gets much nearer to what is probably the truth than Mr Packe:

The more common way of representing Mrs Mill's ascendancy [he says] is to say that she imbibed all his views, and gave them back in her own form, by which he was flattered and pleased. This is merest conjecture: the authors of the surmise never saw Mill and his wife together; and, in all probability misconceived the whole situation. As I have just remarked, it was comparatively few of his ideas that she could render back in an intelligent form. But farther, it is not the true account of Mill to say that he was pleased by the simple giving back of his own thoughts. Of course, this would have been preferable to contradicting him at every point, or to gross misconception of his meaning. Judging from my own experience of him, I should say that what he liked was to have his own faculties set in motion, so as to evolve new thoughts and new aspects of old thoughts. This might be done better by intelligently controverting his views than by merely reproducing them in different language. And I have no doubt that his wife did operate upon him in this very form. But the ways of inducing him to exert his powers in talk, which was a standing pleasure of his life, cannot be summed up under either agreement or opposition. It supposed independent resources on the part of his fellow-talker, and a good mutual understanding as to the proper conditions of the problem at issue.[1]

It is only fair to say that Mr Packe alludes to this passage and says that 'Bain came closest to the mark' (p. 316) in estimating the nature of Harriet's influence. But, with great respect, to say that

[1] *John Stuart Mill: A Criticism* (1882) p. 173.

she possessed 'independent resources' and that there was 'a good mutual understanding of the conditions of the problem at issue' and that for this reason she was able to set 'his faculties . . . in motion', is not the same as saying that she was responsible for the principles underlying all the important works except the *Logic*.

IV

It is perhaps useful to ask in what respects all the information which has come to light since the publication, shortly after Mill's death, of the *Autobiography* and Bain's sketch really modifies the general impression of the man himself which emerges from these books and from a perusal of Mill's main works themselves.

In my judgement not much modification is involved by the publication of the love letters. We knew that Mill was infatuated; and as regards the partnership, as I have just indicated, Bain's verdict seems to me to be appropriate. In spite of their great intrinsic interest as evidence bearing on the problem of his relationship, the letters serve chiefly to vindicate this view against others. The actual substance of most of them does not seem very astonishing. It is a limited view of human nature to be surprised that, under the influence of passion, logicians and economists are capable of such words as 'darling', 'adored one', etc., etc. The intimate spectacle of Mill in love is just what might have been inferred from the *Autobiography*.

Much less expected, in my judgement, is the aspect which is revealed by the correspondence with Comte, well written up by Mr Packe, whose habit of slightly guying characters with whom he is not in complete sympathy is not inappropriate in this connection. Here we are confronted with the spectacle of the frank, generous, Utilitarian philosopher vis-à-vis as pathological an egocentric as ever strutted the stage in a Strindbergian madhouse. All the traditional paraphernalia of the *soi-disant* genius are there: the bland assumption of superiority over all predecessors and entitlement to unquestioning intellectual (and financial) support from followers, the world which is contemptibly impervious, the enemies who are constantly conspiring, the wife who does not understand, the mistress who does – and, for a time, poor Mill is completely taken in. He, whose mind was so infinitely more subtle and sensitive than this boring and arrogant system-monger's, humbly acknowledges intellectual indebtedness. Hearing that Comte is financially embarrassed, he offers a share of his own purse. He procures a subsidy from Grote and Molesworth; and when that comes to an end, has to put up with a terrific outburst of rage from the major prophet – 'mon appréciation philosophique de l'ensemble de la conduite tenue envers moi dans un cas aussi décisif'. Only when the correspondence touches on what Comte calls 'la question des femmes' does the ingenuous Mill begin to smell a rat; and only after extensive attempts at reason and persuasion – needless to say, wasted on a man who, on the ground that women's heads are smaller than men's, had legislated them for ever out of the affairs of his revolting totalitarian Utopia – does he sadly conclude that it has all been rather a mistake, and, twenty years after, produces the most devastating critique of the Comtean system ever written. No wonder Harriet, with her much stronger hold on reality, seems to have felt a certain sense of embarrassment when she was shown the letters and let Mill know that she thought he had rather let himself down. 'I am surprised in your letters to find your opinion undetermined where I had thought it made up – I am disappointed at a tone more than half apologetic with which you state your opinions. . . . This dry root of a man is not a worthy coadjutor; scarcely a worthy opponent' (p. 278). The whole episode has a peculiar pathos about it. If Mill's biography is the biography of the Saint of Rationalism, then this chapter must be headed 'The Saint as Sap'.

On the whole I do not think any substantial reappraisal is called for. Professor Hayek and Mr Packe have added greatly to our knowledge and our enjoyment. But the picture which emerges, although much larger in scale, is not radically dissimilar to the picture which already existed. I think that Mill has been under-rated as an economist, particularly perhaps in the oral tradition of the London School of Economics, myself a bad culprit at one stage.

But this is a side issue, and Professor Stigler has dealt with it very effectively in a recent number of this journal.[1] Speaking broadly, in the light of this recently discovered material, the impression jointly conveyed by Bain and the *Autobiography* seems to me to be about right. Not so original nor so well equilibrated as Hume, not so sure in judgement or literary skill as Smith, and lacking the profound analytical vision and genial personality of Ricardo, Mill yet stands out as one of the great figures of the Classical tradition, not unworthy to be mentioned in the same breath as these giants: a man of massive powers of intellectual synthesis and of burning idealism and integrity, willing to follow thought wherever it led him, somewhat over-solemn and not a very good judge of men but courageous, generous and sensitive – a rare spirit, conspicuous even in his own great age, with a message of candour and humanity which, as Mr Packe so rightly emphasises, has still much relevance for ours.

ANNEX

I have reproduced here two reviews of works, appearing after the publication of Mr Packe's book, which throw additional light on its subject matter.

(i) *The Early Draft of Mill's Autobiography*[2]

At last the first draft of John Stuart Mill's *Autobiography* is available in printed form. From Mill's death until the death in 1918 of Mary Taylor,

[1] 'The Nature and Role of Originality in Scientific Progress', *Economica*, XXII (Nov 1955).

[2] A review of the book of that name, ed. Jack Stillinger (Urbana, Ill.: University of Illinois Press, 1961), *Economica*, XXIX (May 1962). Reproduced by courtesy of the London School of Economics and Political Science.

his stepdaughter Helen Taylor's niece, the manuscript was in the possession of members of the family. Then, after being auctioned in 1922 at Sotheby's to Maggs Bros. (£5 5s!), it was sold to Jacob Hollander in whose library it remained inaccessible until his death in 1940. In 1941 it was examined by Professor Levi who made it the basis of two articles which were used by Professor Hayek in his important study of the relationship of Mill and Harriet Taylor, and also by Mr St John Packe. But, pending the disposal of the estate, it again became inaccessible until its acquisition, together with the rest of Hollander's library, by the University of Illinois in 1958. Now it is published, more or less as a whole, with an extensive apparatus of comment and references by Professor Stillinger of that university.

Now doubtless if this were the only possible way in which it could be hoped that this important document could hope to see the light, its publication in this form must be regarded as a good thing. But I hope I shall not appear churlish if I say that in publishing it thus Professor Stillinger and the University of Illinois have failed to rise to the height of the scholarly opportunity with which they were presented. Indeed, it might be said that, with the best intentions, they have done some disservice. For it is very improbable that this manuscript, incomplete as it is compared with the final revision, and lacking Mill's final polishing and emendations, will ever be published again. It is not a commercial proposition. Its interest must necessarily be confined to those who are interested to trace the *minutiae* of Mill's psychological and intellectual evolution – necessarily a small minority. Hence, surely, if it was to be published at all – and in view of the intrinsic interest of Mill's spiritual pilgrimage and his importance in the history of thought, it was certainly well worth publishing – it was desirable that this should be done in a form which should make comparison with the final version as easy as possible: only an edition which reproduced this *and* the final version with the corresponding passages on opposite pages would really satisfy the needs of scholarship. But this has not been done. Admittedly, Professor Stillinger, working within the limitations of a mere reproduction, has made considerable effort, by notes and references at the top of each page to the World's Classics and the Columbia editions, to facilitate such comparisons: and his somewhat rueful reference to printing costs suggests regrets in this connection. But this solution is very definitely inferior to immediate juxtaposition, as exemplified, for instance, in Selincourt's great edition of the first and last versions of Wordsworth's *Prelude*. This was a model for all editors of first drafts; and it is a great pity that it has not been followed in this instance.

As had already been revealed by Dr Levi, Mill's first draft contains a good deal more adverse comment on his father than in the end he thought it expedient, or perhaps, just to preserve for posterity. James Mill's harshness as a tutor, his lack of understanding as a father, the repulsiveness of the manner of the polemic against Mackintosh – these and other aspects are explicitly mentioned in the first draft and disappear later on. We learn, further, of the actual suppression, in the review article on Sidgwick, of passages which James Mill considered as an attack on Bentham and on himself. There are judgements on others, too, which were later omitted, presumably for the same reasons of discretion or revision of earlier judgements. It is difficult to believe that Mill ever revised his judgement of Roebuck 'entrapped in the petty vanities and entanglements of what is called society', or Mrs Austin's very mischievous tongue. But the omission of the harsh verdict on Grote – 'when brought face to face with an audience opposed to his opinion, when called upon to beat against the stream, he was found wanting . . .' (p. 155), etc. – seems to have been the result of a more mature review of past history and, perhaps, the persistence or recrudescence of ancient friendship. All these in one way or another are valuable additions to the materials with whose aid history must form judgement on the various personalities involved.

It must not be thought, moreover, that all the omitted passages had this pejorative flavour. There are others where the omission is presumably to be explained in terms of intention to eliminate superfluity or to suppress personal detail – in particular, the moving description of the walk by the Thames at the time of his mental crisis, and the delightful account of life at Ford Abbey with Bentham and his father:

> Mr Bentham and my father studied and wrote in the same large room (a different room, however, in summer and in winter). My father commenced at about seven, summer and winter: and as Mr Bentham did not make his appearance till some time after nine, I and the other children worked at our lessons in the same room during those two hours. The general hour of breakfast was nine, but Mr Bentham always breakfasted at one o'clock among his books and papers, his breakfast being laid early in the morning on his study table. The party at the general breakfast consisted of my father and mother, Mr Bentham's amanuensis for the time being, and the visitors, if as not unfrequently happened, any were staying in the house. Before his one o'clock breakfast Mr Bentham regularly went out for the same invariable walk, a circuit of about half an hour, in which my father almost always joined him. The interval between breakfast and this walk my father [. . .] employed in hearing lessons, which when weather permitted, was always done in walking about the grounds. The hours from one to six my father passed in study and this was the time

regularly allotted to us children for learning lessons. Six was the dinner hour, and the remainder of the evening Mr Bentham passed in social enjoyment, of which he had a keen relish. I was never present on these evenings except a few times when Mr Bentham good-naturedly sent for me to teach me to play at chess (pp. 68–9, n.).

Fragments of this sort all have an interest today which makes their preservation and reproduction very worth while indeed.

In the course of his Introduction, Parts III and IV of which are a somewhat puzzling attempt at once to report the nature of the omissions and revisions and to comment on the significance of events in Mill's life, Professor Stillinger goes out of his way to make an effort finally to put Harriet Mill in her place – which, in his judgement, is not very exalted. This seems to me as uncalled for and as unsuccessful as Mr St John Packe's attempt to vindicate Mill's own estimate. In this connection I am clear that the sanest judgement is that of Bain who, recognising the extravagance of Mill's panegyrics, was yet prepared to contend against Harriet's detractors that she set Mill's faculties to work 'by intelligently controverting his ideas' Professor Stillinger actually quotes this contention, but then blurs it completely by quoting Laski to the effect that Bain told Morley that she 'repeated to . . . Mill in the morning what he had said to her the night before and astounded him by the depth of her grasp' (p. 24). I am afraid I attach very much more weight to what Bain actually says in his book than to what Laski said he said to Morley. For Bain weighed his words carefully – the whole temper of his book shows that – whereas Laski – for all his erudition and amiable qualities, which were extensive – was the least reliable man I have ever known when it was a matter of casual anecdote or attribution; I do not believe for a moment that Bain said to Morley exactly what, in his book, he went out of his way explicitly to deny.

(ii) *Mill's Earlier Letters*[1]

These two books inaugurate a notable academic enterprise. For many years it has been a reproach to scholarship in the English-speaking

[1] A review of *The Collected Works of John Stuart Mill*, vols XII–XIII: *The Earlier Letters of John Stuart Mill, 1812–1845*, ed. Francis E. Mineka (Toronto: University of Toronto Press, 1963), *Economica*, XXXII (Nov 1965). Reproduced by courtesy of the London School of Economics and Political Science.

world that there existed no collected edition of the works of John Stuart Mill; for, whether or not there are enduring elements in his contribution to economics and philosophy, there can be no doubt of his dominating influence on the thought of his age; any study of that period must be incomplete without continual reference to his letters and his publications. The filling of this gap has now been undertaken by a distinguished committee at Toronto University and these two handsomely produced volumes are the first fruits of their project.

The collection which they contain is a joint product of the labours of two scholars. The conception of an assemblage of Mill's earlier letters and the discovery of the larger fraction of the unpublished material is due to Professor Hayek, who had set himself this task long before the present enterprise was contemplated. The editing of the material thus collected and the further discovery of a substantial number of manuscripts is the work of Professor Mineka, to whom in the early fifties Professor Hayek handed on his papers. The result is a work of outstanding importance and distinction. Of the 534 letters in the main text 238 are published for the first time, and in addition 72 letters have previously unpublished passages; and throughout the editing is quite superb. It is difficult to conceive it done better. There is an introduction by Professor Hayek explaining, with characteristic *Fingerspitzengefühl*, the history of the Mill papers and his attempts to rediscover them, and a Preface by Professor Mineka setting forth the methods and objectives of his editorial apparatus. Altogether, a splendid achievement on the part of each collaborator.

The series begins with a letter to Jeremy Bentham, written in Mill's seventh year in 1812, asking for a loan of the third and fourth volumes of Hooke's *Roman History* – the process of 'recapitulating' the first and second volumes having been nearly completed. It concludes with a letter written in December 1848 to Émile Littré, enclosing a bill for 250 francs as a contribution to a fund for Comte, by which time the *Principles of Political Economy* had been published and was already attracting reviews. It thus covers the more formative period of Mill's life; and while it is true that many of the more important letters have been published before – the letters to d'Eichthal, Carlyle, Tocqueville and Comte, for instance, this is the first time that there has been an opportunity of reading them in chronological order together with the unpublished material. In this form they are an invaluable supplement to the *Autobiography*. At the same time, because of the wide range of persons to whom they were addressed and topics discussed, they cast important light on the history of thought and events in the period which they cover.

The *Autobiography* is essentially the story of a questing spirit, breaking away from the restricted outlooks of early youth, seeking always for fresh contacts and fresh vistas, open to new impressions, sometimes carried away by them, then recoiling and reformulating – essentially the opposite of the dogmatist and the system-maker. These earlier letters provide documentation for these vicissitudes. They show the to-ings and fro-ings which underlay the famous essays on Bentham and Coleridge, the warming to and retreat from the extremes of Saint-Simonism and Carlylian romanticism. There is an extraordinary letter to Sterling in which Mill actually says apropos of Wordsworth 'All my differences with him, or with any other philosophical Tory, would be differences of matter of fact or detail, while my differences with the radicals and utilitarians are differences of principle . . .' (p. 81) and an equally significant letter to Carlyle in which he confesses that 'there has been on my part something like a want of courage in avoiding or touching only perfunctorily with you, points on which I thought it likely that we should differ' (p. 153). The variations in his relations with Comte and his estimates of the importance of the Comtean system are perhaps even more remarkable.

In interpreting such changes, the correspondence itself affords clues not otherwise available. It would be easily possible to compile a list of utterances showing pure inconsistency: and some inconsistency there undoubtedly was. But the letters also reveal, what is not revealed by the *Autobiography*, a certain chameleon-like quality of sympathy which led him, in writing to his various correspondents, insensibly to adapt his words and rhythms to their style of thought and exposition. Thus, 'and this is one eternal and inestimable pre-eminence (even in the productions of pure intellect) which the doings of an honest heart possess over those men of the strongest and most cultivated powers of mind when directed to any other and in preference to, or, even in conjunction with, Truth' (p. 111). Who wrote that typical piece of ranting Carlylese, the major prophet himself? Not at all: his sympathetic and humble correspondent, the temperate and rational John Stuart Mill. Such a capacity, however amiable, had the defects of its virtues and was apt to create a false impression of agreement or even discipleship which, when the first excitement of discovery had spent itself and Mill was once more master of his intellectual destiny, involved much disillusion for the other party. Comte clearly completely underrated Mill's intellectual eminence and his toughness, regarded him just as an intellectual camp-follower and was obviously disconcerted, not to say high and mighty, when disagreement developed; and we know to what degrees of denigration Carlyle eventually descended. Of course this undue adaptability was not always present: the letters to Tocqueville, for instance, are marked by fraternal independence and plain speaking. It was when, deep down, there was incipient incompatibility co-existing with the superficial enthusiasms born of new insights that excessive identification was apt to appear. Fundamentally, Mill was an empirical rationalist; and that centre kept his circle just.

There are other aspects of Mill's character revealed in these letters which do not appear so strongly in the *Autobiography*, or do not appear at all. His generosity, for instance – the infinite pains, in a busy official life, which he took with his various correspondents, important or unimportant, his gifts and the amazing offer to share his purse with Comte whom he had never seen – his modesty and his candour and, above all, his deep human sympathy. I know few things in biographical literature more affecting than the letter which he wrote to John Sterling when the latter was on his deathbed. It is perhaps worth transcribing a section thereof as some countervailing evidence to the still prevalent view of Mill as a characteristically bloodless intellectual, untypical only by reason of his peculiar passion for Harriet Taylor:

There is one thing which cannot be said to you too often [he wrote] because I have seen before that there was real need of saying it. If there should be but little chance of your recovering anything like solid or perfect health, or even of your possessing permanently and safely such a degree of it as you have sometimes had for considerable periods together, in the last few years, I am afraid you will think that anything short of this is not worth having or worth wishing for – that you will be useless and helpless and that it is better to be dead. I enter most perfectly into such a feeling and should very likely feel the very same if I were as I have several times thought I might be, in your circumstances – but I cannot conceive anything more completely mistaken as in your case such a feeling would be. If you were never able to go through any active exertion, or to write a single line, except an occasional letter, or to exercise any influence over mankind except the influence of your thoughts and feelings upon your children and upon those by whom you are personally known and valued, you would still be, I sincerely think, the most useful man I know. It is very little that any of us can do, except doing good to those nearest to us – and of what we *can* do the smallest part, in general, is that which we calculate upon and to which we can attach our name. There are certainly few persons living who are capable of doing so much good by their indirect and unconscious influence as you and I do not believe you have ever had an adequate conception of the extent of influence you possess and the quantity of good which you produce by it. Even by your mere existence you do more good than many by their laborious exertions. I do not speak of what the loss of you would be, or the blank it would make in life even to those who like me have except for short periods had little of you except the knowledge of your existence and of your affection. None of us could hope in our lives to meet with your like again – and if we did, it would be no compensation. And when I think how many of the best people living are at this moment feeling this, I am sure that you have much to live for. . . (p. 629).

7

Mill's *Essays on Economics and Society*[1]

I. INTRODUCTION: NATURE OF THE COLLECTION

THE papers collected in this volume have a twofold value. They provide important insights into the evolution of the views of their author on economic and social problems; and, since they come from one of the world's outstanding economists and social philosophers, they still possess great intrinsic interest. John Stuart Mill's *Principles of Political Economy* is one of the great synthetic works of Classical economics; anything which throws light on its propositions and their development is therefore of considerable historical importance. The views of the author of *On Liberty* on any aspect of social and economic policy have still great significance at this stage of human history.

For good scholarly reasons the papers here reproduced are printed in chronological order. For purposes of discussion, however, they are better classified according to subject matter. From this point of view, they may be considered under six main headings: General Economic Theory (other than money and banking); Money and Banking; Public Finance; Labour; Property and Its Social Control; and Socialism. It is under these headings and in this order that they will be discussed in this Introduction.

II. GENERAL ECONOMIC THEORY

Juvenilia

THE papers relating to non-monetary general economic theory begin with a set of three which may be regarded as exposition on

[1] Being an Introduction to the *Essays on Economics and Society*, vols IV and V of the *Collected Works of John Stuart Mill*, ed. J. M. Robson (Toronto: University of Toronto Press, 1967). Reproduced by courtesy of the University of Toronto Press.

the part of the youthful John Stuart of an outlook which he inherited from his father and Ricardo. Their chief value consists in their revelation of the position from which he set out. The review of McCulloch's *Discourse on the Rise, Progress, Peculiar Objects and Importance of Political Economy* (reprinted in an Appendix because it was jointly composed with William Ellis) is pure propaganda for the School; it is fairly clear that the eulogy of McCulloch would not have been written later on.[1] The paper on 'The Nature, Origin, and Progress of Rent', a straightforward exposition of Ricardian theory, was written as an Appendix to McCulloch's edition of Smith's *Wealth of Nations* and well explains the Ricardian critique of Adam Smith's views on rent. But the most notable thing about the reprint is the footnote on p. 178 where Professor Robson reproduces a marginal note from Mill's copy, now at Somerville College, in which he shows dissatisfaction with the dogmatic insistence on the doctrine that rent does not enter into cost of production, thus foreshadowing possibly the concessions in this respect appearing in the *Principles*.[2]

The article from the *Westminster Review*, 'The Quarterly Review on Political Economy', which is the earliest of the three, is also the most extensive. It is an episode in the war between the two Reviews. The article which it attacks – a review of McCulloch's *Discourse* – was actually written by Malthus. But Mill's review, which was obviously written with this knowledge, pretends that the article in the *Quarterly Review* was written with a view to making Malthus look ridiculous. As a piece of debating, it is excellent rough stuff. As usual, outside his writings on population, Malthus had put his points so poorly that it was not difficult to make logical mincemeat of them; and this the youthful reviewer does with great relish. The article contains no indication that he

---

[1] See a letter to Professor Rau (20 Mar 1852), reprinted in Hugh S. R. Elliot, (ed.), *The Letters of John Stuart Mill* (London: Longmans, Green, 1910) I 168–70.

[2] *Principles of Political Economy with Some of Their Applications to Social Philosophy*, ed. J. M. Robson, in *Collected Works* (Toronto: University of Toronto Press, 1965; London: Routledge & Kegan Paul) III 498.

was yet aware of the vulnerable point in the crude assertions of Say's and his father's arguments about the impossibility of general gluts. And to those who have read the thorough trouncing from Torrens, evoked by an earlier effort to sustain his father's preposterous view that differences in the period of investment might all be reduced to labour,[1] the attempt to minimise the differences between this view and Ricardo's must have interest as almost the one instance in the whole corpus of his writings where Mill was not entirely ingenuous. For any who are interested in the finer shades of the disputes between Malthus and the Ricardians, this article is required reading. For the rest, it is chiefly notable as an exceptionally clear exposition of what the Ricardian theory of value really asserted.

Papers on General Theory written before 1848

Next comes a central group of essays and reviews in which Mill is to be seen working out his own views on general theory in forms later to appear in the *Principles*. Of these, the five included in the separate volume entitled *Essays on Some Unsettled Questions of Political Economy* are by far the most important. Their actual publication did not take place until 1844 and seems to have been stimulated by a desire to set before the world a more systematic and temperate exposition of the role of demand in international trade theory than was being expounded with great debating brilliance, but considerable overemphasis, by Torrens in the famous, or notorious, *Budget* letters. But they were written in 1829 and 1830 and therefore come first in chronological order, as they do in the order of intellectual importance.

The first of the series is the most famous. The background is fairly well known. The theory of comparative cost, invented by Torrens and Ricardo and expounded by Mill's father, had indi-

---

[1] See my *Robert Torrens and the Evolution of Classical Economics* (London: Macmillan, 1958) pp. 70–2. This, Mill's earliest essay in economic theory, will appear in the forthcoming volume of his works devoted to contributions to newspapers.

cated the nature of the advantages of territorial division of labour and the limiting cost ratios (in a two-commodity model) between which exchanges advantageous to both parties could take place. But it did not decide at what rate these exchanges would actually take place and therefore the way in which the gains of trade would be divided. Indeed, in the first edition of James Mill's *Elements* the exposition actually involved a double counting of the gain, only corrected in the third edition after representations by his son and his son's friend, George Graham. It was doubtless in the course of attempts to fill this gap that there took place those conversations which, as Mill relates in his *Autobiography*,[1] eventually resulted in the writing of the essay 'Of the Laws of Interchange Between Nations; and the Distribution of the Gains of Commerce among the Countries of the Commercial World'.

This essay is surely one of the most powerful contributions ever made to the evolution of economic analysis. The idea of demand as a function of price was not, of course, entirely new: it is easy to find perceptions of this relationship in earlier literature. But this was the first case in which it was systematically set forth and made the analytical basis of important propositions.[2] Moreover, there is involved in this essay the first systematic presentation of the Classical theory of international trade in all its main implications. Ricardo, with the theory of comparative costs and the theory of the distribution of the precious metals, had provided two of the most basic ingredients. But until the demand element was explicitly introduced, the theory was necessarily incomplete. In this essay Mill not only meets this need, in models involving both barter and money, but he also provides a systematic working out of the corollaries as regards tariffs and the terms of trade, the export of machinery, the problem of two countries competing in a third, and the payment of international tribute. Not all the solutions are comprehensive. But for the first time the general outline of a

[1] *Autobiography*, 1st ed. (London: Longmans, Green, 1875) p. 85.

[2] It was first published by Cournot in his *Recherches sur les principes Mathématiques de la théorie des richesses* (Paris, 1838). But whereas Mill's essay was not published until 1844, as stated above, it was written much earlier.

comprehensive analysis is set forth; and, although there was some elaboration in the *Principles*, we have the authority of Edgeworth for the view that not all this was an improvement.[1]

The second essay, 'Of the Influence of Consumption on Production', is scarcely less remarkable. Classical teaching on this subject had hitherto been represented by Adam Smith's proposition that 'What is annually saved is as regularly consumed as what is annually spent, and nearly in the same time, too',[2] or by the even more doctrinaire Law of Markets, as it was thought to be propounded by J. B. Say and certainly was by Mill's father, which flatly asserted the identity of aggregate supply and aggregate demand and flatly denied the possibility of general overproduction – a principle which, as we shall see later, Mill himself, as a young man, was not unwilling to adduce in a dispute about war expenditure.[3] Mill's essay begins with an assertion of the broad principle that 'What a country wants to make it richer, is never consumption, but production' (I 263). But in searching for 'scattered particles of important truth' amid 'the ruins of exploded error' he is led to reformulations which in fact amount both to a refutation of Say's Law as usually applied to a money economy, and to a view of the operations of the speculative motive which affords what is in effect a theory of the trade cycle. 'In order to render the argument for the impossibility of an excess of all commodities applicable to the case in which a circulating medium is employed, money must itself be considered as a commodity. It must, undoubtedly, be admitted that there cannot be an excess of all other commodities, and an excess of money at the same time.' He continues: 'But those who have . . . affirmed that there was an excess of all commodities, never pretended that money was one of these commodities; they held that there was not an excess, but a deficiency of the circulating medium.' What this amounted to was

[1] F. Y. Edgeworth, *Papers Relating to Political Economy* (London: Macmillan, 1925) II 22–3.

[2] *The Wealth of Nations*, ed. E. Cannan (London: Methuen, 1904) p. 320.

[3] [See above, p. 12]. Subsequent references to the present volumes (the *Collected Works*) are given in the text.

that persons in general, at that particular time, from a general expectation of being called upon to meet sudden demands, liked better to possess money than any other commodity. Money, consequently, was in request, and all other commodities were in comparative disrepute. . . . But the result is, that all commodities fall in price, or become unsaleable. When this happens to one single commodity, there is said to be a superabundance of that commodity; and if that be a proper expression, there would seem to be in the nature of the case no particular impropriety in saying that there is a superabundance of all or most commodities, when all or most of them are in this same predicament (i 277).

For some reason or other this remarkable reconstruction of the Classical position has seldom received explicit recognition. It can be detected between the lines in the treatment of speculation in the *Principles*, but it is nowhere so overtly developed; and from that day to this, the neat side-tracking of the crudities of Say's Law has passed very little noticed. Yet, as Messrs Baumol and Becker remark, in their excellent résumé of the historical treatment of the issues, 'In reading it one is led to wonder why so much of the subsequent literature (this paper included) had to be written at all.'[1]

The remaining three essays in this collection are not of the same path-breaking importance, but they have considerable interest nevertheless. The third essay, 'On the Words Productive and Unproductive', is devoted to making clear that the use of these words, in the sense in which they had been employed by the English Classical economists – as distinct from the Physiocrats – was to indicate the difference between the production of capital in some form or other, and the rendering of pure services leaving directly or indirectly no lasting sources of enjoyment behind. Attention to such elucidations should have saved many purely semantic polemics in the literature of the hundred years after they appeared.

The fourth essay, 'On Profits and Interest', consists first of a clarification and amendment of the Ricardian proposition that

[1] Gary S. Becker and William Baumol, 'The Classical Monetary Theory: The Outcome of the Discussion', *Economica*, xix (Nov 1952) 355–76.

profits depend upon wages, and then a discussion of the relation between profits and interest, and the influences on the determination of the latter independent of the influence of the former. This part is conspicuous for a very clear exposition of the process of 'forced accumulation', as Mill calls it, through inflationary movements of cash or credit – an exposition which is explicitly stated to be no palliation of the iniquity of the process. 'Though A might have spent his property unproductively, B ought not to be permitted to rob him of it because B will expend it on productive labour' (1 307).

The subject matter of the last essay in this series is sufficiently indicated by its title, 'On the Definition of Political Economy; and on the Method of Investigation Proper to It'. A scrutiny of earlier definitions and successive refinements of tentatives of his own eventually leads Mill to the conclusion that political economy is best defined as 'The science which traces the laws of such of the phenomena of society as arise from the combined operations of mankind for the production of wealth in so far as those phenomena are not modified by the pursuit of any other object' (1 323); and what he calls the *a priori* method of reasoning from general assumptions is declared to be the only legitimate method of reaching general conclusions, although these conclusions need continually to be tested by reference to specific experience. These conceptions have sometimes been thought to have been discarded in the writing of the *Principles*. But it is doubtful if this is so. The essay makes it abundantly plain that, for purposes of practical recommendations, the use of the abstract propositions of the science as its author conceived it needed to be supplemented by other knowledge. In the world of reality there are many disturbing circumstances which do not fall within the province of political economy, 'and here the mere political economist, he who has studied no science but Political Economy, if he attempted to apply his science to practice, will fail' (1 331). The scope of the *Principles* was intended to cover not only theory but also applications, as is evident even in its full title, *The Principles of Political Economy with Some of Their Applications to Social Philosophy*, and it is difficult to believe that Mill would have admitted any incompatibility between this objective and his earlier discussion of scope and method. This is not the only time in the history of economic thought that attempts to clarify logical distinctions have been mistaken for prohibitions of catholicity of interest.

There are two other papers, published before the writing of the *Principles*, which are concerned with questions of general theory.

The first is a review of the concluding number of Harriet Martineau's *Illustrations of Political Economy*, that entitled *The Moral of Many Fables*. Mill did not always speak kindly of this lady – he once referred to her as 'a mere tyro'[1] – but here, while making plain its limited pretensions, he treats her little book with a measure of respect. But he brings against it the reproach which by that time (1834) he had begun to feel against the political economy he had inherited from his father and his father's circle, namely that it took the existing institutional framework as a permanent feature of the human situation:

> Thus, for instance, English political economists presuppose, in every one of their speculations, that the produce of industry is shared among three classes, altogether distinct from one another. . . . They revolve in their eternal circle of landlords, capitalists, and labourers, until they seem to think of the distinction of society into those three classes, as if it were one of God's ordinances, not man's, and as little under human control as the division of day and night (1 225-7).

It is easy to see in these strictures the beginnings of the distinction that plays such a predominant role in the *Principles* between the laws of production which were immutable and the laws of distribution which were contingent on human institutions.

The second paper is a review of De Quincey's *Logic of Political Economy*. This was written very shortly before the commencement of the *Principles* and it can well be believed that, in the writing

---

[1] Letter to Walter Coulson (22 Nov 1850), in Elliot (ed.), *Letters of John Stuart Mill*, 1 157. This was not one of Mill's more urbane utterances; presumably some of Harriet's tittle-tattle about Mrs Taylor and himself had come to his ears: 'Mr Kingsley's notions must be little less vague about my political economy than about my socialism when he couples my name with that of a mere tyro like Harriet Martineau.'

thereof, some of the stimulus of De Quincey's lively exposition was still present in his mind. De Quincey's politics were antipathetic to Mill, who candidly avows that he found it difficult 'to reconcile this wretched party invective with the respect we sincerely wish to feel' (1 404). But he takes De Quincey's discussions of the theory of value very seriously and reproduces at length the charming parable of alternative sales of a musical box in London and on a boat on Lake Superior with which De Quincey attempts to illustrate the respective influence of difficulty of attainment and usefulness.[1] The paper is also noteworthy for a repudiation of the view, expressed by De Quincey and wrongly attributed by many (including no less an authority than Schumpeter) to Ricardo, that supply and demand are irrelevant to the determination of value.[2]

Papers on General Theory written after 1848

Mill published very little on general economic theory once the *Principles* had appeared; his interest thereafter was focussed upon more detailed applications. There are two papers appearing in this period which might legitimately be brought under this heading, the review of Newman's *Lectures on Political Economy* of 1851 and the review of Thornton's *On Labour and its Claims* of 1869. Each of these, however, has its centre of gravity in another universe of discourse. The review of Thornton will accordingly be dealt with below under the heading of Labour, and that of Newman under Socialism.

III. MONEY AND BANKING

Mill's papers relating to money and banking fall into two clearly marked groups. There is a group dealing with the controversies and events of the twenties and early thirties – the left-overs, so to speak, of the great Bullionist debate; and there is a group, dealing with banking policy and the conduct of the Bank of England, which

[1] This passage is retained in the *Principles*; see II 462–3.
[2] See above, p. 61–2.

is part of the controversy concerning the expediency and results of the Bank Act of 1844. As we shall see, there is some evidence of continuity of thought between the two groups. But there is sufficient difference in content to make it useful to deal with them separately.

Papers of the Twenties and Early Thirties

The first paper of the earlier group is a review of the pamphlet, *Observations on the Effects Produced by the Expenditure of Government during the Restriction of Cash Payments*, by William Blake. At the height of the Bullion controversy Blake had published a short treatise in which the main principles of Bullionist orthodoxy were forcibly expressed,[1] but he had changed his mind, and in the pamphlet under review had urged that the rise of prices during the war and the subsequent fall were all attributable to the increase and diminution of government expenditure. This pamphlet had been the subject of critical comment by Ricardo shortly before his death[2] and had been the subject of an exchange of views between the author and McCulloch.[3] It was only to be expected that it should be singled out for critical examination in the *Westminster Review*, which in this connection, through its association with James Mill and his circle, stood for the unqualified Classical position; and it was in character with this position that the task should have been assigned to John Mill.[4]

It is a crude article, imbued with the youthful combativeness and occasional arrogance which we have already noticed in the review

[1] *Observations on the Principles which Regulate the Course of Exchange; and on the Present Depreciated State of the Currency* (London: Lloyd, 1810), which Huskisson described as containing 'the most complete exposition of the whole doctrine of exchange that I have met with in any language': *The Speeches of the Rt. Hon. William Huskisson* (London: Murray, 1837), I 56 n.

[2] See P. Sraffa (ed.), *The Works and Correspondence of David Ricardo*, IV (Cambridge University Press, 1951) 325–56.

[3] Ibid., IX (Cambridge, 1952) 302.

[4] For a thorough discussion of Blake's pamphlet and the controversy arising therefrom, see B. A. Corry's invaluable *Money, Saving and Investment in English Economics, 1800–1850* (London: Macmillan, 1962) pp. 162–8.

of Malthus of about the same period. It begins with a denial of general distress after the war – 'We neither saw nor heard it, except in the cant of the agriculturists' (1 3) – and relies on Tooke's attempts[1] to exhibit the Blakean thesis as wholly mistaken. 'No general reasoning could have added to the conviction which everyone must feel, who has perused Mr Tooke's detail of facts, that Mr Blake's theory is totally erroneous' (1 21). The attitude is not sympathetic to this modern reader. Historical scholarship, at the present day, would probably hold that Blake had overstated his case. Moreover, at times his arguments are muddled and do not carry conviction. But to contend that there was nothing in the view that the great variations in government expenditure played some part in the inflationary and deflationary movements of prices is implausible to the modern outlook; and it must be admitted that there is something slightly repellent about the confidence with which the youthful reviewer asserts this point of view.

Moreover, Mill's own view at this stage cannot be regarded as free from error. He regards it as a fallacy to suppose that 'expenditure, as contradistinguished from saving, can by any possibility constitute an additional source of demand'; and he similarly denounces the conception that 'capital which being borrowed by government becomes a source of demand in its hands, would not have been equally a source of demand in the hands of those from whom it is taken' (1 13), neither of which views can in fact be taken to be inevitably fallacious. We have seen already that, in the essay 'On the Influence of Consumption on Production', Mill was to break the impasse created by the proposition that all that is saved is consumed and in about the same time. It is clear that at the time of this early review he was still in the bondage of this kind of thinking. As a critique of Blake's general position his paper is radically inferior to the section devoted to that subject in Matthias Attwood's *Letter to Lord Archibald Hamilton*.[2]

---

[1] Thomas Tooke, *Thoughts and Details on the High and Low Prices of the Last Thirty Years* (London: Murray, 1823).

[2] *A Letter to Lord Archibald Hamilton on Alterations in the Value of Money* (London, 1823).

The same spirit of somewhat combative dogmatism inspires the paper, written in 1833, entitled 'The Currency Juggle'. This is a violent polemic directed chiefly against the position of Thomas Attwood who, in a recent debate with Cobbett, had advocated currency depreciation as a means for lightening the burden of debt and increasing the volume of employment. It is clear from the opening paragraphs of the paper that the object in writing it was to disassociate the radical movement from this propaganda, which it was felt was likely to bring the cause of reform into discredit; and, given the facts that the restoration of a metallic standard had taken place more than twelve years before and that the country was tired of controversy about the currency, it is not difficult to understand this motive. It is not difficult, moreover, to understand the view that Cobbett's desire for an overt scaling down of debt, although in Mill's view a mistaken position, should have been regarded as morally superior to a proposal to bring about the same thing by measures which were likely to rob all existing holders of money, whether or not they were creditors, of some of the value of their holding. What, however, is more difficult to understand is the tone of the argument and the apparent unwillingness to admit any force or quality in the position of the writers attacked. After all, from the point of view of modern analysis, during the period before the restoration of the metallic standard when the economy was being crippled by deflation, the position of the Attwoods seems considerably more defensible than that of the contemporary Classical orthodoxy; and although by 1833 the economic situation had changed and the balance of argument was then probably against unorthodox changes, it is difficult to regard all their arguments as being as contemptible as they are made to appear in Mill's attack. At first sight there is lacking the fairness, the willingness to do justice to opposing points of view, characteristic of Mill in his prime. But in fact, where any question of inconvertible paper was concerned, this attitude persisted till the end, as is shown not only by *obiter dicta* in the *Principles*, but also by the preservation of this particular effusion in *Dissertations and Discussions*. Apparently the traumatic experience of

E

inconvertible paper during the Restriction period had left such a deep imprint on the members of the Classical school that one and all seem to have been incapable of calm argument rather than of denunciation in this connection – which was a pity, for it left a gap in the literature not well filled even at the present day.

The last paper in this group is the article on 'Paper Currency and Commercial Distress' from the *Parliamentary Review* for the session of 1826. This paper, although somewhat prolix and rambling in form, is probably the most significant of the three, both as regards positive content and as an indication of the lines on which Mill's future thought was to evolve.

The positive value of the paper consists in its explanation of the course of a speculative boom and its eventual collapse. The vivid account of the origin of such movements in anticipation of shortages of supply, their extension so that the 'speculative purchases produce the very effect, in anticipation of which they were made' (1 75), the repercussions of this state of affairs on manufacture, the arrival of increased supplies, and the unloading of swollen stocks – all this is without parallel in the earlier literature; and it is possible to read into it some anticipation of the essay 'On the Influence of Consumption on Production' with its masterly invocation of fluctuations in willingness to hold money rather than commodities. Certainly it contains the germs of much of the content of the chapter (III xii) on the 'Influence of Credit on Prices' in the *Principles*.

At the same time, in its criticisms of the Government's decision to prohibit the issue of pound notes and the arguments by which that decision was supported, there are to be discovered, at times in a somewhat extreme form, anticipations of Mill's subsequent position in the controversy between the so-called Banking and Currency Schools. Thus, for instance, he maintains that until paper money has entirely displaced metal there can be no talk of excess. 'So long as there remains a sovereign in the country, three has been no over-issue' (1 83). To the suggestion that such displacement takes time and that, in the interval, the total circulation may legitimately be described as excessive, he replies by a virtual denial of the existence of any appreciable lags. And he goes on to argue that if there were no paper circulation capable of depreciation in speculative periods, the same effect would be produced by the multiplication of other forms of credit. 'It appears, that in periods of speculation, the addition to the circulating medium and the depreciation of its value, are no greater with a local bank paper than without it' (1 96). Finally he denies that the movement of interest rates had been in the least influenced by the increased issue of notes.

Certainly the main positions of the Banking School are all here in embryo. But this brings us to the papers bearing directly on the controversy concerned.

The Controversy about the Principles of the Bank Act of 1844 and its Operation in Practice

This controversy related specifically to the principles appropriate to the regulation of a convertible paper currency. Both the schools of thought involved repudiated any connection with propaganda for inconvertible paper and insisted on the need for convertibility. But, given this degree of common ground, they differed root and branch concerning the need for regulation beyond this requirement. The Currency School, led by Overstone, Norman and Torrens, argued that regulations were necessary in order that the movements of a mixed circulation might be similar to those which would take place if the currency were wholly metallic: to this end they proposed what was embodied in the famous Bank Act of 1844, a separation of the function of issue from the function of banking in the organisation of the Bank of England, and a rule which brought it about that, beyond a fixed fiduciary issue of an amount smaller than the minimum needs of trade, each note outstanding should be covered by an equivalent gold reserve. The Banking School argued that no such regulation was necessary and further that the separation of the departments imposed undesirable limitations on the proper discharge of the functions of the central bank.

Beyond these practical issues there lay deeper divisions of view regarding the working of the monetary mechanism and the objectives of monetary policy.[1]

Thus the Banking School regarded the size of the note issue as completely passive to the movement of prices. It did not determine prices; it was determined by them. They contended that it was impossible for bankers to bring about an increased circulation of notes: any attempt to do so was believed to be frustrated by the celebrated Principle of Reflux. They regarded bank credit as having exactly the same status as convertible notes, not only in relation to prices and incomes but also as part of the total system of circulating media. Their remedy for any menace to the convertibility of the note issue was to increase the central banking reserve. And they argued against the alleged desirability of a system which brought it about that the active circulation was influenced, as the plans of the Currency School held that it should be, by the state of the balance of payments.

Against this, their opponents planted themselves firmly on the norms indicated by the Ricardian theory of the distribution of the precious metals. They urged that the movements of a mixed circulation should be similar to those which would take place were it wholly metallic. They ridiculed the idea that prices were indifferent to the volume of convertible paper. They maintained that the banks could vary the circulation of notes by variations in the terms of lending and contended that, unless the reflux of notes was instantaneous, the fact of a time-lag necessarily involved the possibility of temporarily increased issues. They argued that the possibility of variations in the note issue, other than those similar to what would take place if the currency was purely metallic, increased the possibility of adverse variations in bank credit. And they held that the use of a reserve to insulate the circulation from fluctuations which otherwise would be caused by variations in the state of the balance of payments was likely to delay readjustment and increase the danger to convertibility of a prolonged external drain. They denied the accusation that they regarded absolute

[1] For a fuller discussion of these issues, see my *Robert Torrens and the Evolution of Classical Economics*, chap. v.

increases in the note circulation as necessarily the initiating cause of fluctuations in prices and the external balance, contending that the focus of their precautions was on the prevention of *relative* over-issue – a state of affairs as likely to result from changes originating on the side of goods as from those on the side of money.

As happens so often, the verdict of time on this controversy has not been unequivocally in favour of one side or the other. It is clear that the Currency School erred gravely in regarding control of the note issue as a sufficient control of the volume of credit: there are indications that Torrens at least was beginning to see this by the end of his career.[1] The Banking School had more sense of contemporary reality in this respect. It is also clear that, having regard to the possibility of sudden movements on capital account, there was much weight in their plea for a larger reserve. But on matters of deeper analysis, in my judgement, the balance of merit is reversed. The Banking School were wrong about the passivity of issue and the significance of reflux; and they preached a perilous doctrine in urging that the internal circulation should be insulated from changes in the external position. And although it is easy to pick holes in the rigid prescriptions of the Currency School, focused on the current account and relying too heavily on control of the note issue, it is arguable that, given fixed exchange rates, their assumption of a connection between the internal and external position, only to be violated at peril of continuing disequilibrium, is one which still has relevance to the problems of the present age.

In this dispute, Mill's general position was that of the Banking School. His connections with Tooke inclined him to a similar mode of approach; and although, as can be seen in 'The Currency Question', he was not unaware of the vulnerability of some of Tooke's formulations vis-à-vis Torrens's expert guerrilla warfare, he tended to accept the broad implications of his general position. The chapter in the *Principles*, 'Of the Regulation of a Convertible Paper Currency' (III xxiv), makes some concession to the Currency

[1] See his unsigned article, 'Lord Overstone on Metallic and Paper Currency', *Edinburgh Review*, cvii (Jan 1858) 248–93.

School in regard to the possibility of increasing note issues in times of buoyant speculation and therefore, in regard to the effectiveness of the Act of 1844, in arresting speculative extensions of credit. But in the main it is the pure milk of the Banking School. Thus, apart from the exception just noted, it minimises throughout the importance of the note issue and its relation to the creation of credit in general. It endorses Fullarton's conception of the central role of 'hoards' in the settlement of disparities of international indebtedness. And it disputes the desirability of arrangements which seek to make the general movements of the circulation vis-à-vis the outside world approximate to what would be the case were it entirely metallic. It was not by accident that it was singled out for a paragraph by paragraph critical examination in Torrens's major polemic.[1]

The three papers here reprinted afford useful insights into the evolution and consolidation of this attitude. The first, entitled 'The Currency Question', which appeared in the *Westminster Review* when the controversy relating to Peel's proposals for the renewal of the Bank's charter was at its height, is in effect a defence of Tooke against Torrens. The pamphlet, *An Enquiry into the Currency Principle*, by the respected author of the *History of Prices*, which was a frontal attack on the whole intellectual basis of these proposals, had elicited a reply from Torrens, *An Enquiry into the Practical Working of the Proposed Arrangements for the Renewal of the Charter of the Bank of England*; and Mill's article was an attempt to defend Tooke's position from what was certainly a highly ingenious and resourceful attack. The main purport of the argument is to demonstrate that 'it seems not easy to understand how an increased creation of the written evidences of credit called bank notes, can, of itself, create an additional demand or occasion a rise of price. . . . What does the person do who issues them, but take so much from the third element of purchasing power, namely

---

[1] See the 2nd and 3rd editions of his *Principles and Practical Operation of Sir Robert Peel's Act of 1844 Explained and Defended* (London: Longman, Brown, Green, Longmans, & Roberts, 1857 and 1858). See also my *Robert Torrens and the Evolution of Classical Economics*, pp. 336–41.

credit, and add it to the first element, money in hand – making no addition whatever to the total amount?' (I 354). It protests that the separation of the departments will increase rather than diminish the violence of commercial fluctuations, and reaches the conclusion that

> the proposed changes in the mode of regulating the currency will be attended with none of the advantages predicted; that, so far as intended to guard against the danger of over-issue, they are precautions against a chimerical evil; that the real evil of commercial vicissitudes, of 'cycles of excitement and depression', is not touched by them, nor by any regulations which can be adopted for bank notes or other mere instruments of credit; and that in what Mr Tooke justly calls (next to solvency and convertibility) 'the main difference between one banking system and another', namely, 'the greater or less liability to abrupt changes in the rate of interest and in the state of commercial credit', the present arrangements, under the condition of a larger bank reserve, have a decided advantage over the new system (I 361).

The two remaining papers, 'The Bank Acts' (evidence before the Select Committee on the Bank Acts of 1857) and 'Currency and Banking' (replies to the questions of the French Enquête sur les principes et les faits généraux qui régissent la circulation monétaire et fiducière), come from a date when the Peel Act had been some time in operation; and they exhibit the views and arguments characteristic of the chapter in the *Principles* which had remained and continued to remain substantially unaltered.

'The Bank Acts', which is much the longer and more important of the two, involves much repetition, as might be expected when the witness was cross-examined in turn by different members of the committee. But certain positions stand out. Mill is against the separation of the departments because he thinks it inhibits the flexibility of credit policy. He admits the usefulness of the Act in imposing a curb on the expansion of credit at times of speculative excitement. But he urges that in every other respect it is destabilising. The right way to safeguard convertibility, he urges, is not the separation of the departments but, as Tooke had urged, the keeping of a larger reserve. As for the claim that the movements of a mixed system should conform to the movements which would take place if the currency were wholly metallic, he repudiates it:

> no currency can be good of which the permanent average value does not conform to the permanent average value of a metallic currency; but I do not admit the inference that in order to enable it to do this, its fluctuations in value must conform to the fluctuations in the value of a metallic currency; because it appears to me, that fluctuations in value are liable to occur from anything that affects credit; and I think that a metallic currency is liable to more severe revulsions of credit, than a mixed currency, such as ours was before the Act of 1844; and therefore, that a paper currency of the permanent value of metallic currency, and convertible, but without any other restriction, is liable to less fluctuation than we now have under the Act of 1844 (II 544).

And, developing this point, he argues that the advantage of the absence of restriction is that the Bank 'will not be obliged to contract credit in cases in which there had been no previous undue expansion of it' (II 544).[1]

The replies to the questions of the Enquête add very little to all this. They are, however, notable for a particularly forceful statement of the case where, an external drain having been caused by excessive speculation, the authorities of the central bank are under an obligation to contract their issues to prevent a cumulative breakdown:

> L'écoulement ainsi produit n'a pas de limite naturelle, et n'a aucune raison de s'arrêter avant la cessation des causes qui l'ont amené. Il ne cesse et ne peut cesser que lorsque les hauts prix qui lui ont donné lieu ont pris fin par un mouvement de baisse, c'est-à-dire lorsque la spéculation a cédé à une réaction. En ce cas, l'écoulement du numéraire est le remède naturel et indispensable de la maladie, et parvint-on à le retarder, on ne réussirait qu'à prolonger le mal et à aggraver la crise finale. Si, en ce cas, la Banque s'abstenait d'agir pour défendre son encaisse, si elle continuait d'escompter aussi largement qu'auparavant, en laissant s'écouler sa réserve métallique, les spéculateurs, trouvant à emprunter au cours ordinaire, ne seraient pas réduits à

---

[1] It is interesting to see that in this evidence Mill speaks out against the issue of small notes, which he had defended so passionately in his youthful paper on the crisis of 1826, his ground now being that the prohibition of issue retained in the country a quantity of gold which could be used to replenish the reserve in case of necessity. See II 509–10.

vendre: ils pourraient prolonger pendant quelque temps encore leur lutte contre les lois naturelles; les prix surhaussés ne baisseraient pas, et partant l'écoulement suivrait son cours jusqu'à ce que la réserve même la mieux fournie y eût passé tout entière. A l'approche de cette catastrophe, la Banque, pour ne pas faire faillite, serait dans la nécessité de produire d'un seul coup la réaction qu'elle aurait dû préparer graduellement. Une diminution des escomptes et une élévation du taux de l'intérêt, qui eussent suffi pour arrêter la spéculation dans les commencements de la sortie des métaux précieux, ne suffiraient plus: il faudrait une action non-seulement plus brusque, mais plus excessive et plus violente. De là, écoulement général du crédit, la panique et la peine, qui est loin de frapper seulement les spéculateurs dont l'imprudence a amené le mal (II 604).

All of which would have delighted the hearts of Colonel Torrens and the others of his persuasion. But they would have added that there were other cases when to allow an external drain to continue without affecting the internal circulation might lead to equivalent dangers. And if we have regard to the possibility of adverse turns in the terms of trade and to the Ricardian theory of the distribution of the precious metals, it is not at all certain that they would not have been right.

IV. PUBLIC FINANCE

The papers on public finance in this collection fall into two entirely distinct groups: a group written in the twenties attacking various aspects of the protective duties of the day, and a group chiefly consisting of evidence on income and property taxation tendered to government committees in the years after the publication of the *Principles*.

Protective Duties

The two principal papers in the first group are both concerned with the Corn Laws and may be regarded as a repository of the Classical doctrine on these duties. The first, taking for granted the interest of the community as a whole in cheap imports, makes great use of standard Ricardian analysis to isolate the interests of the landlords in this respect from those of all other classes. It might be thought that protection to agriculture benefited the farmers. But, in so far as the farmer is a capitalist, in the long run he suffers with the rest, other than the landlords: a high price of corn means higher wages to cover the higher costs of subsistence, and this in turn leads to a lower rate of profit. Moreover, a lower rate of profit, it is noted, means a lower rate of accumulation; and 'it is on the accumulation of capital that the advancement of the national wealth is *wholly* dependant' (I 50; italics added). It is therefore only the landlords who gain from this kind of protection, and the high rents they receive are not merely a transfer from other classes. In order that they may receive this kind of benefit, the community has to suffer the losses due to using resources to produce high-cost corn rather than importing it from lower-cost areas abroad. It would clearly be better to impose direct taxes to provide the subsidy to the landlords.

The second paper, written three years later apropos of the New Corn Law with its sliding scales, continues the attack. The first article had elaborated the proposition that the existing duties aggravated price fluctuations. This one argues that the sliding scales which were intended to deal with this evil will not do so, and that 'the benefit intended to be conferred upon our own consumers by the gradually decreasing scale of duties from 12s downwards, will be reaped principally, if not wholly, by foreigners' (I 146). It goes on to develop a frontal attack on the whole position that there is something especially sacrosanct about agriculture:

Before we offer up our substance to an allegorical idol, let us hear what title it has to our worship. What is this 'agriculture', of which you speak? When you say that no country was ever prosperous without agriculture, do you mean, that no country was ever prosperous without procuring food? If this be all, the truth of the proposition is not very likely to be disputed. But if you mean that no country was ever prosperous unless it procured food by digging and ploughing, instead of procuring it by spinning and weaving, your assertion is altogether destitute of truth: since the Dutch republic, which procured the greater part of its food without digging or ploughing was one of the most prosperous communities which the world ever saw (1 149–50).

He then asks:

when you speak of the necessity of protecting agriculture, do you mean the necessity of protecting the mere turning up of the ground? or the necessity of protecting the procuring of food for the people? If you mean the first, show us, if you can, any reason for desiring to procure food by turning up the ground, when we can procure more with the same quantity of labour in any other way. But if, by protection to agriculture, you mean protection to procuring food, there is no dispute about that. We are as desirous as you are, to afford protection to the procuring of food; provided always, that the procuring of food needs protection. But what is this contrivance of yours for protecting it? Simply this: to force the people to obtain ten bushels of corn by turning up the ground, when with the same degree of labour they might obtain twelve by growing it in their looms and in their cotton mills. If this be *protection* (which it is not, but *privilege*) it is protection only to the owners of the ground. A prohibition of gas-lights might be called, without any great impropriety, protection to the oil-companies: but would the oil-companies be permitted to term it protection for lighting? Yes; if lighting be protected by being rendered more expensive and more difficult. No, if this be, as it evidently is, the very reverse of protection. If agriculture means only turning up the ground, it deserves no protection. Turning up the ground is not a *bonum per se*. If it means procuring food, it is protected by excluding cheap corn, precisely in the same manner as the lighting of the streets of London would be protected by imposing a heavy duty upon gas (1 150).[1]

The remaining papers in this group, the article on 'The Silk Trade' and the 'Petition on Free Trade', have not the same intellectual interest. The 'Petition' exemplifies Mill's capacity for lucid and forceful draftsmanship; the disquisition on the silk duties, his capacity for bringing general principles to bear on the

---

[1] This second paper is also notable for the high praise awarded Perronet Thompson's *Catechism on the Corn Laws*, one of the leading vehicles of the more popular propaganda on the subject. 'Mr Thompson is master of his subject, and has disposed of the fallacies with great philosophic accuracy' (1 152). But Mill goes out of his way to repudiate any endorsement of Thompson's pamphlet on rent, which had criticised Ricardo on palpably superficial grounds.

argument of particular instances. The only addition to the general position developed in the papers on the Corn Laws is the argument in the paper on the silk trade that 'the high rate of wages occasioned by our corn laws, though highly prejudicial to all classes of capitalists, by lowering the general rate of profit, is not more prejudicial to those who are exposed to foreign competition than to those who are not; and that nothing, therefore, can be more utterly unwarranted than the claim of the silk manufacturers to peculiar protection on account of it' (1 135).

Income and Property Taxation

The bulk of the material in this collection which relates to income and property taxation is in the form of evidence before the two Parliamentary Committees of 1852 and 1861 – the review of Baer of 1873, although valuable as evidence of Mill's continued capacity to consider new ideas, is not of great significance. This material is intensely interesting as providing a spectacle of Mill under cross-examination by some of the acutest intellects of the day, from Gladstone downwards. But it is extremely unsystematic. The questions and answers pass from one aspect of the subject to another as the interrogation is passed round the members of the committees; and these in turn choose their own order and focus of attention. To realise the significance of what is going on it is necessary, with the aid of the relevant chapters of the *Principles*, to have a more systematic picture of Mill's main positions on this group of subjects.[1]

There are three outstanding features of Mill's attitude to the problems of the taxation of incomes and property. First, he opposed the graduation of taxes on incomes. Secondly, he favoured the exemption of savings. Thirdly, he favoured stringent limitations on inheritance and steep graduation of death duties.

Mill's opposition to the graduation of the income tax was based both on grounds of equity and incentive. He was in favour of

[1] On the contemporary discussion of such issues, Dr Shehab's useful monograph, *Progressive Taxation* (Oxford, 1953), may be consulted.

exemption at the lower end of the scale – which, of course, arithmetically involved a certain degree of graduation since the lump sum exempted must be a diminishing proportion of the actual income taxed. But beyond 'the amount . . . needful for life, health, and immunity from bodily pain',[1] he saw no equitable reason for differentiation. The doctrine that £100 from £1,000 was a heavier (proportionate) impost than £1,000 from £10,000 seemed to him 'too disputable altogether, and even if true at all, not true to a sufficient extent, to be made the foundation of any rule of taxation'. But beside that, he argued that to 'tax the larger incomes at a higher percentage than the smaller, is to lay a tax on industry and economy; to impose a penalty on people for having worked harder and saved more than their neighbours'.[2]

This did not mean that he opposed *any* differentiation of tax rates. As will be seen from his evidence before the two government committees, he devoted much thought and energy to the search for a just differentiation between 'earned' and 'unearned' incomes. And this search led him to the conclusion which is the second of the salient features of his principles of taxation, that a just income tax would exempt all savings. He argued this on the ground that what distinguishes the recipients of temporary incomes from those who enjoy incomes in perpetuity is the necessity governing the planning of the former, of saving to provide for themselves and their families when their temporary incomes cease. But he also argued it on the general ground which, despite the opposition of the protagonists of 'common sense', has been argued since by so many high authorities, from Irving Fisher downwards, that the taxation of savings in fact hits income twice. That a non-graduated income tax which exempted savings would be in effect a proportional tax on expenditure did not worry him in the least, since his conception of justice in the taxation of income was exactly that.[3]

---

[1] *Principles*, III 809–10.
[2] Ibid., 810–11.
[3] So far as I am aware, he made no reference to the minimum standard in this connection. This might have presented difficulties at that time, but in our own day it is easy to conceive of alleviations through the pension system or the issue of vouchers for tax-free goods.

But while considerations both of equity and incentive led Mill to oppose graduation where the direct results of work and saving were concerned, they led him in just the opposite direction when it was a matter of property passing at death. He believed in freedom of bequest. But he did not believe in freedom of inheritance. He believed with Bentham that, if anything was to be done to diminish inequality, the moment of death was the appropriate time. And in this connection he went further than any of his predecessors, and most of his successors, in this field. He was in favour of setting an absolute upper limit on the amount which might be received by inheritance or gift. But failing this, he regarded progressive duties as highly appropriate. 'The principle of graduation (as it is called,) that is, of levying a larger percentage on a larger sum, though its application to general taxation would be in my opinion objectionable, seems to me both just and expedient as applied to legacy and inheritance duties.'[1]

It is the appearance of these principles and their defence under cross-examination which lend continuing interest and importance to these records of Mill's evidence.

V. LABOUR

We now come to papers in which, in contrast to his more technical preoccupations in the items already discussed, Mill is concerned with economic organisation and its evolution in the light of general social philosophy. The first group of these is concerned with labour and its future.

Mill's fundamental attitude on this problem is enshrined in the famous chapter 'On the Probable Futurity of the Labouring Classes' in the *Principles* (IV vii). This chapter, according to his account,[2] owed much to the influence of Harriet Taylor, who eventually became his wife. But whatever the inspiration, it must always be regarded as one of the most authoritative statements of

[1] *Principles*, III 811–12.   [2] *Autobiography*, p. 174.

his general social philosophy and his hopes and fears for the future. The opening sections, with their fine contrast between what he calls the theory of dependence and protection and the theory of self-dependence,[1] are indeed among the most outstanding pronouncements on the fundamental principles of Classical liberalism; and the fact that in the present age we seem to have chosen as a basis of social policy the former principle rather than the latter does not render them any less relevant. But the two essays here reprinted and to be discussed under this heading throw much useful supplementary light on the thought underlying the chapter.

The germs of such thought are very clearly to be discerned in the article, from the *Edinburgh Review* of 1845, on the then fashionable handbook of benevolent paternalism, Arthur Helps's *The Claims of Labour*. The intentions of this article are well stated in an extract from a letter from Mill to Macvey Napier which is reprinted with the editorial note prefatory to the present reproduction. However well intentioned, the tendency of works such as Helps's book, Mill argues, is 'to rivet firmly in the minds of the labouring people the persuasion that it is the business of others to take care of their condition, without any self control on their own part', and he goes on to maintain that it is 'very necessary to make a stand against this sort of spirit while it is at the same time highly necessary . . . to shew sympathy in all that is good of the new tendencies, & to avoid the hard, abstract mode of treating such questions which has brought discredit upon political economists & has enabled those who are in the wrong to claim, & generally to receive, exclusive credit for high & benevolent feeling' (I 364).

The article certainly fulfils these intentions. After a preliminary survey of the influences from Malthus to Carlyle and the revelations of the great commissions which had led to increased interest in the 'condition of the people question', he plunges into a statement of the paternalist theory which he was proposing to criticise:

Their theory appears to be, in few words, this – that it is the proper function of the possessors of wealth, and especially of the employers of

[1] *Principles*, III 758–66.

labour and the owners of land, to take care that the labouring people are well off: – that they ought always to pay good wages; – that they ought to withdraw their custom, their patronage, and any other desirable thing at their disposal, from all employers who will not do the like; – that, at these good wages, they ought to give employment to as great a number of persons as they can afford; and to make them work for no greater number of hours in the twenty-four, than is compatible with comfort, and with leisure for recreation and improvement. That if they have land or houses to be let to tenants, they should require and accept no higher rents than can be paid with comfort; and should be ready to build, at such rents as can be conveniently paid, warm, airy, healthy and spacious cottages, for any number of young couples who may ask for them.

He contends that it 'is allowable to take this picture as a true likeness of the "new moral world" which the present philanthropic movement aims at calling into existence' (1 372–3).

Now, if things are to be run this way, he asks, are we prepared to accept the inevitable accompaniments? The states of society which have assumed such duties on the part of the wealthy have been states in which the condition of the poor has been one of virtual unfreedom. Paternal care implies paternal authority:

The higher and middle classes might and ought to be willing to submit to a very considerable sacrifice of their own means, for improving the condition of the existing generation of labourers, if by this they could hope to provide similar advantages for the generation to come. But why should they be called upon to make these sacrifices, merely that the country may contain a greater number of people, in as great poverty and as great liability to destitution as now? If whoever has too little, is to come to them to make it more, there is no alternative but restrictions on marriage, combined with such severe penalties on illegitimate births, as it would hardly be possible to enforce under a social system in which all grown persons are, nominally at least, their own masters. Without these provisions, the millennium promised would, in little more than a generation, sink the people of any country in Europe to one level of poverty. If, then, it is intended that the law, or the persons of property, should assume a control over the multiplication of the people, tell us so plainly, and inform us how you propose to do it (1 375).

The fact is, he contends, that until there is proper restraint upon numbers, there can be no hope of permanent relief of poverty:

And how is this change to be effected, while we continue inculcating [upon the working classes] that their wages are to be regulated for them, and that to keep wages high is other people's business and not theirs? All classes are ready enough, without prompting, to believe that whatever ails them is not their fault, but the crime of somebody else; and that they are granting an indemnity to the crime if they attempt to get rid of the evil by any effort or sacrifice of their own. The National Assembly of France has been much blamed for talking in a rhetorical style about the rights of man, and neglecting to say anything about the duties. The same error is now in the course of being repeated with respect to the rights of poverty. It would surely be no derogation from any one's philanthropy to consider, that it is one thing to tell the rich that they ought to take care of the poor, and another thing to tell the poor that the rich ought to take care of them; and that it is rather idle in these days to suppose that a thing will not be overheard by the poor, because it is not designed for their ears. It is most true that the rich have much to answer for in their conduct to the poor. But in the matter of their poverty, there is no way in which the rich *could* have helped them, but by inducing them to help themselves; and if, while we stimulate the rich to repair this omission, we do all that depends on us to inculcate upon the poor that they need not attend to the lesson, we must be little aware of the sort of feelings and doctrines with which the minds of the poor are already filled. If we go on in this course, we may succeed in bursting society asunder by a Socialist revolution; but the poor, and their poverty, we shall leave worse than we found them (I 375–6).

The remainder of the article is devoted to the author's own proposals for improvement of the condition of the people. It expatiates on the need for education, both at school and beyond, and, with a footnote reference to the experiments of M. Leclaire which figure so largely in the pivotal chapter in the *Principles*, it hints at Mill's own solution, 'raising the labourer from a receiver of hire – a mere bought instrument in the work of production, having no residuary interest in the work itself – to the position of being, in some sort, a partner in it' (I 382).

It is arguable that the very uncompromising nature of parts of this article is different in tone and temper from what it would have been if written after the movement towards some sort of socialism which took place in Mill's thinking after the events of 1848. But on the essential core of the argument against paternalism, there is no reason to believe that Mill's position altered greatly, and it is a very significant circumstance that he should have still thought it worthy of preservation and re-publication when in 1859 he came to collect his papers in *Dissertations and Discussions*.

The second paper here reprinted, the article on Mill's friend Thornton's book *On Labour*, is of much greater historical significance, for it contains both the celebrated retractation regarding the wages fund and Mill's most mature reflections on the ethics and economics of collective bargaining and trade unionism.

The retractation of belief in the existence of a determinate wages fund caused some sensation at the time of its appearance, and indeed it may be held to be one of the influences bringing about the end of the ascendancy of Classical theory in Great Britain. The treatment of wages in the *Principles* had followed Classical tradition in this respect. In the long run, wages depended on the tendencies of population increase; in the short run, given the labour force, they depended upon a fund of determinate size destined for the employment of labour. Now, confronted with Thornton's argument that if individual employers' demand for labour was not thus inelastic, the aggregate demand could not be inelastic either, Mill abandoned this position, saying: 'The doctrine hitherto taught by all or most economists (including myself), which denied it to be possible that trade combinations can raise wages, or which limited their operation in that respect to the somewhat earlier attainment of a rise which the competition of the market would have produced without them, – this doctrine is deprived of its scientific foundation, and must be thrown aside.' Thornton's critique had destroyed

a prevailing and somewhat mischievous error. It has made it necessary for us to contemplate, not as an impossibility but as a possibility, that employers, by taking advantage of the inability of labourers to hold out, may keep wages lower than there is any natural necessity for; and *e converso*, that if work-people can by combination be enabled to hold out so long as to cause an inconvenience to the employers greater than that of a rise of wages, a rise may be obtained which, but for the combination, not only would not have happened so soon, but possibly might not have happened at all. The power of Trades' Unions may therefore be so exercised as to obtain for the labouring classes collectively, both a larger share and a larger positive amount of the produce of labour; increasing, therefore, one of the two factors on which the remuneration of the individual labourer depends. The other and still more important factor, the number of sharers, remains unaffected by any of the considerations now adduced (II 646).

It is clear that the practical implications of this admission fully justified the sensation which it caused. Its intellectual status, however, in the history of economic analysis, is not so impressive. Thornton's critique had been preceded by a general attack on current formulations of the laws of supply and demand; and in dealing with this, Mill had shown masterly insight and analytical ability. But when he comes to the matter of the wages fund, it is as though the realisation that his earlier formulations had been wrong deprived him of his habitual critical insight and compelled merely a bold admission of error. As Taussig has well shown, the analysis at this point becomes faltering and jejune.[1] Of course, it was right to admit that the money demand for labour at any moment was much less determinate than the rigid formulations of the wages-fund theory had assumed. But it was not helpful to speak as if all that had been said of the dependence of real wages on the real accumulations of the past lost all relevance in the light of Thornton's strictures; and it is arguable, from the theoretical, as distinct from the practical point of view, that the retractation brought as much confusion as clarification. It is not without significance that in the seventh edition of the *Principles*, the last to appear in his lifetime, Mill made little alteration of what he had said before. A sentence on the power of combinations to raise wages, which earlier had predicted that unemployment would follow any attempt to raise the rate of wages above that which 'distributes the whole circulating capital of the country among the entire working population', was rewritten in terms of the narrow limits 'of obtaining . . . an increase . . . at the expense of profits'.[2] And in the Preface there is a reference to recent 'instructive discussion'

[1] F. W. Taussig, *Wages and Capital* (New York: Appleton, 1899), chaps xi and xii.   [2] *Principles*, III 930.

between himself and Thornton, the results of which, 'in the author's opinion, are not yet ripe for incorporation in a general treatise on Political Economy'.[1]

After the drama of the retractation, the second part of the paper, with its reflections on the ethics and economics of collective bargaining and trade unionism, comes as something of an anticlimax. But it is valuable, nevertheless, as affording a more extended treatment than elsewhere of the difficult questions with which it deals. The opening sections, with their illuminating contrast between the *a priori* and the Utilitarian approaches to the problems of productive organisation and distributive justice, are as good as anything Mill ever wrote on this matter. And the statement of his attitude to the various problems presented by the activities of combinations of labourers is more thorough and systematic than the treatment of these matters in the *Principles*. There are no conspicuous departures from the views expressed in that treatise, but there is much more elaboration; and the total effect is a complex one. Mill is desperately anxious to be fair; and because he felt that the unions of that time performed valuable functions in raising the self-respect of their members and providing (perhaps) organisations which might eventually transcend the status of mere sellers of hired labour in the form of self-governing associations of co-operative producers – 'a transformation' which 'would be the true euthanasia of Trades' Unionism' (II 666) – he was prepared to find excuses for practices which one would expect him to condemn. Practices restrictive of output are indeed roundly denounced. But in contrast, practices which raise wages in some sectors at the expense of the general body of workers receive a qualified extenuation: 'all such limitation inflicts distinct evil upon those whom it excludes – upon that great mass of labouring population which is outside the Unions; an evil not trifling, for if the system were rigorously enforced it would prevent unskilled labourers or their children from ever rising to the condition of skilled' (II 662). But it is urged that there are 'two considerations, either of which, in the mind of an upright and

[1] *Principles*, II xciv.

public spirited working man, may fairly legitimate his adhesion to Unionism'. The first is the educational and evolutionary value of unionism; the second, 'a less elevated, but not fallacious point of view', namely the Malthusian, is that the unions at least preserve something which would otherwise be swallowed up by the indiscriminate increase of the unreflecting: 'As long as their minds remain in their present state, our preventing them from competing with us for employment does them no real injury; it only saves ourselves from being brought down to their level' (II 664).

Similarly, while violence, defamation of character, injury to property, or threats of any of these evils in the course of trade disputes is condemned, there is a defence of the social compulsions exercised to induce workers to form a union or take part in a strike:

> As soon as it is acknowledged that there are lawful, and even useful, purposes to be fulfilled by Trades' Unions, it must be admitted that the members of Unions may reasonably feel a genuine moral disapprobation of those who profit by the higher wages or other advantages that the Unions procure for non-Unionists as well as for their own members, but refuse to take their share of the payments, and submit to the restrictions, by which those advantages are obtained. It is vain to say that if a strike is really for the good of the workmen, the whole body will join in it from a mere sense of the common interest. There is always a considerable number who will hope to share the benefit without submitting to the sacrifices; and to say that these are not to have brought before them, in an impressive manner, what their fellow-workmen think of their conduct, is equivalent to saying that social pressure ought not to be put upon any one to consider the interests of others as well as his own. All that legislation is concerned with is, that the pressure shall stop at the expression of feeling, and the withholding of such good offices, as may properly depend upon feeling, and shall not extend to an infringement, or a threat of infringement, of any of the rights which the law guarantees to all – security of person and property against violation, and of reputation against calumny (II 659–60).

All of which, in the twentieth century, sounds rather naïve from the author of *On Liberty* who foresaw so many inimical trends. But it is a revealing picture of the frame of mind of men of goodwill in the sixties and seventies, when defence of combinations of workers seemed to be defence of one of the better hopes of humanity; and it does not in the least settle the question of what Mill's attitude would have been to more recent manifestations of what such combinations can do when given special privileges by the law.

VI. PROPERTY AND ITS SOCIAL CONTROL

Next comes a group of papers which, in one way or another, spring from Mill's interest in various aspects of the institutions of property and their susceptibility to social control. This is a sphere in which his thought was avowedly tentative and experimental. He believed firmly that throughout the greater part of civilised history private property in various forms had served positive functions, functions which must be performed somehow if there is to be order and progress – the preservation of peace, the safeguarding of the fruits of accumulation, the reward of enterprise and initiative. But he did not believe that these institutions were immutable. They depended on opinion and volition and were capable of variety and development. They were also perhaps capable of being superseded by other arrangements, if these arrangements were such as to secure the same fundamental desiderata. The distinction, to which he attached such importance, between the laws of production which partook 'of the character of physical truths'[1] and the laws of distribution which were of human origin, was fundamental to his thinking here; and as is well known – and as we shall be discussing further in the next section – he was not unwilling to contemplate the eventual emergence of certain forms of collectivist ownership and control. But within the sphere of existing institutions, he believed in development and improvement:

> The principle of private property [he argued] has never yet had a
> fair trial in any country; and less so, perhaps, in this country than in

---

[1] *Principles*, II 199. See also *Autobiography*, pp. 174–5.

some others. The social arrangements of modern Europe commenced from a distribution of property which was the result, not of just partition, or acquisition by industry, but of conquest and violence: and notwithstanding what industry has been doing for many centuries to modify the work of force, the system still retains many and large traces of its origin. The laws of property have never yet conformed to the principles on which the justification of private property rests. They have made property of things which never ought to be property, and absolute property where only a qualified property ought to exist. They have not held the balance fairly between human beings, but have heaped impediments upon some, to give advantage to others; they have purposely fostered inequalities, and prevented all from starting fair in the race. That all should indeed start on perfectly equal terms, is inconsistent with any law of private property: but if as much pains as has been taken to aggravate the inequality of chances arising from the natural working of the principle, had been taken to temper that inequality by every means not subversive of the principle itself; if the tendency of legislation had been to favour the diffusion, instead of the concentration of wealth – to encourage the sub-division of the large masses, instead of striving to keep them together; the principle of individual property would have been found to have no necessary connexion with the physical and social evils which almost all Socialist writers assume to be inseparable from it.[1]

We have seen already, in the discussion of Mill's attitude to problems of taxation, his willingness to alter existing arrangements in regard to the law of inheritance. The papers discussed in the present section illustrate further in various ways this essentially empirical approach to the possible evolution of various aspects of the institution of property.

The minutes of evidence here entitled 'The Savings of the Middle and Working Classes', together with the short note on 'The Law of Partnership', are a product of Mill's lively interest in the reform of the law so as to permit industrial investment and association without commitment to unlimited liability of the property of the persons concerned. It was his belief that reform of this sort would serve the double purpose of making available for development a larger volume of saving, and at the same time facilitating, on a much larger scale than that then prevailing, the active participation

[1] *Principles*, II 207–8.

of the working classes in the organisation of industry. This involved changes both in the law relating to partnership and the law relating to joint-stock companies, and to both these movements Mill lent the weight of his support. In the papers here reprinted, the main burden of his argument is directed to the law of partnership, in respect of which he contended that the prohibitions of associations *en commandite*, as in the French law, had as little justification as the ancient laws against usury. On the larger question of the desirability of limited liability for investors in joint-stock companies, he expresses here some slight reserve on the ground that the privilege involved, if granted, should be extended to all individuals. But we know from his discussion of this question in the *Principles* that he was indeed thoroughly in favour of it. Indeed, his statement of the justification of such arrangements may well be regarded as the classic formulation of the principle:

> If a number of persons choose to associate for carrying on any operation of commerce or industry, agreeing among themselves and announcing to those with whom they deal that the members of the association do not undertake to be responsible beyond the amount of the subscribed capital; is there any reason that the law should raise objections to this proceeding, and should impose on them the unlimited responsibility which they disclaim? For whose sake? Not for that of the partners themselves; for it is they whom the limitation of responsibility benefits and protects. It must therefore be for the sake of third parties; namely, those who may have transactions with the association, and to whom it may run in debt beyond what the subscribed capital suffices to pay. But nobody is obliged to deal with the association: still less is any one obliged to give it unlimited credit. The class of persons with whom such associations have dealings are in general perfectly capable of taking care of themselves, and there seems no reason that the law should be more careful of their interests than they will themselves be; provided no false representation is held out, and they are aware from the first what they have to trust to.

When the law has 'afforded to individuals all practicable means of knowing the circumstances which ought to enter into their prudential calculations in dealing with the company, there seems no more need for interfering with individual judgement in this sort of transactions, than in any other part of the private business of life'.[1]

The next set of papers falling within this group are 'Leslie on the Land Question' and the manifesto on 'Land Tenure Reform'. It is well known from famous passages in the *Principles* that Mill regarded property in land as needing a justification different in kind from the justification of other forms of property. 'The essential principle of property being to assure to all persons what they have produced by their labour and accumulated by their abstinence, this principle cannot apply to what is not the produce of labour, the raw material of the earth.'[2] This is not to say that he was hostile to all forms of private land ownership; on the contrary, he attached great, probably exaggerated, value, for instance, to peasant proprietorship. But it does mean that he regarded land, or what Ricardo would have called the original powers of the soil (including position), as having a special significance in economic analysis and a special position in social philosophy: 'with property in moveables, and in all things the product of labour . . . the owner's power both of use and of exclusion should be absolute, except where positive evil to others would result from it: but in the case of land, no exclusive right should be permitted in any individual, which cannot be shown to be productive of positive good'.[3] Thus he favoured in certain instances the break-up (with proper compensation) of large estates and their redivision among small proprietors. He favoured special provisions in the law safeguarding the position of tenants. He was fiercely against exclusive rights of access to scenic areas. And he supported special kinds of taxation designed to take from landowners the element of unearned increment in the value of their holdings. 'They grow richer, as it were in their sleep, without working, risking, or economising,' he said. 'What claim have they, on the general principle of social justice, to this accession of riches?'[4]

The two papers reprinted in this collection, although by no means exhausting Mill's contribution to this subject, for which it

[1] *Principles*, III 898. [2] Ibid., II 227.
[3] Ibid., II 231-2. [4] Ibid., III 819-20.

is necessary also to go to the *Principles* and to the speeches, provide a very fair indication of this general attitude. The review of Cliffe Leslie's *Land Systems* is devoted largely to illustrations of the principle that the 'maxims of free trade, free contract, the exclusive power of everyone over his own property, and so forth' are not applicable, or not applicable without serious limitations, to the control of landed wealth. As Professor R. D. C. Black has shown in his notable study, *Economic Thought and the Irish Question,*[1] Mill had a much better record than other economists of the day in correct insight into the nature of the economic problems of Ireland, and this paper is perhaps especially valuable as a concise statement of his attitude in this respect.

The second paper, the *Explanatory Statement of the Programme of the Land Tenure Reform Association* – the title used on its initial publication – is valuable as an explicit statement of the actual reforms in the law relating to property in land which Mill's general views on the subject led him to support. Its content is best summarised by the reproduction of the ten points of the programme on which Mill's paper is a running commentary:

I. To remove all Legal and Fiscal Impediments to the Transfer of Land.

II. To secure the abolition of the Law of Primogeniture.

III. To restrict within the narrowest limits the power of Tying up Land.

IV. To claim, for the benefit of the State, the Interception by Taxation of the Future Unearned Increase of the Rent of Land (so far as the same can be ascertained), or a great part of that increase, which is continually taking place, without any effort or outlay by the proprietors, merely through the growth of population and wealth; reserving to owners the option of relinquishing their property to the State at the market value which it may have acquired at the time when this principle may be adopted by the Legislature.

V. To promote a policy of Encouragement to Co-operative Agriculture, through the purchase by the State, from time to time, of Estates which are in the market, and the Letting of them, under proper regulations, to such Co-operative Associations, as afford sufficient evidence of spontaneity and promise of efficiency.

[1] (Cambridge University Press, 1960.)

VI. To promote the Acquisition of Land in a similar manner, to be let to Small Cultivators, on conditions, which, while providing for the proper cultivation of the land, shall secure to the cultivator a durable interest in it.

VII. Lands belonging to the Crown, or to Public Bodies, or Charitable and other Endowments, to be made available for the same purposes, as suitable conditions arise, as well as for the Improvement of the Dwellings of the Working Classes; and no such lands to be suffered (unless in pursuance of the above mentioned ends, or for peculiar and exceptional reasons) to pass into Private hands.

VIII. All Lands now Waste, or requiring an Act of Parliament to authorise their inclosure, to be retained for National Uses: Compensation being made for Manorial rights and rights of Common.

IX. That while it is expedient to bring a large portion of the present Waste Lands under Cultivation for the purposes and on the principles laid down in the preceding articles, it is desirable that the less fertile portions, especially those which are within reach of populous districts, should be retained in a state of wild natural beauty, for the general enjoyment of the community, and encouragement in all classes of healthful rural tastes, and of the higher order of pleasures; also, in order to leave to future generations the decision of their ultimate uses.

X. To obtain for the State the power to take possession (with a view to their preservation) of all Natural Objects, or Artificial Constructions attached to the soil, which are of historical, scientific, or artistic interest, together with so much of the surrounding land as may be thought necessary; the owners being compensated for the value of the land so taken.

The two papers next to be considered, that on 'Corporation and Church Property' and that on 'Endowments', are concerned not only with the question of the right of the state to modify the conditions of foundations and endowments but also with the question of the support and control of higher education. Separate in the time of their writing by more than thirty-five years, the emphasis of the argument differs; but the essential content remains the same.

'Corporation and Church Property' is chiefly concerned to show that 'there is no moral hindrance or bar to the interference of the Legislature with endowments, though it should even extend to a total change in their purposes', and then to enquire 'in what spirit, and with what reservations, it is incumbent on a virtuous

Legislature to exercise this power' (1 195). As a Utilitarian, believing that, in the end, only consideration of the happiness of individuals should influence moral judgement, Mill is clear that it is intolerable that the wishes of dead men should be allowed to bind the dispositions of resources for more than a limited period after their death. If circumstances change, rendering their instructions no longer appropriate, then it is in the general interest that the legislature should intervene and impose new conditions. If there is proper compensation to the expectations of any persons enjoying benefits under the original dispensation, then it cannot be argued that anyone is injured by such intervention; the corporation as such has no grievance. If the law assumes 'that a man cannot know what partition of his property among his descendants, thirty years hence, will be for the interest of the descendants themselves', it cannot be assumed that 'he may know (though he have scarcely learnt the alphabet) how children may be best educated five hundred years hence; how the necessities of the poor may then be best provided for; what branches of learning, or of what is called learning, it will be most important to cultivate, and by what body of men it will be desirable that the people should be taught religion, to the end of time' (1 199).

This, however, does not mean that endowments and foundations are in themselves undesirable. Much as he admired him, Mill was not in agreement with Turgot, who had taken this view. On the contrary, he urged that they had functions to fulfil particularly in regard to education, in respect of which their existence was a positive good. It was indeed the duty of governments to provide funds for such purposes. But it 'is impossible to be assured that the people will be willing to be taxed for every purpose of moral and intellectual improvement for which funds may be required'. If, however, there were 'a fund specially set apart, which had never come from the people's pockets at all, which was given them in trust for the purpose of education, and which it was considered improper to divert to any other employment while it could be usefully devoted to that, the people would probably be always willing to have it applied to that purpose. There is such a fund, and it consists of the national endowments' (1 216). While, therefore, it is incumbent on the state to interfere with the conditions of endowments when these have ceased to serve a useful purpose, it is desirable that the interference should involve, not appropriation of the funds for the general purposes of public expenditure, but rather a better discharge of the useful functions originally intended.

Mill returns to this theme in the second paper and develops at greater lengths the argument for the existence of decentralised initiative in regard to education and research. A certain Mr Fitch, an authority on the abuses of endowments, had made statements which almost implied the abolition of centres of this sort – 'a doctrine breathing the very spirit, and expressed in almost the words, of the apologies made in the overcentralised governments of the Continent for not permitting any one to perform the smallest act connected with public interests without the leave of the Government' (1 616). But the 'truth needs reasserting, and needs it every day more and more, that what the improvement of mankind and of all their works most imperatively demands is variety, not uniformity' (II 617).

> Because an endowment is a public nuisance when there is nobody to prevent its funds from being jobbed away for the gain of irresponsible administrators; because it may become worse than useless if irrevocably tied up to a destination fixed by somebody who died five hundred years ago; we ought not on that account to forget that endowments protected against malversation, and secured to their original purpose for no more than two or three generations, would be a precious safeguard for uncustomary modes of thought and practice, against the repression, sometimes amounting to suppression, to which they are even more exposed as society in other respects grows more civilised (II 621).

Beyond this, in this paper Mill is led to argue the positive benefits, especially to higher education, of the existence of suitably constituted endowments. He is not sanguine that free competition in education will provide what is desirable without the help, example, and stimulus of education provided this way:

> It must be made the fashion to receive a really good education. But how can this fashion be set except by offering models of good

education in schools and colleges within easy reach of all parts of the country? And who is able to do this but such as can afford to postpone all considerations of pecuniary profit, and consider only the quality of the education . . .? The funds for doing this can only be derived from taxation or from endowments; which of the two is preferable? Independently of the pecuniary question, schools and universities governed by the State are liable to a multitude of objections which those that are merely watched, and, in case of need, controlled by it, are wholly free from; especially that most fatal one of tending to be all alike; to form the same unvarying habits of mind and turn of character (II 623).

It is not clear to me that in the twentieth century, with the drying up of so many sources of private endowment, Mill would necessarily have frowned on extensive support of higher education from state sources. But it is very obvious that he would still have been foremost among those who seek, by one means or another, to insulate it as far as possible from direct operation and control from parliaments and ministers; and I suspect that he would have shown more approval to a tax system such as that of the United States, which provides direct and powerful incentives to gifts for educational and cultural endowments through its death duties, than that of Great Britain, which actively resists any movement in that direction.

Finally in this group there comes the short but important paper on 'The Regulation of the London Water Supply'. Here is an instance where, the technical conditions of production rendering impossible the existence of such a degree of competition as in his opinion justified the private property system as an agent of supply, Mill was prepared to recommend thoroughgoing municipalisation. In such circumstances, he argued, the case for government regulation of some sort was indisputable. Whether this should take the form of control of existing companies or of direct governmental operation, he held, was a matter to be decided on consideration of the technical circumstances in each case arising. So far as London water was concerned, in the absence of a suitable organ of London government, he favoured the appointment of a commissioner with elastic powers of reorganisation and control. Had there existed a suitable municipal authority, he would have had 'no hesitation in expressing an opinion, that to it . . . should be given the charge of the operations for the water-supply of the capital' (II 435).

VII. SOCIALISM

The two papers bearing on socialism which appear in this collection are of very different importance. The review of Newman's *Lectures on Political Economy*, written as Mill was moving into his phase of greatest sympathy with socialism, is important principally as a demonstration of Mill's strongly negative reaction to what he thought to be unfair criticism of socialist plans and principles; it is of some interest also as the sole example in the Classical literature of any discussion of the problem of pricing under socialism. In contrast, the 'Chapter on Socialism', written towards the end of his life, are of major importance as an indication of his final views on the subject.

The vicissitudes of Mill's attitude to socialist proposals for the future organisation of society are reasonably well known so far as the documentation is concerned.[1] There is a phase of considerable sympathy, coinciding with the period of his revulsion from Benthamism: this is mentioned in the *Autobiography*, but the authentic contemporary expression thereof is to be found in a letter to Gustave d'Eichthal.[2] This is followed by a mood of greater distance exhibited in the relevant chapter (II i) in the first edition of the *Principles* – an exposition which, to Mill's annoyance but not altogether without justification, impressed some readers as

[1] There is a chapter discussing these vicissitudes in some detail in my *The Theory of Economic Policy in English Classical Political Economy* (London: Macmillan, 1961).

[2] *Autobiography*, pp. 161-4; Francis E. Mineka (ed.), *The Earlier Letters of John Stuart Mill, 1812–1848*, in *Collected Works* (Toronto: University of Toronto Press, 1963; London: Routledge & Kegan Paul) pp. 88-9.

being definitely anti-socialistic. Then under the influence of the aftermath of 1848, Mill, now very much under the influence of his wife in this respect, moves into the position of overt, if cautious, sympathy as expressed in the third edition of the *Principles* – a phase which in the *Autobiography* Mill said would class them both 'under the general designation of Socialists'.[1] Finally, in 1869, he sat down to write the chapters here reproduced, which were published after his death by his stepdaughter, Helen Taylor, who can certainly be trusted not to have released anything which did not do justice to his most mature views; and these certainly show much greater reserve than is shown in the phase represented by this third edition of the *Principles*. But the chapters are incomplete, and the question remains: what does this latest phase amount to?

It is very clear that there had been a sharp recoil from any sort of sympathy with revolutionary socialism in its totalitarian aspects. There is a sharp denunciation of all this in these chapters (see especially II 748–9), and there is a letter to Georg Brandes, of March 1872, on the goings-on of the First International, which makes quite clear the persistence of this mood.[2]

So far as the more moderate and limited proposals for piecemeal experiment are concerned, I do not doubt that Ashley is right when he contends that there has been some retreat from the position of the chapters in the third edition of the *Principles*. It would be wrong to suggest that there is now no sympathy: that is certainly not the case. But there is certainly much more caution and, I would judge, more inclination to insist on what can be done by reform within the institutional framework of the private property system. I am reasonably clear that if the details of the treatment of the main problems of socialist organisation discussed respectively in the *Principles* and in these 'Chapters' were placed in parallel columns and shown to some outside investigator, ignorant of the context of the query, he would judge the second column to show a position much less positive, much more sceptical, than the first.

[1] *Autobiography*, p. 162.
[2] Elliot (ed.), *Letters of John Stuart Mill*, II 334–5.

In the last analysis, however, more important than these nuances is the fact that the position of the third edition is by no means so strong as might be judged, either from the indications of change in the Preface or in the relevant passage in the *Autobiography*. The discussion of socialism in the chapter on property is not to be judged in isolation. It must be evaluated in conjunction with the chapter 'On the Probable Futurity of the Labouring Classes', a chapter to which we know Mill attached peculiar importance, the more general sections having been written in close conjunction with his wife. And in that chapter, it is clear that Mill's Utopia is not nearly so much in duodecimo editions of the new Jerusalem (to use the contemptuous phrase of the *Communist Manifesto*), which he had discussed with such fairness and attempt at sympathetic understanding in the chapter on property, but in the development of workmen's co-operatives – self-governing corporations foreshadowed, as he thought, by the experiments of Leclaire and others in Paris and elsewhere. In the last analysis, that is to say, Mill's socialism proves to be much more like non-revolutionary syndicalism than anything which would be called socialism at the present day.

And that, after all, should not be so surprising if we remember the famous passage in *On Liberty* alluding to these matters. As we have seen, where there was no competition, Mill was not unwilling to experiment with municipal ownership and control. But on a future in which state ownership had become widespread, his verdict was unequivocal:

> If the roads, the railways, the banks, the insurance offices, the great joint-stock companies, the universities, and the public charities, were all of them branches of the government; if, in addition, the municipal corporations and local boards, with all that now devolves on them, became departments of the central administration; if the employés of all these different enterprises were appointed and paid by the government, and looked to the government for every rise in life; not all the freedom of the press and popular constitution of the legislature would make this or any other country free otherwise than in name. And the evil would be greater, the more efficiently and scientifically the administrative machinery was constructed – the more skilful the

F

arrangements for obtaining the best qualified hands and heads with which to work it.[1]

VIII. CONCLUSIONS

The papers collected in these volumes are undoubtedly best read in conjunction with the *Principles* and the essay *On Liberty*: they throw light on the evolution and significance of these masterpieces, and are in turn illuminated by them. But taken by themselves, they would still represent a very significant achievement, a body of pronouncements on economic theory and the relations between economics and social philosophy which has no obvious rival among the productions of other writers on these subjects in the literature of the period. As to the main essays in *Some Unsettled Questions*, the papers on 'Thornton on Labour and Its Claims', 'Corporation and Church Property', and the unfinished 'Chapters on Socialism' – we should have to look far to discover productions of parallel weight and stimulus.

When Mill lay dying, it is reported that he said, 'My work is done.' By this he obviously did not mean that all the causes he stood for, all the propositions he had advanced, had been triumphant. He meant, rather, that he had had his say, that the circumstances of his life had permitted him adequately to set forth his views on the various matters on which he wished to make a contribution. And that was surely true. He had indeed developed and elaborated a system of thought so comprehensive and impressive that it came to dominate, perhaps more than it should have done, the thought of his generation, and it is not surprising that eventually there should have been some reaction against it, a reaction which we can now see went much too far and ran the risk of losing much of great value. Yet, in the end, the historic value of Mill's contribution did not reside either in the range or in the finality of the elements of the system; it was rather in the spirit

[1] *On Liberty* (London: Parker, 1859) pp. 198–9.

thereof. It is for this reason that for a generation disillusioned with systems, he once more appears as a highly admirable figure: a man with a firm hold on the ultimate values of truth and justice and liberty, with strong principles and a strong belief in their applicability; yet, once the high spirits and arrogance of youth had been transcended, fair in argument, willing to learn from experience, empirical in practical judgement, experimental in action.

8

Mill's *Principles of Political Economy*[1]

THIS new edition of the *Principles of Political Economy* is the second item to appear in the University of Toronto's projected collection of the works of John Stuart Mill, the *Earlier Letters*, reviewed in a recent number of *Economica*, being the first. The text is that of the seventh edition, together with variant readings from the previous six. There is an Introduction by the editor describing the history of the successive editions and explaining his technique of presentation; and there are nine Appendices reproducing not only the variant readings which are too long for footnote reproduction, but also correspondence relevant to the writing and revision of the *Principles* with Harriet Taylor (eventually Harriet Mill) and J. E. Cairnes. There is also a most helpful Bibliographical Index of persons and works cited, in addition to – what Mill never provided – an index of subjects.

It is safe to say that this edition is quite definitive. Professor Robson has done his work so thoroughly that no future scholar will need to do it again; and, in so doing, he has placed all those who are interested in Mill scholarship under a considerable debt. It is true that the earlier labours of Miss Ellis and Ashley had brought to light most of the more conspicuous variations. But even Ashley indicates only 16 per cent, on Professor Robson's counting, of the variant readings, whereas it is difficult to believe that the 3472 shown in the present edition will ever be significantly increased. Altogether it may be said that the editing both of these two volumes, as of the two volumes which preceded them, puts

[1] A review of *The Collected Works of John Stuart Mill*, vols II–III: *Principles of Political Economy with Some of Their Applications to Social Philosophy*, ed. J. M. Robson (Toronto: University of Toronto Press, 1965), *Economica*, XXXIII (Feb 1966). Reproduced by courtesy of the London School of Economics and Political Science.

them on the same plane as that of Mr Sraffa's Ricardo – than which there could be no higher praise.

The substantial changes in successive editions of the *Principles* revealed by Professor Robson's labours fall into three main groups: changes involving revision of perspective regarding policy and the possibilities of future development; changes amplifying or restating particular bits of analysis; changes incorporating new factual material not available, or not known, at the time of publication of earlier editions. Of these there can be no doubt that it is the first group which has the greatest historical interest. The significance of the changes in Mill's views on property and socialism is still a disputed question; and it is a great convenience to have at hand in this edition the opportunity of exact comparison between successive formulations. But it would be a great mistake to ignore the importance of the analytical changes. Not only in the chapter on international values, but also in the chapters on credit and the relations of money and interest, there are developments and restatements of considerable significance, in the former in relation to contemporary controversies, in the latter in relation to the intensely interesting correspondence with Cairnes, the inclusion of which has already been mentioned. The importance of the changes in factual material is naturally considerably less. But they have none the less value, both as an indication to the sort of evidence which weighed with Mill and as a reflection of the topics of contemporary discussion. The value should also be emphasised of the bringing to light of the hundreds of smaller changes, often only of single words or phrases, which do not fall into these broad categories. Individually they may be insignificant; cumulatively, however, they add up to a most impressive demonstration of intellectual fastidiousness and moral scruple which cannot but enhance both understanding of the way Mill's mind worked and admiration for his integrity.

It is an interesting experience to be compelled, as a conscientious reviewer, to re-read this great Classical work from beginning to end. It is also a salutary experience if, like the present reviewer, you were brought up as a student slightly to look down on Mill's contribution. For, on the whole, Mill's successors have tended to be critical rather than appreciative. Jevons and Cannan were outspoken in their denigration; and in spite of Marshall's obvious respect and Edgeworth's tribute, with one or two exceptions, historians of economic thought have tended to treat him as, at best, a worthy systematiser and, at worst, as a rather muddled bore.

But this is really all wrong. It is true that the *Principles* has not the appearance of novelty of synthesis of the *Wealth of Nations*, nor its classic objectivity. Mill was too concerned with the possibilities of improvement to be able to contemplate the springs of action with Smith's somewhat salty detachment; and his style, although not incapable of fine eloquence, has not the same magic. Nor does it show the soaring imagination which enabled Ricardo from a few simple assumptions to construct a whole system of analysis. But it is still one of the great books in the history of economic thought – great both in its analytical contribution and in its marriage of analysis and social philosophy.

So far as analysis is concerned, the business of rehabilitation has already been carried far by Professor Stigler in his notable reappraisal of Mill's contribution to the theory of value.[1] Never has an author so misrepresented himself as Mill did with his dictum that 'happily there is nothing in the laws of value which remains for the present or any future author to clear up; the theory of the subject is complete'. As Professor Stigler has shown, Mill's own treatment is marked by conspicuous originality and improvement – demand as function of price, value with joint production, rent as opportunity cost, economies and diseconomies of scale, the theory of non-competing groups . . . and the same grasp and forward-looking innovation is conspicuous throughout. The treatment of international values is indeed, to use Edgeworth's words, 'stupendous' – nearly all Marshall's contribution is here except the curves – and we know now that the propositions on capital, although somewhat implausibly expressed, were at least

[1] 'The Nature and Role of Originality in Scientific Progress', *Economica*, XXII (Nov 1955).

groping after something which had completely eluded most of their critics. It is true that the treatment of aggregate demand lacks the clarity and force of the remarkable earlier paper 'On the Influence of Consumption on Production' – it is something of a puzzle in the history of thought why in this respect Mill's cutting edge became dulled. But, for all that, the arrangement and treatment of the problems of money and credit is fuller than in any earlier work except Thornton's masterpiece; and it is necessary to come much further forward in time before anything so systematic and well integrated is to be discovered.

As to the applications, here surely is the Classical exposition of nineteenth-century liberalism at its zenith – undogmatic, historically sensitive, alive to the possibilities of change, yet firm in its grasp of the fundamentals. Mill lived in an environment vastly different from ours – how different comes out with great vividness from the series of chapters on taxation. He certainly made many mistakes in his appraisal of tendencies: he vastly overestimated the future of co-operative production; and his sense of the nearness of the stationary state, though sometimes recurrent among more recent thinkers, has proved to be historically inappropriate. But how *factually correct* he was in his general perspective as regards the menace to human improvement of population pressure; and how *morally right* he was on the position of women. To read the *Principles* today is still a liberal education in the art of political economy.

In a lively and interesting Introduction, Professor Bladen, expatiating with like approbation and quoting Ashley, seems almost to claim for the *Principles* contemporary value as a textbook. In great sympathy with much of what Professor Bladen says, I find it difficult to go quite that far. I could wish indeed that the study of the history of economic thought were sufficiently widespread for a substantial proportion of the graduates of economic faculties to have at least a first-hand *smell* of the great classics of the past – Mill's work not least among them. But for the central teaching of the subject, for good or for bad, we have chosen another way – and it is doubtful if we can go back. Not for us the comprehensive synthesis, the central treatise embodying both analysis and social applications – rather the austerities of pure analysis and the patient footslogging of empirical testing, all value judgements and appraisals of social and political practicability left ostentatiously to other departments and to other writers. The most we seem to be able to do in that direction is to hope that by a suitable arrangement of complementary subjects in degree requirements – as at L.S.E. in the B.Sc.(Econ.) – we may put the student on the way to his own synthesis and prevent the more acrobatic emerging as pure barbarians. Unavoidable? It looks like it. But when we read a work such as the subject of the present review, it is very patent how much of civilising educational value has dropped out.

9

The Place of Jevons in the History of Economic Thought[1]

I

WILLIAM STANLEY JEVONS, whose centenary we are met to commemorate, is not one of those economists whose merits have failed to achieve due recognition. In his own lifetime his work on various practical questions gave him a reputation far transcending the limits of his own profession. Since his death he has been recognised universally as one of the most outstanding figures in the history of economic thought. Not merely as economist but also as logician, philosopher, reformer, he stands out as one of the most remarkable men of the age in which he lived. He is one of the great Englishmen of the nineteenth century.

Yet if one is asked precisely to define the exact nature of his achievement, the answer is not easy. He formed no school. He created no system. He died early, and few of his many brilliant ideas were worked out with the care and precision which, in our treacherous and elusive subject, alone can assure permanent validity. Marshall has said that he was a Classic, in that he originated ideas which were capable of becoming the basis for long trains of systematic development.[2] Mr Keynes has described him as a

[1] A paper read before the Manchester Statistical Society, 27 Feb 1936. Reproduced by courtesy of the Manchester Statistical Society.

[2] *Memorials of Alfred Marshall*, ed. A. C. Pigou (1925) p. 374. An author 'is not for me classical unless either by the form or the matter of his words and deeds he has stated or indicated architectonic ideas in thought or sentiment which are in some degree his own, and which once created can never die, but are an existing yeast ceaselessly working in the cosmos . . . I incline to regard Petty and Hermann and Von Thünen and Jevons as classical but not Mill.' Marshall's verdict is especially significant. His earlier estimate of Jevons's place was by no means so favourable. See the *Academy* review reprinted ibid. pp. 93–100.

F 2

pamphleteer in that he flicked his ideas at the world, not waiting for their full elaboration.[1] Both verdicts are just. It is the totality of his achievements, the wide range of his activities, the fertility of his imagination, the marvellous lucidity and attack of his expository style, rather than the perfection of any one of his constructions, which gives him his place in history.

II

Jevons's main contribution to theoretical economics is to be found in his *Theory of Political Economy* (1871).[2] The posthumous *Principles of Economics* (1905) is a fragment – and a rather disappointing fragment at that. The *Primer of Political Economy* (1878) and the *Money and the Mechanism of Exchange* (1875) are elementary textbooks, devoted chiefly to descriptive matter; what theory they contain has no particular novelty. But the *Theory of Political Economy* is a great seminal work.

[1] *Essays in Biography* (1933) pp. 188, 211.
[2] Jevons has been fortunate in the critics of his theoretical work. At the present day there is a wealth of important commentary available for the serious student. The following are especially valuable:

A. Marshall, 'Mr Jevons' *Theory of Political Economy*', *Academy*, 1 Apr 1872, reprinted in *Memorials of Alfred Marshall*, pp. 93–100. See also Appendix 1 to the *Principles of Economics*, 8th ed. (1920) pp. 813–21.

E. H. Darwin, 'The Theory of Exchange Value', *Fortnightly Review*, XVII (1875) 243–53 (a defence of Jevons against Cairnes).

F. Y. Edgeworth, 'On Professor Jevons' Formulae of Exchange', Appendix V of *Mathematical Psychics* (London School of Economics reprint, 1932).

P. H. Wicksteed, 'On Certain Passages in Jevons' *Theory of Political Economy*', *Quarterly Journal of Economics*, III (1889) 293–314, reprinted in the *Common Sense of Political Economy and Selected Papers and Reviews on Economic Theory* (1933) II 734–65.

K. Wicksell, *Über Werte, Kapital und Rente* (London School of Economics reprint, 1933) pp. 20 ff.

A. A. Young, 'Jevons' *Theory of Political Economy*', *American Economic Review*, II 3 (1912), reprinted in *Economic Problems New and Old* (Boston, 1927) pp. 213–31.

F. H. Knight, 'Relation of Utility Theory to Economic Method in the Work of William Stanley Jevons and Others', in Stuart A. Rice (ed.), *Methods in Social Science* (Chicago, 1939) pp. 59–69.

To appreciate its historical significance, it is necessary to go back a little. In the years following the publication of Mill's *Principles of Political Economy* a certain stagnation had overtaken the world of economic thought. The Classical ferment had ceased to work. Yet the Classical system, beautiful as it was, was incomplete. In default of new constructions, it was inevitable that attention should be drawn more and more to its deficiencies. It was inevitable that, if analytical economics failed to fill the gap, appeal should be made to other principles. In Germany, the sterility of theoretical speculation led to a definitely anti-theoretical reaction. It was not to be expected, said the leaders of the Historical School, that abstract analysis should yield knowledge of a living and developing social reality. The true instrument of sociological research was not analysis but history. In England this reaction never went so far. The Classical system had been further developed and – what is seldom sufficiently recognised – the historical reaction over here was inspired, save perhaps in the case of Cunningham, by a much greater sense of proportion. Still, the reaction was considerable. Cliffe Leslie may have been justified in protesting that Jevons was mistaken in suggesting that he wished altogether to abolish the deductive part of economics.[1] But it is quite clear, as he went on to admit, that he regarded the urgent want of the time as induction and viewed with great suspicion long trains of deductive reasoning. There can be no doubt that this was typical of an important tendency. Some of the liveliest minds of the time were beginning to distrust theory or to lose interest in it; and with the exception of Cairnes, the representatives of the Classical tradition seemed to lack the intellectual vigour to defend their methodological position. It is true that Marshall was working away in the background elaborating the system which was to reverse these tendencies. But he had not yet published.

In such an atmosphere, the *Theory of Political Economy* was at once a challenge and a portent. Its author was a man who had already won a public reputation by the excellence of his work in

[1] *Essays in Political and Moral Philosophy*, 2nd ed. (1888) p. 72.

applied economics. The tract on the *Serious Fall in the Value of Gold* (1863) and the more ambitious *Coal Question* (1865) satisfied the most rigorous criteria of the anti-theoretical school. Indeed, as we should expect, the methods which he had devised in this connection – the systematic use of index numbers and logarithmic curves – were infinitely superior to anything devised by the traducers of theory. Yet here was a work by the same author in which the necessity for general theory was proclaimed with the utmost emphasis and which itself was devoted almost entirely to curves and equations having no precise quantitative content. It was true, said the author, that the widest possible development of separate specialisms was desirable. 'There will arise various sciences, commercial statistics . . . systematic descriptive economics, economic sociology and fiscal science. . . . The whole subject is so extensive, intricate and diverse that it is absurd to suppose that it can be treated in any single book or in any single manner.' But at the same time a general theory was indispensable. 'As all the physical sciences have their basis, more or less obviously, in the general principles of mechanics, so all branches and divisions of economic science must be pervaded by certain general principles. The establishment of such a theory is a necessary preliminary to any definite drafting of the superstructure of the aggregate science.'[1] Beyond this, and outraging even the feelings of some of the supporters of the Classical methods,[2] it was contended that such a theory must necessarily be mathematical:

> *Our science must be mathematical* [it said] *simply because it deals with quantities.* Wherever the things treated are capable of being greater or less, there the laws and relations must be mathematical in nature. The ordinary laws of supply and demand treat entirely of quantities of commodity demanded or supplied and express the manner in which the quantities vary in connection with the price. In consequence of this the laws are mathematical. Economists cannot alter their nature

---

[1] *Theory of Political Economy*, 4th ed. (1911) p. xvii. (Throughout this paper the references are to this edition.)

[2] See, e.g., the protest of Cairnes in his *Character and Logical Method of Political Economy*, 2nd ed. (1875) pp. 4–5, a work which in other respects has been unjustly neglected.

by denying them the name: they might as well try to alter red light by calling it blue.

If it were only for its apology for the mathematical method, which, as Allyn Young has remarked, is probably still the best statement of the matter,[1] the *Theory of Political Economy* would still be memorable.

But it was not merely as a vindication of abstract methods that the book was a challenge. In that respect indeed it could be regarded as a continuation of the main tradition. It challenged also the content of existing theory. There is no doubt that Jevons believed that his discoveries were completely revolutionary. 'In the last few months,' he had written to his brother eleven years before, 'I have fortunately struck out what I have no doubt is the *true theory of economy*, so thorough and consistent that I cannot now read other books on the subject without indignation.'[2] And at the conclusion of his book, there is a celebrated plea against the 'Noxious influence of Authority' as represented by 'David Ricardo, the two Mills, Professor Fawcett, and others who have made the orthodox Ricardian School what it is'[3] – a plea so vigorous that it can only have sprung from the most overwhelming conviction. At the present day, with the superior lights of more than half a century's development to guide us, this attitude may seem extreme. From our point of view, the development of theory may seem in some ways to have been much more continuous. But it is clear that, to Jevons, his book seemed almost a complete break with the tradition.

And indeed there can be no doubt that his great idea, the idea that the origin of the objective exchange values of the market was to be traced to the subjective valuations of individuals, was very revolutionary. However much we emphasise the continuity of analytical tradition, we must admit that the vindication of this idea has shifted the emphasis of analysis in such a way as to deserve the name of revolution.

[1] 'Jevons' *Theory of Political Economy*', cited above, p. 170.
[2] *Letters and Journals of W. Stanley Jevons, Edited by His Wife* (1886) p. 151.
[3] *Theory of Political Economy*, pp. 275, 277.

There are three aspects of this shift which it is desirable to underline explicitly.

In the first place it puts the individual – the economic subject – in the centre of the analytical picture. It has been said that the Mercantilists are preoccupied with gold, the Classical economists with goods and the modern economists with men. Like most short statements about history, this puts too sharp an edge on it. Of course, it is not true that the Classical economists regarded goods as having value without possessing utility; and we know that they were passionately preoccupied with the conditions of human improvement. But it is true that they tended to take the demand side as unimportant and in consequence got into all sorts of analytical difficulties. And it is true that they never even attempted to go behind demand to the more fundamental subjective valuations that underlie demand, that they moved all the time in the world of goods without enquiring further concerning their significance to the individual. The subjective theory of value changed all that.

In the second place, just because of this change, the new theory provided the basis for a far-reaching unification of the concept of the very subject matter of economics. My friend, Professor Hayek, has stated that Menger, Jevons's great contemporary, was the first to base the distinction between free and economic goods on the idea of scarcity.[1] I confess I find it hard to believe that some of the earlier English writers at least, even if they did not use the actual term 'scarcity' in this connection, had not some inkling of the distinction in question. But no one who has perused those passages in which the Classical writers were wont to preface their exposition of the theory of value with distinctions between goods which derive their value from scarcity and goods which are capable of indefinite multiplication, will question for a moment that the Classical analysis left considerable room for doubt on this matter.[2] The subjective theory of value changed all that too. All

[1] *The Collected Works of Carl Menger* (London School of Economics reprint, 1934) I 13.

[2] In the Classical theory of distribution, only land is specifically designated as scarce. There is no ultimate scarcity of labour: only the

goods which are limited in relation to demand, all goods, that is to say, whose marginal units possess specific importance, are economic goods and have value. The question of their mode of reproduction is a minor question of technical coefficients.

In the third place, as regards the actual causation of value, the subjective theory did, as it were, stand the Classical explanation on its head. According to the Classical economists, granted that commodities possessed utility, their value was determined by their cost, that is to say by the value of the factors of production which went to make them. According to the subjective theory, given the quantities of the factors and their technical substitutability, their values (and hence the cost of production of particular commodities) must be regarded as determined by the preferences of the economic subjects.[1] These were not merely different ways of putting the same thing, to be reconciled by emphasis on 'mutual determination'. Save in the case of land, the Classical economists did not recognise the influence of demand on the prices of the factors of production, still less on costs. The theory of distribution was separate from the theory of value. In John Stuart Mill's system, it was even prior to it. In the post-Jevonian treatment, whether Marshallian or Austrian, it is simply its most general case. Goods would have value if there were no such thing as production, provided only they were scarce. The process of production has significance only in so far as it modifies the possibilities of choice.

All this and much more must have been surging vaguely in Jevons's head when he made the passionate challenge I have quoted. Yet it would be wrong to say that it was all clearly worked out in his book. If Jevons were to return to earth and to examine

---

scarcity of food (which derives from the scarcity of land) limits its indefinite multiplication.

[1] This way of putting things is designed to side-track the objection of those who object to describing the conditions of supply of factor services (as distinct from the total potential quantity) as determined by demand. The fundamental distinction is between the preferences of the economic subjects whether as consumers or producers on the one hand, and the technical conditions on the other.

an up-to-date version of the theory of value such as we find, e.g., in Messrs. Allen and Hicks's recent essay, he would find indeed that the fundamental substance of his central idea – that the ratio of final degrees of utility is proportionate to the ratio of exchange – remained. But he would find many – perhaps to him sometimes disconcerting – changes in formulation.

He would find, for instance, that the link with psychological hedonism which he went to such pains to establish – he prefaced his theory of utility with a theory of pleasure and pain – had been not merely ignored but even deliberately repudiated. Modern economics has followed Menger rather than Jevons here. We do not draw curves with ordinates of absolute utility; we express the significance of one commodity in terms of another at different margins. The idea of measuring utility cardinally tends more and more to disappear. Nor do we not conceive of the diminution of relative utility in terms of psychological satiation. Jevons illustrated his theory to his brother by means of a dinner-table illustration. 'The decrease of enjoyment between the beginning and end of a meal may be taken as an example.'[1] We would avoid doing this. We consider merely the diminishing substitutability of one good for others, in regard to the whole hierarchy of prospective uses – again a Mengerian rather than a Jevonian construction. There is no theory of pleasure and pain in modern economics; we are concerned simply with the logic of choice.

He would find too that his theory had acquired much greater generality. We no longer think of the marginal utility (significance) of a good as dependent only on the quantity of that good we possess. We think of it as depending on the quantities of all the commodities in our possession. The accusation that the utility analysis is 'atomistic', that by regarding the significance of marginal units of particular commodities as dependent on the supply of those commodities alone, it ignores the 'organic' interconnections of our system of values, is irrelevant to modern analysis. Since the time of Edgeworth we have learnt to make utility a function of all the goods concerned. The indifference

[1] *Letters and Journal of W. Stanley Jevons*, p. 151.

curve technique which we owe to Edgeworth, Fisher and Pareto[1] has been developed for this specific purpose.

But with all this, the fundamental discovery remains. The principle laid down as far back as 1862 in the paper presented to the British Association, that it is the marginal increment whose valuation is significant, is the basis of all subsequent development.

III

It is interesting to observe how Jevons fared in the attempt to apply this theory in detail and to develop a theory of distribution which should be consonant with its main requirements.

He was not very successful in elaborating a satisfactory theory of exchange. His celebrated equations of exchange[2] certainly showed one condition of equilibrium, namely, that in equilibrium, for each party to exchange, what he called final degrees of utility must be proportionate to price. This is right enough so far as it goes – on the simple assumptions Jevons was making. But it does not explain the formation of price under competitive conditions; and the so-called Law of Indifference and the very clumsy device of the 'trading bodies' do not really help. The idea of relating marginal utility to demand *at a price* is due to Walras rather than Jevons.[3] And it was Edgeworth[4] who finally worked out the exact

---

[1] It is desirable to emphasise the debt to Fisher. I do not think that it is sufficiently appreciated that his *Mathematical Investigations into the Theory of Value and Prices*, first published in 1892, contains nearly all the innovations in this connection which we are accustomed to regard as characteristically Paretian.

[2] Namely, $$\frac{\phi_1\,(a-x)}{\psi_1\,(y)} = \frac{y}{x} = \frac{\phi_2\,(x)}{\psi_2\,(b-y)}\,,$$

where a and b represent the quantities of two commodities initially held by the two economic subjects, x and y the quantities exchanged, and ϕ_1 and ψ_1 and ϕ_2 and ψ_2 final degrees of utility to the economic subjects concerned: *Theory of Political Economy*, p. 100.

[3] The conception is clearly stated in the first memorandum presented by Walras to the Academy of Moral and Political Science in 1873, reprinted in the *Théorie mathématique de la richesse sociale* (Paris, 1877).

[4] See especially the illuminating and sympathetic critique of Jevons in *Mathematical Psychics*, Appendix V.

conditions which must be fulfilled if the price, the ratio of exchange, is to be completely determinate.

He was even less successful in developing a theory of distribution which should be coherent with his general theory of value. The very stern review of the *Theory of Political Economy* which Marshall wrote for the *Academy* is just, at least in this respect. He nowhere shows any real appreciation of the interdependence of the various elements determining the prices of the factors of production. Time and time again he seems to be on the brink of the modern theory. He sees that wages can be treated as rents.[1] He sees that the earnings of fixed capital are susceptible of a rent analysis.[2] He insists that wages and rents are determined by the size of the produce. But he does not develop a general productivity theory.[3] He accepts the Classical theory of land rent without developing its implications as regards productivity; and, like Walker at a slightly earlier date, he treats wages as a mere residuum. All of which is very disappointing. For the idea that the value of ultimate commodities comes from their utility leads directly, as Menger emphasised, to the idea that the value of factors of production depends on the value of their products. All that is needed is the development of a technique for identifying marginal products.

But there is one section of his distribution theory which, I think, has often received less than justice. I refer to his theory of capital and interest. There is no doubt that he himself attached great importance to it. In the paper presented to the British Association it receives an emphasis equal to that accorded to the marginal theory of value itself, and there is evidence in his letters that he regarded it as being of almost co-ordinate importance.[4] But it suffered from its association with the rest of his distribution

---

[1] *Theory of Political Economy*. Preface, p. 1.

[2] Ibid., p. 1 and Appendix II.

[3] Indeed, there are places where he definitely denies the possibility of attributing to each factor its specific contribution to the product. See, e.g., *The State in Relation to Labour* (1882) p. 91.

[4] *Letters and Journal of W. Stanley Jevons*, p. 155. There is an interesting passage in a letter to his sister written as early as 1859, in which the whole doctrine is anticipated: 'I think you do not duly appreciate the

theory. Marshall saw the defectiveness of its setting. But he did not realise its intrinsic originality; and it was shamefully misunderstood by Böhm-Bawerk, who certainly ought to have known better.[1] The misunderstanding was probably enhanced by Jevons's own habit of repudiating connection with the Classical writers.[2] So that, even at the present day, there are many who have not appreciated the importance of his contribution here.[3]

The substance of the theory is that the rate of interest is *inter alia* a function of the time for which factors of production are invested before yielding their final product. The essence of capitalistic production is resort to roundabout processes which yield a higher – that is, a more desired – product than more direct methods, but which necessitate a period of waiting before the yield of investment accrues. Capital is, therefore, to be defined as that which enables us to undertake such processes – in Jevons's view, 'the aggregate of those commodities which are required for sustaining labourers of any kind of class engaged in work'. And the rate of interest is *the rate at which the product is increased as the*

---

comparative importance of preparation and performance, or perhaps, as I may illustrate it, of capital and labour. You desire to begin and hammer away at once, instead of spending years in acquiring strength and skill, and then striking a few blows of immensely greater effect than your unskilled ones, however numerous, would be. We enter here into one of those deeply-laid and simple propositions of economy which I hope some day to work out in a symmetrical and extensive manner hitherto unattempted even by Mill and Adam Smith.' The discovery of the Jevonian theory of capital is thus anterior to the discovery of the marginal utility theory.

[1] Böhm-Bawerk's error is sufficiently exposed by Wicksell, *Über Werte, Kapital und Rente*, pp. 118–19. A translation is now available: *Value, Capital and Rent* (1954). The relevant passage is on pp. 142–4.

[2] He admitted kinship with Ricardo (*Theory of Political Economy*, p. 222) but denounced the wage-fund theory most emphatically (ibid., p. 268). And in his *Principles of Economics* he goes out of his way to criticise Mill's fundamental propositions respecting capital in a most unsympathetic manner (pp. 120–33).

[3] As usual, Professor Taussig is outstanding among English-speaking economists for having got things in their proper perspective. See his very just appreciation and criticism in his *Wages and Capital*, pp. 303–9, published as long ago as 1897 (reprinted by the London School of Economics, 1933).

period of production is extended, divided by the total product.[1] It is thus time which is the central figure in the picture. This comes out very clearly in a letter which Jevons wrote to Edgeworth in the last year of his life – a letter which, curiously enough, seems hitherto to have completely escaped attention.

> I have read your remarks on capital with care and interest: you will excuse my saying that you seem to be still deep in the fallacies of Mill. I fear you have not yet approached to a comprehension of my theory of capital as involving solely the element of time. I now see that the whole theory of the matter is implied in the expression for the rate of interest as given on p. 266 of my 2nd edition, some of the other expressions may be misleading. Indeed, as long as you speak of 'capital', instead of capitalisation I think you are pretty sure to go wrong.[2]

If that does not constitute a fairly strong claim to be regarded as one of the founders of the modern theory of capital, I do not know what does. There is no doubt that it is not set out with very great clarity. In the *Theory of Political Economy*, as distinct from the letter and the posthumous fragment, there are formulations of the capital concept which still bear too wage-fundish a complexion to be wholly free from objection. In all sorts of ways the exposition is incomplete and incorrect. But the main formula is there. The essence of the use of capital is time. And the formula for the rate of interest, though framed on exceedingly narrow assumptions, is correct. It is substantially the same as Wicksell's.[3]

Now, of course, this theory, much more than the subjective

---

[1] If $F(t)$ be the product and $F^1(t)$ the rate of increase, the rate of interest is $\dfrac{F^1 t}{Ft}$, *Theory of Political Economy*, p. 246.

[2] *Letters and Journals of W. Stanley Jevons*, p. 439. There is an equally trenchant passage in the fragment on capital, reprinted as Appendix II to the 4th ed. of the *Theory of Political Economy*: . . . 'to avoid confusion of ideas we ought not to speak of capital, but of capitalisation. Capital, if it consists of concrete wealth, is simply a thing and involves no idea of time: whereas we can have no reference to the use of capital without introducing time as the essence of the matter' (p. 295).

[3] In his essay on 'Jevons' *Theory of Political Economy*', cited above, Allyn Young urges that the Jevonian theory of interest is to be regarded as an incomplete marginal productivity theory. This, I think, is correct.

theory of value, is still to be regarded as an open question. It is quite clear that in the form propounded by Jevons it is in many respects too simple. It neglects compound interest, which is a phenomenon which itself vitiates the idea of the casual significance of any single average period of production.[1] It fails to provide a solution of the problem of durable goods. It considers only labour and not the vast multiplicity of different kinds of factors of production which in any full treatment of the problem must be worked into the picture. All this is painfully clear from recent controversy on the matter. But I confess that, in my judgement, the critics of this theory have not really grasped its significant bearing. They pick away at unrealistic deficiencies in the first approximation and think that they have vitiated the central idea. It is, indeed, very easy to pick holes in almost any existing formulation of this theory of capital and interest. But I do not believe that anything which has been said, or indeed, that can be said, will vitiate the central notion that the essence of capitalistic production is the use of factors in processes which only yield their fruit after the lapse of time, and that the rate of interest is determined on the technical side by differences between the productivity of factors used for longer and for shorter processes. And that was the central thesis of the Jevonian theory of capital.

IV

I have lingered over Jevons's contribution to pure theory because it is there, in my judgement, that his work has greatest contemporary interest and significance. But a sketch of his significance

---

But the essence of the marginal productivity theory, as it seems to me, is its emphasis on the interdependence of factors – the marginal products are partial differentials – and this is conspicuous from its absence in the Jevonian theory. The essence of capital theory, on the other hand, is its emphasis on the productivity of lengthy investment, and this Jevons emphasises. Hence, while I should say he perceived the main thing about capital theory, he was still some way off the central feature of the general marginal productivity theory of distribution.

[1] See F. A. Hayek, 'Investment and Output', *Economic Journal*, XLIV (June 1934).

as an economist would be ill-drawn, however slight it was, if it took no account of his work in the fields of applied economics and economic policy. For there was no field in which his touch showed greater evidence of sheer genius than in his capacity for handling facts, for marshalling large bodies of statistical evidence in a clear and succinct manner, and in extracting the utmost significance from them. Indeed, there have been some – I am not sure that Marshall was not one of their number[1] – who have held this to be his most conspicuous claim to fame. And if it is true – as I believe it is – that the occurrence of really great ability in applied economics is even rarer than ability in pure theory, then this claim may well be supported. For there have been few who have showed more ability here than the author of the *Serious Fall in the Value of Gold*.

But at the same time, by its very nature, the *substance* as distinct from the *method* of work in this field must have a more ephemeral significance than the discovery of general principles. The one remains, the many change and pass. The detailed facts of the fleeting day alter and a new generation is confronted with new data. Many of the investigations which interested Jevons most have ceased to have significance, save as history. We are left with the example of a method so fresh, so lively, so powerful that even when the substance it deals with is dead, we can contemplate its form with profit.

Jevons's most important incursions into these fields were three: his investigation of the trend of prices in the fifties and the sixties; his investigation of the coal question; and his investigation of the trade cycle. There were many others, the investigation of seasonal pressure in the money market, the census of the gold coinage, the match tax, for example, which would have brought fame to a lesser man. But in his work they are of smaller importance. In one of these major investigations he was completely right; in one as right as it is possible to be, predicting over more than half a century; in one, so far as we can see, quite wrong.

[1] See the letter to Jevons, reprinted in *Memorials of Alfred Marshall*, p. 371.

He was dead right about the movement of prices. *The Serious Fall in the Value of Gold* is one of the most beautiful investigations in applied economics ever made, and its contentions have been vindicated up to the hilt by subsequent researches. He was right about the increase of prices as against those who said that no increase had taken place. He was right as regards its probable limits, as against those who held that the increase in the supply of gold must lead to a catastrophic inflation.

We cannot speak so decisively about the contentions of the *Coal Question*. It is clear that many of Jevons's estimates have been found to be defective.[1,2] It is clear, too, that, at the present day, the availability of other sources of energy renders many of his fears much less urgent. But his main thesis, that the rate of increase of the middle of the last century could not be maintained without rising costs of production, was surely correct. And he was correct, too, in supposing that, as time went on, the competition of other sources of supply of coal would become increasingly difficult to meet. Of course, the fact that we have reached a period of competitive difficulties does not prove that these difficulties are all of the kind that Jevons predicted. Some are pretty obviously not. But can it really be denied that some at least of our troubles have been due to the growing age and inaccessibility of some of our older coalfields?

It is in regard to the investigation of the trade cycle that we have to record Jevons's one comparative failure. It might have been hoped that, as the author of by far the best pure theory of capital that had up to then been propounded, and that as a member of

[1] On all this, the comments of Sir Alfred Flux should be consulted in the edition which he edited (3rd ed., 1906).

[2] There is one analytical error in his arguments which has some practical significance. He argued that it was analytically wrong to suppose that the discovery of substitutes for coal could ever result in a slower rate of consumption, on the ground that the demand for coal was on the same footing as the demand for labour, and the discovery of substitutes for labour had always, in the end, increased the demand for it: *Coal Question*, 3rd ed., pp. 140 ff. But this is not certain; it is not excluded *a priori* that the discovery of ways of economising fuel may lead to a diminished rate of consumption.

your society, which, as Mr Ashton has recorded, was the scene of some of the best work in the early investigations of business fluctuations, he would have proceeded to solve this problem, too. And, if we look at the *Serious Fall in the Value of Gold*, there is one passage which does, indeed, offer the highest promise of fruitful developments. 'The remote cause of these commercial tides,' he says, 'seems to lie in the *varying proportion which the capital devoted to permanent and remote investment bears to that which is but temporarily invested to reproduce itself.*'[1] There surely you have a text which neither Robertson nor Hayek would be ashamed of – a jumping-off point for nearly all that is most exciting in the modern theory of the trade cycle.[2] Unfortunately it was not to be. Having ascertained the existence of the cycle – there was nothing very new about this – and having thrown out this path-breaking suggestion, Jevons was beguiled into attempting to establish a correlation between the fluctuations of trade and certain astronomical phenomena – the sunspot cycle – using the price of corn either in England or in India as the connecting link ! There is really little that can be said for this construction. The cycles did not always fit; two of the biggest crises of the century fell outside the series. The sunspot cycle was revised; and the list of crises was found to be so elastic that it was possible to revise it too.[3] Few authorities take Jevons's periodicities very seriously now. In any case the methodological basis of the whole speculation was weak. It is quite possible that there may exist rhythms of temperature or solar activity

[1] *Investigations in Currency and Finance*, 1st ed. (1884) pp. 27–8.

[2] The passage is quoted by Hayek as an anticipation of recent views on this matter in an historical appendix to the second edition of *Prices and Production* (1935) p. 102.

[3] Professor Wesley Mitchell's comment may be quoted: 'Jevons had an admirably candid mind: yet in 1875, when the sunspot cycle was supposed to last 11.1 years, he was able to get from Thorold Rogers' *History of Agriculture and Prices in England*, a period of 11 years in price fluctuation, and when the sunspot cycle was revised to 10.45 years he was able to make the average interval between English crises 10.466 years. To get this later result Jevons purposely left out from his list of crises 'a great commercial collapse in 1810–11 (which will not fit into the decimal series)'; he also omitted the crisis of 1873, and inserted a crisis in 1878 which other writers do not find': *Business Cycles*, 2nd ed. (1927) p. 384.

affecting crop yields and economic activity generally. But is there any probability that they are the *only* disturbing forces? Is there any evidence that *only* this kind of shock can be transformed into cyclical fluctuation? How much better if, instead of chasing this statistical will-o'-the-wisp, Jevons had settled down to give a solid account of the way in which 'variations in the proportion between fixed and circulating capital' can give rise to crises and the *many* ways in which these variations can be occasioned.[1]

There is one other of Jevons's suggestions in these fields which deserves notice even in the wide survey we are taking. In the *Theory of Political Economy*, he suggested that by the examination of trade statistics it should be possible to discover the demand functions for particular commodities, as Gregory King had attempted to do in regard to the price of corn. He was quite aware of some of the limitations of such functions when obtained. 'The subject is too complex to allow of our expecting any simple precise law. Nevertheless, their determination will render economics a science as exact as any of the physical sciences – as exact, for instance, as meteorology is likely to be for a very long time to come.'[2] He did not follow up the suggestion, save by one or two very sketchy examples, and it is arguable that even with all the qualifications he made he was too optimistic of results. Nevertheless, he is to be held as one of the chief pioneers of such attempts to make closer the relation between statistics and the general theory of value.

V

Jevons's interest in the application of economic theory was not limited to the investigation of the relations of facts; he was intensely interested in the prescription of policy also. His lively imagination was continually playing upon the leading problems of the day – bimetallism, ideal money, the management of posts

[1] The account in the *Primer* is fresh and interesting, but has no theoretical interest.
[2] *Theory of Political Economy*, p. 147.

and telegraphs, the position of married women in factories, trade unions and industrial co-operation. And he touched nothing that he failed to invest with new interest.

Most of these issues are now dead. But the general issue of the place of the state in economic life is, if anything, more urgent than ever. As we should expect, this was not an issue which Jevons neglected. The opening chapter of the *State in Relation to Labour* contains a long discussion of the question whether we can frame general criteria of the desirable limits of state activity – a discussion which I fancy has had great influence on the subsequent thought on this subject. The conclusion is reached that no such criteria are possible. Jevons examines the desirability of non-interference in regard to the conditions of labour. He has no difficulty in showing that there are cases – the use of dangerous machinery is a case in point – where there seems an obvious utilitarian justification for bringing about certain results by direct regulation rather than by leaving them to be secured by the slower-moving forces of the market. From these and similar considerations he reaches the conclusion that there are no general rules – that every case must be examined separately. 'The outcome of the inquiry is that we can lay down no hard and fast rules, but must treat every case in detail on its merits. Specific experience is our best guide or even express experiment where possible, but the real difficulty consists in the interpretation of experience. We are reduced to balance conflicting probabilities of good and evil.'[1]

I confess I find this very unsatisfactory. It is easy enough to see why it was written. The Duke of Wellington, reviewing his troops, is reported to have said, 'I don't know what impression these make on the enemy; but, by God, they make me afraid.' It is easy to see that Jevons, the enlightened Utilitarian, must have felt much the same, reviewing the way in which popular advocacy of economic freedom, then, as now, was wont to prejudice a good cause, by opposition to measures which were obviously expedient, and by appeal to dogmas which were obviously indefensible. It is easy to understand the strong urge to repudiate all that. As against that

[1] *The State in Relation to Labour*, p. 6.

wooden view of social life which sets up dogmatic rights to unlimited freedom of the individual and dogmatic limitations of
government authority, without regard to their utilitarian justification, the Jevonian case is unanswerable; and it can hardly be better
stated. But as the last word on the principles of industrial legislation, it is surely most inadequate. We do not believe that we can
prescribe, out of the blue, detailed forms of industrial legislation
which shall fit every conceivable state of industrial technique, and
every conceivable type of population. But we do believe that there
are certain principles which must be invoked if we are correctly
to analyse each case on its merits. And we do believe further that,
given the general structure of different forms of society, and given
a knowledge of what people want, it is not impossible to frame
rules about the desirability of different *types* of action. We are
really not always compelled to start from scratch whenever we are
confronted with new proposals.

Now, of course, it is highly improbable that if things had been
put this way Jevons would have made any objection. He states
very clearly that he is considering the relation between science and
practice, not the status of scientific generalisations themselves. He
is very careful to say that 'all effects of the proposed act, whatever
be their remoteness or uncertainty, must be taken into account.
There may be collateral or secondary effects which will not be
apparent for years to come.'[1] It is obvious that such effects cannot
be detected save with the aid of analytical principle. And he goes
out of his way to say 'in order to prevent the possible misapprehen-
sions into which a hasty reader might fall, I may here state that I
am a thorough-going advocate of free trade',[2] which is a position
he could only have reached by considerations very much transcending the merits of particular cases. But I do not think it is
unfair to state that the net effect of his discussion here, however
unintentional, is certainly to leave the impression that all questions
of practice are completely open questions, and that there are no
rules of any degree of generality which social science, combined
with the Utilitarian norms, may enable us to devise. Yet if this

[1] Ibid., p. 6. [2] Ibid., p. 13.

were to be regarded as the last word on the subject it would surely be very much to be regretted. Whatever may have been the case in Jevons's day, it is certainly not true today that the claims of general rules are overemphasised. We do not need any exhortation to be empirical. On the contrary, indeed, it is the lack of any body of generally recognised rules which constitutes one of our main difficulties. We have got into the most dreadful muddle dealing with each case 'on its merits'. No doubt this is because we have neglected to observe that this involves considering 'the remoter as well as the more immediate consequences of action' – the Jevonian precepts might have seen us through if only they had been faithfully interpreted. But, as Jevons himself urged, the suitability of precepts can be tested experimentally, and we have had a long period of experimentation. Today, at least, it seems that if we are to get out of our present difficulties it will be, not by dispensing with general rules, but by seeking to reconstruct them on a sounder basis. Today, at least, we render homage to Jevons, not as destroyer, but as creator, not as one who loosened the hold of the old rules, but as one who, by his general services to economic science, prepared the way for a more rational formulation of the new.[1]

---

[1] On p. 183, in the paragraph dealing with *The Coal Question*, I have expunged a sentence appearing in the original paper, which suggested a prospective decline in population. I was not aware till I re-read my paper that I had committed myself in writing to endorsement of this delusion, so fashionable in the late 1930s. But I certainly often did so in conversation.

10

Philip Wicksteed as an Economist[1]

I

PHILIP HENRY WICKSTEED, the author of the *Common Sense of Political Economy* and the other works collected in these volumes, was one of the most remarkable intellectual figures of the half-century which has just passed. He was a leading member of the Unitarian ministry. He was one of the foremost medieval scholars of his time. He was an economist of international reputation. He was a savant who made contributions of permanent value to highly technical branches of knowledge. He was a teacher who, without vulgarisation, succeeded in making intelligible to many the main significance of the various fields of learning in which he moved. Few men of his time so successfully combined such a wide range of intellectual pursuits with such conspicuous excellence in each of them.

The main facts of his external career are soon told.[2] The variety of Wicksteed's experience lay in the world of thought rather than in the world of action. He was born in October 1844 at Leeds in Yorkshire. His father, Charles Wicksteed, was a Unitarian minister; on completing his undergraduate studies at University College, London, he himself decided to enter that ministry. In 1874 he was appointed successor to James Martineau at Little

---

[1] An Introduction to the *Common Sense of Political Economy*, reprinted by Messrs Routledge & Sons (1933). Reproduced by courtesy of Messrs Routledge & Kegan Paul Ltd.

[2] For a full account of Wicksteed's life and literary achievements, see C. H. Herford, *Philip Henry Wicksteed: His Life and Work* (1931). In preparing this Introduction, I have drawn liberally on a chapter on Wicksteed's economic writings, which I contributed to that work. But I have expanded it considerably, and in certain places where, in the light of further reflection or information, it seemed desirable, I have slightly altered the emphasis.

Portland Street Chapel, and in this position for the next twenty years he played a leading part in Unitarian circles in London. But, from a very early date, his activities had begun to extend beyond this rather limited sphere. His philosophical interests led him to Dante and the Middle Ages. His interest in ethics and sociology led him to economics. He had a genius for teaching, and he became one of the most successful of the early University Extension lecturers. In 1897, his theology having become more and more unorthodox and his literary and philosophical preoccupations having become more and more pressing, he resigned his position at Little Portland Street and henceforward supported himself and his family by lecturing and by writing. In this period he produced the *Common Sense of Political Economy* and many of his most important works on the Middle Ages. He died of an obstruction in the throat on 18 March 1927. It is characteristic of his whole life-work that until two days before his death he was engaged in the dictation of a translation of Aristotle.

II

According to Dr Herford, Wicksteed's interest in economic problems was first aroused by a perusal of Henry George's *Progress and Poverty*. But unlike so many who have been stirred by that powerful but essentially wrong-headed manifesto, he was moved, not merely to propaganda, but to further enquiry. He embarked upon an examination of the meaning of economic phenomena in the large. All his life he retained a sympathy for the idea of land nationalisation, although the reasons by which he justified this attitude, and the practical measures he was willing to support, differed *toto caelo* from the arguments and measures usually associated with that cause.[1] But the main significance of his early

[1] See the very cautious paper on 'Land Nationalisation' read before the Political and Economic Circle of the National Liberal Club (*Transactions of the National Liberal Club Political and Economic Circle*, III (1901) 214–238): 'It is indeed impossible', he wrote, 'that we should follow out Henry George's delightfully simple plan of seizing the land straight away and leaving the landlords to find their compensation in the happier order

acquaintance with this movement was, not that it led him to believe in the desirability of public bodies acquiring, out of the proceeds of taxation, certain forms of landed property, but that, in the course of the enquiries thus initiated, he was led to the study of Jevons.

By the beginning of the eighties, the Jevonian innovations in pure economics were beginning to emerge from their initial obscurity. They had received favourable notice abroad; and at home, in spite of Cairnes's hostility and Marshall's very cold water, they were beginning to attract the attention of the educated public. From his first acquaintance with them, Wicksteed seems to have realised their immense force and revolutionary significance. In order to be in a position to understand them to the full, he supplemented his own mathematical training by taking lessons in the differential calculus. A copy of the second edition of the *Theory of Political Economy*, which was purchased by Wicksteed in 1882, is in the possession of the present writer; the marginal annotations on almost every page show how profoundly and extensively he had meditated on its doctrines. In the utility theory of value, which was Jevons's main contribution, he discovered a foundation on which he believed there could be built a system of

---

of society in which they would find themselves living. Land has been freely recognised as private property for generations past. It has changed hands backwards and forwards; and even if a great deal of it has been stolen within the historic memory of man, the thieves have long ago sold out under the direct sanction of the community and gone to their reward. We cannot make social reform a mere game of hunt-the-slipper, and ask the last man who passed on the article to help us in seizing and despoiling the man to whom he has just passed it. And if we pay him compensation, then we must either raise money at once out of the present generation; that is to say, we must call upon the possessors of wealth of every kind to endow the State by a huge act of self-renunciation – a call to which it is to be feared they will not respond – or else we must borrow the money with which to buy out the landlords, and saddle ourselves with a debt which may for many years absorb the whole revenue we derive from the land.' Wicksteed's hope seems to have been that land should gradually be acquired by the State out of the proceeds of taxation and that there might be enacted certain modifications in the law regarding property rights in minerals discovered in the future.

economic analysis, more far-reaching in its scope and more exact in its detailed development than any that had yet been possible.[1]

Wicksteed's first contribution to theoretical economics was an application of the Jevonian analysis to the criticism of the Marxian theory of value – an article on *Das Kapital* which appeared in the socialist journal, *To-Day*, in October 1884. The article is not merely a criticism; it is an independent exposition of the new theory which carried it further forward and, on more than one point, adds important new corollaries. The labour theory is declared to be false. The cases which it appears to explain are explained more convincingly as special instances of a more comprehensive theory. 'A coat is not worth eight times as much as a hat to the community because it takes eight times as long to make it. . . . The community is willing to devote eight times as long to the making of a coat because it will be worth eight times as much to it' (p. 718). It was the first scientific criticism of Marx's theory – written years before Böhm-Bawerk's or Pareto's – and in some respects it remains the most decisive. The argument is developed with the ease and certainty of a man who is completely sure of himself, not because of any self-deception or premature synthesis, but because he has mastered the essential material. Mr George Bernard Shaw, at that time a Marxian Socialist, made a controversial reply; but as Mr Shaw, who, as he has subsequently related,[2] was eventually persuaded by Wicksteed that he was wrong, would be the first to admit, the significance of his reply lay not so much in what it itself contained, but rather in the fact that it elicited further elucidations of Jevons.[3] It is perhaps worth noting that Wicksteed's rejoinder contains one of the earliest recognitions of the relative nature of the concepts invoked by the utility theory of value.

In 1888, Wicksteed began to venture on more constructive

[1] See the Preface to the *Common Sense* (pp. xxxi, xxxii) and the articles on Jevons contributed to *Palgrave's Dictionary of Political Economy* and the *Economic Journal* (pp. 801–13, below; subsequent references to the present work [the *Common Sense*] are given in the text.

[2] *The Times*, 25 Mar 1927.

[3] 'The Jevonian Criticism of Marx: A Rejoinder' [below, pp. 731–3).

exposition. In that year he published his *Alphabet of Economic Science* – an attempt to restate and to elaborate positively the central guiding principles of the theory he had learnt from Jevons. The book is avowedly an introduction. Forty pages of careful mathematical illustration of the notion of limiting rates preface the attempt to apply this notion to the explanation of exchange values, and copious and minute illustrations accompany every step in the subsequent argument. In the history of theory, the book is, perhaps, chiefly notable for its introduction of the term 'marginal utility' – a rendering of the Austrian *Grenznutzen* – as a substitute for the Jevonian 'final utility', which, for obvious reasons, had tended to lead to confusions. But the book is not merely of historical interest. It still preserves considerable pedagogic value. Much as has been written on the subject with which it deals since that date – not least by Wicksteed himself – it still remains one of the best available introductions to the subject. Other introductions may be easier to read and perhaps more entertaining to the student; but none is more calculated to give him real grasp and comprehension. In broad outline, of course, nothing can be simpler than the general notion of diminishing marginal utility. But in closer application to the problems of price determination, the notion is apt to prove elusive, at least to the non-mathematician; and more than one economist of standing has been betrayed into grotesque misconstructions. It is the great merit of Wicksteed's work that, starting from a point at which no knowledge of the calculus is assumed in his readers, he succeeds in expounding the theory with such minuteness and precision that misconstructions of this sort should be impossible for anyone who has read it with normal attention.[1]

The book was an immediate success among economists. With

[1] Some of the main propositions of the *Alphabet*, and of a paper subsequently contributed to the *Quarterly Journal of Economics* – 'On Certain Passages in Jevons's *Theory of Political Economy*' [below, pp. 734–54] – were subsequently restated in articles for the first edition of *Palgrave's Dictionary*. See articles under the general heading 'Elementary Mathematical Economics', 'Dimensions of Economic Quantities', 'Degree of Utility', 'Final Degree of Utility' [below, pp. 755–65].

G

one stride, Wicksteed had secured a place in that limited circle whose pronouncements on pure theory commanded international attention. It was referred to approvingly by Edgeworth; and the great Pareto, most ferocious of critics, most uncompromising guardian of the sanctities of pure theory, gave it a prominent place in the bibliography of works on '*Économie pure*' which appeared in Part I of his *Cours*. With the general public, however, it was not such a success. The severity of its exposition and the uncompromising treatment of difficulties were inimical to its prospects of popularity. It is the one introduction to mathematical economics for non-mathematicians which really does what it promises – conduct its reader by arguments comprehensible to those with no previous knowledge of the calculus to a point at which the central propositions which involve acquaintance with that technique are thoroughly intelligible. But the non-mathematicians who have used it are probably few in number.

The Preface to the *Alphabet* had promised that, if it proved to meet a want among students of economics, it should be followed by similar introductions to other branches of the science. This plan seems to have been abandoned; for the next work was one which by no stretch of language could be described as introductory or simple. This was the celebrated *Essay on the Co-ordination of the Laws of Distribution*, published in 1894.[1]

By the beginning of the nineties, the centre of gravity in theoretical economics had shifted from the narrow problem of commodity value to the wider problem of distribution or, as it is sometimes called, the pricing of the factors of production. Jevons and his fellow innovators abroad had suggested a theory which, as a first approximation, might be held to elucidate the prices which could be secured for 'ultimate commodities'. But the further problem of deciding in what proportions the prices were 'distributed' between the different factors co-operating in the production of these commodities, had not yet reached a satisfactory solution.

[1] This work has been republished as No. 12 in the London School of Economics Series of Reprints of Scarce Tracts in Economics and Political Science.

As early as 1876 Walras had indeed put forward a solution on the very restrictive assumption that the proportions in which productive services could be used were fixed.[1] But although his general framework indicated the lines on which a solution could be found, he quite definitely did not at that time proceed to solve the problem of what happened if the proportions were variable. It was this problem which the *Essay* was designed to solve. The solution offered was what has come to be known as the marginal productivity theory of distribution. If the product to be distributed is P, then, to use Wicksteed's own statement, 'the ratio of participation in the product on which any factor K can insist . . . will be $\dfrac{dp}{dk}$ per unit, and its total share will be $\dfrac{dp}{dk} . K$'.[2]

III

How far this result had been reached independently of the work of others it is difficult to say. Just as, at the beginning of the seventies, the utility theory of value had occurred simultaneously to Jevons, Walras and Menger, so, at the beginning of the nineties, the marginal productivity theory of distribution was 'in the air' and different variants had been put forward by Marshall, Clark and others. It is certain that Wicksteed was acquainted with Marshall's work in this field, for there are footnote references to the *Principles* in the *Essay*. But it is probable that his solution was reached as a result of his studies of Jevons, which were carried out before Marshall had published.[3] This is what seems to follow from Wicksteed's own account of his discovery,[4] and we may be sure that a man so scrupulously honest and so modest about his

[1] At first in his paper 'Équations de la production', read before the Société Vaudoise des Sciences Naturelles in Jan and Feb 1876 and published in the *Bulletin* of that society, XIV 76, pp. 395–430, the substance of which appears in Leçon 41 of that part of the first edition of the *Éléments d'économie politique pure* published at Lausanne in 1877.

[2] Op. cit., p. 9.

[3] *Quarterly Journal of Economics* (1889) 293 ff.

[4] *Essay*, p. 43.

own achievements would have acknowledged any other debt had it existed.[1]

Thus by the time the *Essay* was published, the idea that the notion of marginal productivity might play a part in the explanation of the pricing of the factors of production was becoming widely accepted among the more advanced economists. The same cannot be said, however, of the main propositions of the *Essay* – namely, that if each factor is rewarded according to its marginal productivity, the sum of the remunerations of the separate factors will exactly exhaust the product: in other words, that the marginal productivity analysis is a *sufficient* explanation of distribution in this sense. This bold generalisation has always been associated with the argument of the *Essay*, and it long remained the subject of lively controversy.[2] In later years, Wicksteed himself, as the

[1] At the time of publication, Wicksteed was the subject of a bitter reproach by Walras in the celebrated Appendix to the 3rd edition of his *Éléments* (Lausanne, 1896), 'Note sur la réfutation de la théorie anglaise du fermage de Mr Wicksteed'. The matter, as it appeared to Walras, has been carefully investigated by Professor Jaffé in a masterly monograph, 'New Light on an Old Quarrel' (*Cahiers Vilfredo Pareto*, no. 3, Geneva, 1964), which makes it clear that Walras was not claiming for himself explicit statement of the marginal productivity proposition, but rather having provided a setting in which that proposition suggested itself. It is clear to me, looking at things from Wicksteed's end, that had he been conscious of any such suggestion, he would have acknowledged it – after all, did he not send to Walras a complimentary copy of his book? But Walras, although the soul of honour, as witness his acknowledgements to Jevons and the part he played in the rehabilitation of Gossen, was fantastically touchy about his own priorities and the inadequate recognition he had received in Britain. Moreover, he was justly indignant at the refusal by Edgeworth to print a review of Wicksteed by Barone which at once corrected imperfections in Wicksteed and gave due credit to Walras for the way in which he had posed the problem. Paradoxically enough, it is likely that this refusal was due, not to any predilection on Edgeworth's part for Wicksteed's proposition, which, be it remembered, he subsequently condemned in terms which most would regard as unduly contemptuous, but rather, inexplicable as it may seem, from a fear of offending Marshall [Note added in 1969.]

[2] See the classic treatment of this subject in Professor Stigler's *Production and Distribution Theories* (New York, 1941) pp. 320 ff. Professor Jaffé's monograph, cited above, should also be consulted. [Note added in 1969.]

result of criticism by Edgeworth and Pareto, became dissatisfied
with his own demonstration, declared it to have been a premature
synthesis and, in the *Common Sense of Political Economy*, an-
nounced it to be finally withdrawn. The grounds of his dissatisfaction, however, were technical and mathematical; it would be
wrong to suppose – as has sometimes been the case – that he
renounced the productivity analysis in general.[1] Certainly the
solution offered in its place in the *Common Sense of Political
Economy* does not differ so noticeably from that of the *Essay* as to
suggest that the earlier version was to be regarded as wholly misleading. In fact it is not difficult to reformulate the analysis so as
to make it logically watertight. Wicksteed's proposition was not
untrue; the only criticism to which it is exposed is that the
supporting argument was incomplete. It was not so exhaustive as
its author at first supposed. This is not a very grave defect in a
new theory: we are none of us so near the goal as we believe ourselves to be.

For sixteen years after the appearance of the *Essay*, Wicksteed
published little on economic theory. A couple of reviews in the
Economic Journal – on Jevons's *Principles* in 1905 and on Pareto's
Manual in 1906 – constitute the sum of his published utterances.
But all this time his mind was revolving the terms of a synthesis

[1] What these grounds were, long remained highly obscure. The
fundamental objection to the analysis of the *Essay* was that it assumed
production functions that were linear and homogeneous – an objection
which, as was pointed out by Barone and Wicksell among others, can be
circumnavigated by assuming alternatively that the firms in the competitive economy concerned are operating at least cost – i.e. optimal size –
in which case the main proposition of product exhaustion can be maintained. It now appears, however, from a letter from Wicksteed to J. M.
Clark, written in 1916, and discovered and published by Professor Joseph
Dorfman as recently as 1964 (*Economica*, XXXI, 123 (August 1964)), that it
was Pareto's insistence on the invariability of the proportions of certain
components of particular production processes that occasioned his retractation. It thus seems to have been a somewhat unnecessary gesture;
for, as Sir John Hicks showed many years ago in his article 'Marginal
Productivity and the Principle of Variation' (*Economica*, old series, no. 35
(Feb 1932), on the plane of analysis on which the argument should be
conducted, there are ways round this particular objection. [Note added
in 1969.]

wider than anything he had hitherto attempted, and in 1910 he published his *magnum opus* in this field – the *Common Sense of Political Economy*.

It is not easy in a short space to give an adequate idea of this work. The title conveys less than nothing; indeed, never was a work of this kind more unfortunately named. It is not 'common sense' in the ordinary sense of the term, and it is not *political* economy. It is, on the contrary, the most exhaustive non-mathematical exposition of the technical and philosophical complications of the so-called *marginal* theory of pure economics which has appeared in any language. The chief work with which it can be compared in this respect is Wieser's *Theorie der gesellschaftlichen Wirtschaft*; but even Wieser, like Marshall and other authors of 'systems', really covers a much wider area and does not enter into nearly the same degree of detail.[1]

The aim of the book was twofold. On the one hand, it attempted a systematic exposition of the utility theory of value such that any reader commencing from no previous knowledge of economic analysis would be in a position to achieve 'an intimate comprehension of the commercial and industrial world'. On the other, it involved an attempt to 'convince professed students of Political Economy that any special or unusual features in the system thus constructed are not to be regarded as daring innovations or as heresies, but are already strictly involved and often explicitly recognised in the best economic thought and teaching of recent years' (p. 2). As usual, Wicksteed made no claims to originality. Indeed, he refrained from making claims which might very well have been made. But he did definitely hope that his work would compel recognition of the degree to which economics had been changed by the discussions of the last forty years:

> I believe [he said] that the reconstruction contemplated by Jevons has been carried to a far more advanced point than is generally realised

[1] Another work which may be mentioned in this connection is Sulzer, *Die wirtschaftlichen Grundgesetze* (Zürich, 1895). This remarkable book seems almost wholly to have escaped attention, but in many respects it ranks with Wicksteed's as the forerunner of a school of thought which has come into prominence only in the last few years.

even by those who are themselves accomplishing it. Adhesion to the traditional terminology, methods of arrangement and classification, has disguised the revolution that has taken place. The new temple, so to speak, has been built up behind the old walls, and the old shell has been so piously preserved and respected that the very builders have often supposed themselves to be merely repairing and strengthening the ancient works, and are hardly aware of the extent to which they have raised an independent edifice. I shall try to show in this book that the time has come for a frank recognition of these facts (p. 2).

The book is divided into three parts. In the first comes a systematic exposition of the marginal analysis. This is introduced by an extensive analysis of the economics of household administration, in which the principles of what the Germans call *Naturalwirtschaft* are exhaustively examined. This is followed by a minute explanation of the notions of margins and limiting rates of expenditure, unparalleled in the whole literature of modern economic theory for clarity and precision. 'Nowhere', said the late Professor Allyn Young in reviewing the book for the *American Economic Review*, 'is there so clear a [non-mathematical] explanation of the meaning of marginal significance, or so effective a refutation of those writers who have thought that the existence of indivisible goods puts insurmountable obstacles in the way of the marginal analysis.'[1] The analysis then opens out to include the phenomena of money and exchange. The implications of the economic nexus in the *Verkehrswirtschaft* are expounded. Markets, earnings, interest, are systematically examined, and finally, at a great height, the interrelations of distribution and cost of production are made the basis for an exhibition of the concept of economic equilibrium in its widest possible sense.

The second part of the book, which is described as 'Excursive and Critical', consists of a series of special studies of more technical problems of analysis. The notions of the diagrammatic representations of margins and total utility are investigated with a precision and minuteness which provides a significant contrast to the cursory treatment usually afforded these matters even in respectable textbooks. There follow special studies of the supply curve and markets,

[1] *American Economic Review* (1911) 78–80.

and an examination of the concepts of increasing and diminishing returns and their relation to the theory of rent, in which some of the subsidiary propositions of the *Essay on the Co-ordination of the Laws of Distribution* are expounded and developed. Finally, in Part Three, the general system of analysis elaborated in the earlier chapters is applied to the elucidation of certain practical problems – housing, unemployment, redistribution of wealth, taxation, land nationalisation, socialism, and so on. The treatment here is less detailed, more discursive than before, the Lucretian passage which prefaces this part of the book suggesting perfectly its intention:

> But this faint spoor suffices for an alert mind: so that thou thyself may'st come at all the rest. For just as hounds, when once they have found the true track, full often search out with their nostrils the lair of the mountain-roaming quarry, hidden though it be with foliage, even so may'st thou, in such things as these, see for thyself one thing after another, work thyself into the secret hiding-places and thence drag out the truth.

The book was the culmination of Wicksteed's life-work in this branch of knowledge. Into it he poured all the subtlety and persuasiveness, all the literary charm, of which he was capable. It is a masterpiece of systematic exposition. It is the most complete statement of the implicit philosophy of economic analysis which has been published in our day. It has sometimes been complained that it is too long, that in places the detail of the argument becomes tiring; but, in fact, it is just this exhaustiveness which constitutes one of its main recommendations as a treatise. It explains small points and it refuses to gloss over difficulties. It is true that it makes no concessions to the kind of reader who has been brought up on the modern 'Outline'. You cannot 'get the heart out' of Wicksteed in a couple of hours' reading. It is a work which must be read slowly, conned over diligently – in short, treated with the respect with which any work of careful intellectual architecture must be treated if it is to yield the enlightenment and aesthetic satisfaction which it is capable of yielding. Walter Pater once said very truly that in all great art there is something which small minds find insipid. A failure to sit through the *Common Sense* is a pretty sure sign of intellectual smallness.

IV

The *Common Sense* was the last of Wicksteed's books on economics. But in 1913 he was elected President of Section F of the British Association, and he chose for the subject of his presidential address 'The Scope and Method of Political Economy in the Light of the "Marginal" Theory of Value and Distribution'. This address is probably the best statement in short compass of Wicksteed's main contribution to economic science.[1] There is nothing in it which is not already stated in the *Common Sense*. But by very reason of the necessity for concision, the outline is clearer, the contrasts more vividly pointed. There has never been a better explanation of the methodological significance of the subjective theory of value, nor a more uncompromising rejection of much that still passes for orthodox economics. It is nearly twenty years since Wicksteed demonstrated to the British Association the true nature of the supply curve. Today the majority of economists would accept his demonstration as irrefutable. Yet since the war, there has appeared a great mass of literature on the cost question which, for all the awareness it displays of the essential problem at issue, might for the most part have been the same if Wicksteed had never written.[2] None the less, few things can be more certain than that until the propositions which Wicksteed stressed in this paper are incorporated into the general body of cost analysis, the whole controversy will continue to present an appearance of

[1] Towards the end of his life, Wicksteed made yet one further statement of his views in the short article on 'Final Utility' in the second edition of *Palgrave's Dictionary* [see below, pp. 797–800]. The propositions are so compressed and general that the nuances of expression may well escape notice. But to readers already acquainted with the main body of Wicksteed's work, it is full of interesting suggestions.

[2] The conspicuous exception is Knight, 'Some Fallacies in the Interpretation of Social Cost', *Quarterly Journal of Economics* (1924) 582 ff. It is no accident that Professor Knight is able at once to steer through a great fog of unreality to the essential solution of the problem under discussion.

paradox and unreality – an intellectual backwater, full no doubt of strange fish and queer animalculae, but lacking that relation to the main stream of general equilibrium theory which alone can give it real significance.[1]

Wicksteed's place in the history of economic thought is beside the place occupied by Jevons and the Austrians. The main stream of economic speculation in this country in the last forty years has come via Marshall from the Classics. This is not to say that the work which derives from Marshall any longer has any very intimate relation with the work of Ricardo and his contemporaries, Quite the contrary, indeed; a very good case could be made out for the view that, with all their differences, the systems which seem to make the clearer break with the past are, in fact, nearer in spirit to the Classical system than those which have preserved more closely the Classical terminology and apparatus. The judgement relates merely to origins. In intention at any rate, Marshall's position was essentially revisionist. He came not to destroy, but – as he thought – to fulfil the work of the Classics. Wicksteed, on the other hand, was one of those who, with Jevons and Menger, thought that 'able but wrong-headed man David Ricardo' had 'shunted the car of Economic Science on to a wrong line, a line on which it was further urged towards confusion by his equally able and wrongheaded admirer John Stuart Mill'; and that complete reconstruction was necessary. He was not a revisionist, but a revolutionary. I have cited already the passage from the Preface

[1] It is, perhaps, worth stressing the point that the objection here implied is not to partial equilibrium analysis as such, but to partial equilibrium analysis unrelated to the general theory of equilibrium. It may be quite true that the general theory of equilibrium by itself is often too abstract and general for useful application. But it is equally true – and it is a thing which has often been forgotten in recent dicussions – that partial equilibrium analysis unaccompanied by a continual awareness of the propositions of general equilibrium theory is almost certain to be misleading. It may be asserted without fear of serious contradiction that most of the confusion in the recent cost controversy has sprung from the attempt to make the constructions of partial equilibrium analysis carry more than they can legitimately bear. Cf. Knight, 'A Suggestion for Simplifying the Statement of the General Theory of Price', *Journal of Political Economy*, XXXVI (1928) 353–70.

to the *Common Sense* in which he says that the time has come to recognise that modern economics is not a reconstruction of the old, but a new and independent edifice. The same point of view is very strongly presented in his review of Sir Sydney Chapman's *Political Economy* (pp. 818–22).

The difference is to some extent one of emphasis and conception of theory rather than in the substance of theory itself. But, none the less, it modifies materially the presentation of theory by the representatives of the schools concerned. In spite of considerable agreement on many analytical principles, there is a world of difference between the 'look' of Marshall's *Principles* and Wicksteed's *Common Sense of Political Economy* or Wieser's *Theorie der gesellschaftlichen Wirtschaft*. The difference shows itself most clearly, perhaps, in the use made of the fundamental notion of marginal utility. For Jevons, Menger and their followers, the discovery of the concept of marginal utility meant essentially the revolutionising of the main corpus of analytical economics. In their hands the concept of marginal utility became an instrument whereby the whole statement of the theory of economic equilibrium was altered. The innovation started in the sphere of the theory of exchange. But it was speedily developed and applied to the theories of production and distribution. From 1871 to the present day, the whole development of economics in these quarters has been a steady process of refinement and extension of the application of this concept.[1] This was not so for Marshall, still less for his followers. For Marshall and the Marshallians, marginal utility plays a minor part in the main body of equilibrium theory. It is an embellishment to the theory of the market. If one wants to explain why the demand curve slopes downwards, well, the Law of Diminishing Marginal Utility may be invoked, if you like that sort of thing. It is a ritual to be repeated before the real performance commences. The main substance of Marshall's theory of value and distribution relates to costs – in the first instance to money costs, but in the last analysis to a conception of real costs coming

---

[1] See the article 'Grenznutzen', by Dr P. Rosenstein-Rodan, in the *Handwörterbuch der Staatswissenschaften*, 4. Aufl. (Jena, 1927).

directly from Adam Smith and Ricardo.[1] The Law of Diminishing Marginal Utility becomes of significance for Marshall and his followers only when they pass from considerations of equilibrium to considerations of welfare. It is in the shadow world of consumers' surplus and the constructions based upon that concept that marginal utility assumes for them its main significance. The law is essentially a tool, not of equilibrium analysis, but of 'Welfare Economics'.[2]

Such differences are, perhaps, in part differences of the focus of attention. But there can be little doubt that behind them lie certain differences in the central core of theory. This is especially noticeable in the theory of costs. As is well known, Marshall and (up to a recent date) most of his followers insisted that costs, in the last analysis, were something real and absolute – a conception independent of utility. Wicksteed and the Austrians, on the other hand, denied that they were anything but forgone alternatives. Wieser's Law of Costs becomes – as Wicksteed so magnificently demonstrated – the keystone, as it were, of the whole edifice of the subjective theory of value (pp. 359 ff.).[3] No doubt, in part, this difference of theory was due to a difference of ultimate assump-

---

[1] It can legitimately be argued, I think, that in this respect Marshall was more Ricardian than Ricardo. By the end of his life, Ricardo was certainly far away from a real cost theory of value. It is an interesting circumstance that, in spite of Marshall's continual reiteration of the significance of the time factor, he makes little or no attempt to develop Ricardo's path-breaking treatment of this question (see, e.g., 'letters to McCulloch, in P. Sraffa (ed.), *Works*, VIII (Cambridge, 1952), 791–7). For developments of this sort, we have to go not to Marshall, but to Jevons, to Böhm-Bawerk, and to Wicksell.

[2] It is interesting to observe that the assumption of inter-personal comparisons of wants and desires, on which so much of 'Welfare Economics' is based, was decisively rejected by Wicksteed as early as 1888. 'There is another truth which must never be lost sight of on peril of a total misconception of all the results we may arrive at in our investigations; and that is that by no possibility can desires or wants, even for one and the same thing, which exist in *different minds* be measured against one another or reduced to a common measure': *Alphabet of Economic Science*, p. 68.

[3] See also Mayer, 'Friedrich Wieser, zum Gedächtnis', *Zeitschrift für Volkswirtschaft und Sozialpolitik*, N.F., Bd. 5 (1927) 636.

tions concerning the nature of the conditions of economic equilibrium. But in part it was due to an ultimate difference of opinion concerning what psychological comparisons were *relevant* in the determination of any equilibrium. So far as this was the case, time has decided in favour of the revolutionaries. The conception of real costs as displaced alternatives is now accepted by the majority of theoretical economists, but, as I have suggested already, we are still a long way from making it part and parcel of our daily speculations on those problems to which it is most relevant[1].[2]

The influences which shaped Wicksteed's thought were not confined to Jevons and the earlier Austrians. Himself no mean exponent of the mathematical method, he was deeply influenced by the work of those who carried the application of mathematical methods furthest – by the work of Walras and Pareto. Reviewing the *Manual* of the latter in 1905 (pp. 814–18), he hailed it as 'a work which is likely to modify and stimulate economic thought to an extent quite disproportionate to the number of its readers. It will probably be understood by few, but everyone who understands it will be influenced by it.' *The Common Sense of Political Economy*, written in the years immediately following this review, bears witness everywhere to the extent to which Wicksteed himself had been affected. It is interesting in this respect to compare the theory of the *Common Sense* with the theory of the *Alphabet*. Superficially, the two theories are the same; and no doubt they do belong to the same family. But a closer inspection will reveal important points of difference. The *Alphabet* starts from the idea of the rate at which total utility is increasing; the *Common Sense* from the positions on the relative scale of preferences which marginal units of different commodities occupy. In the *Alphabet*, in spite of the earlier recognition of the relativity of the utility concept, utility is treated as if it were something absolute and

[1] I have tried to exhibit this difference of assumption between Marshall and the Austrians elsewhere. See my article 'On a Certain Ambiguity in the Conception of Stationary Equilibrium', *Economic Journal* (1930) 194–214.
[2] I now think this paragraph to be too cocksure. My present view of this subject is better stated on p. 18 above. [Note added in 1969.]

measurable. In the *Common Sense*, the sole relevance of *relative* utility is emphasised and the idea of *measurability* tends to give place to the idea or *order*. In the *Alphabet*, the analysis is definitely 'one-thing-at-a-time'. In the *Common Sense*, the emphasis on the complementarity of utilities and the simultaneity of the determination of all values is continuous. And so one could go on. There is no feature of the presentation which does not bear evidence of reformulation and improvement.

In all this, the influence of Pareto is very strongly discernible. But it would be a great mistake to regard Wicksteed as a mere expositor of other people's theories. He was much more than that. He was an independent and original thinker. He adopted many of the constructions of Pareto but, as with the other theories by which he was influenced, he developed them further and combined them into a system which was essentially his own. Wicksteed's approach is by no means the same as Pareto's. His analysis of the conditions of equilibrium is much less an end in itself, much more a tool with which to explain the tendencies of any given situation. He was much more concerned with economic phenomena as a process in time, much less with its momentary end-products. In all this, he is to be regarded not so much as a follower of Pareto, but as a forerunner of another line of development. The closest affinities to the doctrines of the *Common Sense* are to be found not in the work of Zawadski, Moret or Pietri Tonelli but in the work of Mayer, Schönfeld and Rosenstein-Rodan.

Apart, however, from his services as exponent of the general theory of equilibrium, there are certain particular contributions for which Wicksteed will always be remembered. I have discussed already his studies in the theory of distribution. Whatever the ultimate decision as to the truth or falsehood of the particular theorem which he advanced with regard to the adequacy of the productivity analysis, there can be no doubt that economists owe him a high debt of gratitude for having focussed attention on this aspect of the problem. It is not always those who are finally right who make the greatest contribution to progress.

A second contribution which must always be associated with

his name is his famous demonstration of the reversibility of the market supply curve. The general proposition that the reservation prices of sellers are, in the ultimate analysis, demands, was one which he continually reiterated with varying shades of emphasis. 'What about the supply price that usually figures as a determinant of price, co-ordinate with the demand curve?' he asked in the address to the British Association in 1913, to which I have already alluded.

> I say it boldly and baldly: there is no such thing. When we are speaking of a marketable commodity, what is usually called the supply curve is, in reality, the demand curve of those who possess the commodity, for it shows the exact place which every successive unit of commodity occupies in their relative scale of estimation. The so-called supply curve is, therefore, simply a part of the total demand curve. . . . The separating out of this portion of the demand curve and reversing it in the diagram is a process which has its meaning and its legitimate function . . . but is wholly irrelevant to the determination of price.[1]

It is safe to say that no one who has followed through his beautiful diagrammatic analysis of this proposition, and realised its wider implication that *all* psychological variables can be exhibited as phenomena of demand acting on fixed stocks – either of products or factors or time or human capacity – will deny that the whole of the analysis of economic equilibrium has received thereby a transforming elucidation.

Finally, in the realm of technical contributions, we must notice his analysis of the relation between the marginal productivity theory of distribution and the Ricardian theory of rent. The discovery that the rent analysis of the Classics is the productivity analysis with, as Edgeworth put it, the relation between dose and patient reversed, was, of course, not peculiar to Wicksteed. By one of those singular coincidences which seem to characterise the progress of our science, the idea seems to have occurred almost simultaneously to at least three writers in the early nineties –

[1] For a very elegant demonstration of this last possibility in relation to the problem of hours of labour, see Wicksell, *Vorlesungen*, Bd. 1 (Jena, 1928) p. 159.

Wicksteed himself, J. B. Clark, and the much neglected H. M. Thompson, author of *The Theory of Wages*.[1] But of the demonstrations of this proposition, Wicksteed's was incomparably the most precise and convincing; and, at the present day, a teacher who wishes to convince some recalcitrant student of the truth of this doctrine cannot do better than refer him to the classic formulation which is to be found in Book II, chapters v and vi, of the *Common Sense of Political Economy* (pp. 527–74).[2]

But apart from these technical contributions, and far transcending them in general importance, come Wicksteed's elucidations of the methodological implications of the subjective theory of value – particularly those discussions of what he called the 'economic relationship', which are to be found in that chapter of the *Common Sense* entitled 'Business and the Economic Nexus' (pp. 158–211). This, if I read him correctly, was the feature of his work to which he himself attached greatest importance, and it is for this above all that he deserves to be remembered. Before Wicksteed wrote, it was still possible for intelligent men to give countenance to the belief that the whole structure of economics depends upon the assumption of a world of economic men, each actuated by egocentric or hedonistic motives. For anyone who has read the *Common Sense*, the expression of such a view is no longer consistent with intellectual honesty. Wicksteed shattered this misconception once and for all. Yet, curiously enough, no aspect of his thought has been more completely neglected. The reason is not far to seek. In England, at any rate, the average economist, secure in the tradition of an analysis which has proved its worth in practice, is apt to be impatient of enquiries which linger on implications and modes of conception. The man in the street, egged on by the inexpert practitioners of other branches of the social sciences, may reproach him for an ingrained materialism and an assumption of a simplicity

[1] See *Co-ordination of the Laws of Distribution*, pp. 18–20; J. B. Clark, 'Distribution as Determined by a Law of Rent', *Quarterly Journal of Economics* (1891) 289 ff.; H. M. Thompson, *The Theory of Wages* (1892) chap. IV, *passim*.

[2] See also the article from *Palgrave's Dictionary of Political Economy*: 'Economics and Psychology' [below, pp. 766–71].

of motive unwarranted by the complexity of the situation to be analysed. But such reproaches leave him indifferent. He knows in his bones that they are unjust. He knows that, unlike his traducers, he is in possession of analytical instruments which do genuinely elucidate the understanding of complicated social relationships, and he regards with impatience those semi-metaphysical enquiries which harp on ultimate assumptions. The instinct, no doubt, is a healthy one and has saved us from the torrents of logomachy which at times have threatened entirely to submerge economic analysis elsewhere. None the less, not all enquiries of this sort are sterile, and it may be contended, I think, that those which have been based on the subjective theory of value[1] have thrown the whole corpus of economic science into an entirely new light – a light in which economics is seen to be a discussion not of the nature of certain *kinds* of behaviour arbitrarily separated off from all others, but of a certain *aspect* of behaviour viewed as a whole. It is perhaps too early to evaluate the individual contributions to this stream of thought, for the movement is by no means exhausted, but when its final history comes to be written, I think it will be found that Wicksteed's exhaustive examination of the 'economic relationship', and his insistence that there can be no logical dividing line between the operations of the market and other forms of rational action, are by no means among the least important or the least original.[2]

---

[1] See von Mises, *Grundprobleme der Nationalökonomie* (Jena, 1933), especially the papers entitled 'Soziologie und Geschichte', pp. 64–121, and 'Vom Weg der subjektivistischen Wertlehre', pp. 137–55; also Strigl, *Die Ökonomischen Kategorien und die Organisation der Wirtschaft* (Jena, 1933).

[2] In my *Essay on the Nature and Significance of Economic Science* (1932) I have endeavoured to bring out some of the implications of this part of Wicksteed's teaching.

I I

Wicksell's *Lectures on Political Economy*[1]

I

JOHAN GUSTAF KNUT WICKSELL, the author of these lectures, is an economist of outstanding achievement whose work has not yet received in English-speaking countries the attention it deserves. In Scandinavia where he taught, and in Central Europe and Italy where he has long been read, his influence has already been extensive and important. But in other parts, even at the time of his death, he was probably less known than any other economist of commensurate rank. In recent years, however, largely as a result of the writings of Professor Hayek and Mr J. M. Keynes, his theories concerning the rate of interest and the price level have become more widely known and his reputation is on the increase. It is safe to say that as the main body of his work becomes available, this process is likely to continue.

II

Wicksell was born in 1851. He was thus nine years younger than Marshall, three years younger than Pareto, and the exact con-

[1] An Introduction to the translation published by Messrs Routledge & Sons (1934). Reproduced by courtesy of Messrs Routledge and Kegan Paul Ltd. In preparing this Introduction I have been greatly helped by articles dealing with Wicksell and his work by Professors Ohlin and Somarin, which appeared in the *Economic Journal*, XXXVI (1926) 503 ff., and the *Zeitschrift für Nationalökonomie*, Bd. II (1930) 221 ff., respectively. A succinct and well-documented account of Wicksell's work on the theory of money and capital and its influence on certain contemporary writers is to be found in an as yet unpublished thesis submitted by Mr Solomon Adler to the University of London for the degree of M.Sc.

temporary of Böhm-Bawerk and Wieser. His interest in economics developed comparatively late: his first important work, *Über Wert, Kapital und Rente*, was not published until 1893. He graduated in philosophy and mathematics, and it was not until after taking his second degree in 1885 that he turned his attention seriously to the subject which became his life-work. After ten years' further study in France, Germany, Austria and England he took his doctorate in economics. In 1900 he was appointed Assistant Professor of Political Economy at Lund. From 1904 to 1916 he held the chair in the same university. He died in 1926.

Wicksell's central contributions to theoretical economics are all outlined, if not fully developed, in three books, all in German, which appeared in rapid succession at the commencement of his career in the nineties: *Über Wert, Kapital und Rente*, which appeared in 1893;[1] *Finanztheoretische Untersuchungen*, which appeared in 1896; and *Geldzins und Güterpreise*, which appeared in 1898. In the first he developed an outline solution of the main problems of the pure theory of value and distribution. In the second he applied certain elements in this solution to the special problems of the theory of public finance and the incidence of taxation. In the third he developed his now celebrated theory concerning the relationship between the money rate of interest and the general level of prices. His *Vorlesungen über National-ökonomie*, of which the present volumes are a translation, were published first in Sweden in two parts, 'General Theory', and 'Money and Credit', in 1901 and 1906 respectively, and contain, with much new material, a systematic restatement of the main theorems of the first and the third of these earlier treatises.

It would be a great mistake, however, to regard Wicksell's work as an economist as limited to these four major publications. He published much on the population problem, played an active part

---

(Econ.) in 1932, and a useful discussion of parts of this theory is to be found in Kirchmann, *Studien zur Grenzproduktivitätstheorie des Kapitalzinses* (Greifswald, 1930).

[1] Some of the matter included in this book had been published in *Conrads Jahrbücher* in the preceding year.

in the discussion of public affairs in Sweden, and throughout his career was a regular contributor to the scientific journals in Sweden and elsewhere. The files of the *Ekonomisk Tidskrift* are full of lengthy articles by Wicksell, tantalisingly inaccessible to those of us who have not the good fortune to possess a sufficient knowledge of Swedish.[1] The German periodicals contain a number of contributions, and the *Economic Journal* and the *Quarterly Journal of Economics*, once at least, each secured an important article from his pen.[2] Few economists of his generation were more productive or – if those articles which are accessible in one or other of the world languages are any criterion – maintained so consistently high a level.

III

It is not easy in a few paragraphs to give a just view of the place in the history of modern economic theory of Wicksell's main achievements. As we have seen, he was the contemporary of men like Böhm-Bawerk and Pareto, whose work falls naturally under the headings appropriate to the so-called schools – the School of Vienna, the School of Lausanne, the School of Marshall. But Wicksell fits into no such classification. No economist of similar rank has been more open to outside influences. But the influences were not all from one quarter. From the outset of his work in the nineties, he stands apart from the disputes of the schools, deriving equally from the good elements in each of them – a pioneer of a generation which stands beyond these early factions and can perceive both the common denominator and the particular contribution in their respective systems. There is no economist whose work more strongly exemplifies both the element of continuity and the element of progress in the central tradition of theoretical economics. Few have known better the works of the English

[1] No longer true. See the review of the collection edited by Lindahl, below, pp. 223–8. [Note added in 1969.]

[2] A short list of Wicksell's principal contributions to foreign periodicals is given by Professor Ohlin, op. cit., p. 512.

Classics or used them to greater advantage. To those brought up in the English tradition of post-Classical Ricardian criticism, his lucid reformulations of their doctrines must come as something of a revelation. But his debt to the later schools is no less evident. In the broad outlines of his value theory, the Austrian influence is strong; and in his capital theory, the influence of Böhm-Bawerk is obvious. But the whole is set in a framework which derives essentially from Walras, and the detail owes not a little to Wicksteed and to Edgeworth. In short, in spite of his dates, Wicksell is of the present generation.

In all this, of course, he bears a strong resemblance to Edgeworth, our own great eclectic. There are indeed many elements in common in their work. Many of the problems which interested them were the same – distribution, public finance, the theory of monopoly – and they both brought to their solution that essential seriousness characteristic of those who are conscious of working with the instruments of an established scientific technique. But there was this important difference. Whereas Edgeworth's eclecticism showed itself mainly in the analysis of particular problems, Wicksell's showed itself even more strongly in a tendency to synthesis. His particular investigations are important. But even more important are his reconstructions of general theory. He had the feeling for broad effects, the capacity for wide abstraction of the great system-makers. But being a scientist and not a mere system-maker, the system he constructed was not specifically his own but the system common to the best work of the past hundred years of economic theory.

In this respect, perhaps, he is more to be compared with Marshall, and more than one critic has made the comparison.[1] But here, too, there are important differences. There can be little doubt that in general knowledge of the details of economic relationships in the modern world, Marshall was greatly Wicksell's superior, as indeed he was the superior of most others of his generation. But as a systematiser of pure theory he had the defects of his qualities. The

[1] See, e.g., Schumpeter, 'Zur Einführung der folgenden Arbeit Knut Wicksell's *Archiv für Sozialwissenschaft*', Bd. 58 (1927) 238–57.

peculiar blend of realistic knowledge and theoretical insight which enabled him to present with such ingenuity the world as he saw it, was not necessarily conducive to clear presentation of abstract theoretical issues. He was so anxious to explain the reality he knew, to make his theory appear *plausible*, that he was apt to be impatient with refinements which, though useless for this purpose, might be fruitful in other connections. Moreover, as Mr Keynes has pointed out, he lacked that aesthetic feeling for order and proportion which is essential to a theoretical synthesis on the grandest scale. It was just here that Wicksell excelled. There is no work in the whole range of modern economic literature which presents a clearer general view of the main significance and inter-relations of the central propositions of economic analysis than these *Lectures*. The arrangement is exemplary. The successive propositions are presented in a setting which emphasises both their implications and – what is just as important – their limitations; and the whole is built up in such a way that at each successive point in the argument attention is always focused upon the new elements in the problem, the rest having been satisfactorily disposed of at an earlier stage. In this no doubt Wicksell learnt much from Walras. But no one would contend that the exposition of the *Éléments d'économie politique pure*, littered up as it is with so much superfluous and somewhat crude mathematics, is a model of expository clarity.

In certain respects, the closest comparison is with Wicksteed. For Wicksteed had the architechtonic instinct, and he too, had derived both from Lausanne and Vienna. He had not, however, Wicksell's feeling for the English Classics, and the development of his thought was on different lines. Strongly influenced by Pareto's modifications of utility theory, in later years he became more and more interested in the philosophical and methodological implications of the general theory of value. Wicksell, on the other hand, who was a bit old-fashioned on pure utility theory, turned his attention more and more to the development of that part of the Jevonian–Böhm-Bawerkian theory of capital, which, just because he rejected the Classical writers so completely, in certain respects

Wicksteed failed to comprehend;[1] and as time went on, his interests became more technical and practical. But the two supplement each other in admirable fashion. The subjective side of modern theory is at its best in Wicksteed, the objective in Wicksell; a combination of the two covers much of the essential ground.[2] I am not clear that Wicksteed was acquainted with Wicksell.[3] But there is ample evidence that Wicksell knew Wicksteed's work and appreciated it long before much was thought of it in England.

IV

Any enumeration of Wicksell's more outstanding contributions to the detail of economic science must commence, if it is to do justice to his own wishes, with his contributions to the theory of population. It was the reproach that his knowledge of the economics relevant thereto was insufficient which first directed his attention to the study of economics; and throughout his life, the population problem in all its aspects retained the strongest hold on his interest and emotions. In 1909, having incurred the penalty of a short term of imprisonment on account of public utterances disparaging certain Christian beliefs, he devoted his time to the preparation of a short book on this subject signed defiantly 'Ystad Prison'. In the statistical field, he did much important work

[1] In this connection a comparison between Wicksteed's article on Jevons's 'Theory of Political Economy' (*Common Sense of Political Economy* (1933), pp. 734–54) and the sections on capital theory in *Über Wert, Kapital und Rente* is very instructive.

[2] But not all. I should be very sorry to be thought to lend any countenance to the view, now apparently gaining ground in somewhat unexpected quarters, that in undergraduate teaching or in advanced studies we are yet in a position to dispense with the most thorough study of Marshall's *Principles*. It would be a sad thing if the uncritical acceptance of this great work, which so long tended to stifle the development of other lines of thought in this country, were to be succeeded by an equally uncritical rejection of all the wisdom and the path-breaking intuitions that it contains.

[3] He must have been aware of *Über Wert, Kapital und Rente*, for it was reviewed together with his own *Co-ordination of the Laws of Distribution* in the *Economic Journal* for June 1894.

on the mechanics of population increase, and in the field of economic theory he was one of the first systematically to develop the concept of an optimum population. Whether it is so easy at any time to assign a specific magnitude to this elusive concept as Wicksell himself supposed, whether indeed we really yet know enough about the application of the laws of returns in this connection to be in a position to describe it in a way which is theoretically satisfactory, are questions on which differences of opinion between reasonable men may yet legitimately arise. But the emphatic pronouncements in the Introduction to the *Lectures* on the place of population theory in a systematic treatment of economic problems are a sufficient indication of the importance Wicksell himself attached to this part of his work.

To the broad outlines of the theory of value Wicksell added little that was completely original. But he fused the main teachings of Walras and the early Austrians with great ingenuity and expository power, giving to the philosophical insight and profundity of Menger and his followers the superior precision and elegance of the mathematical formulation. Seldom have the complications involved in the transition from pure utility theory to the theory of exchange and price been stated with greater clarity and exactitude. To more recent developments of the theory of value he was not very sympathetic, probably on account of the very strong utilitarian bias in his general view of the subject. The student of the theory of public finance, however, should not miss his discussion of the principle of justice in taxation.[1]

In the theory of production, Wicksell displays much greater originality. His statement of the marginal productivity theory is one of the most satisfactory available. As Dr Hicks has shown,[2] the exposition of the *Lectures*, with its express condition that the various firms concerned must be at a stage at which further economies of large-scale production are absent, is immune from

[1] *Finanztheoretische Untersuchungen*, pp. 176 ff. Wicksell's views in this respect have been developed with great ingenuity by his pupil, Professor E. Lindahl, in his *Die Gerechtigkeit der Besteuerung* (Lund, 1919).

[2] *The Theory of Wages* (1932) p. 233.

the strictures which have been passed by Edgeworth and others on the version which is to be found in Wicksteed's *Co-ordination of the Laws of Distribution.* In this he may have been indebted to Barone. But in the light of the discussion of capital theory in *Über Wert, Kapital und Rente,* Wicksell must himself be looked upon as one of the founders of the marginal productivity theory.[1]

Most conspicuous, however, in the sphere of the theory of production is Wicksell's contribution to that part which deals with problems of capital and interest. Here his eclecticism rises to the point of pure genius. By a judicious selection from the best elements in earlier theories he achieved a reformulation of this part of the theory of production from which, it is safe to say, all future work in this field which aspires to be taken seriously must commence. It is worth examining the nature of this achievement in rather more detail.

The part played in the Classical system by the ingredients of a substantially correct theory of capital and interest is by no means so negligible as post-Classical criticism has often assumed. On the one hand in the wage-fund theory, on the other in the Ricardian modifications of the labour theory of value, particularly in the letters to McCulloch, there exist the rudiments of a theory in many essential respects not dissimilar from that which is to be found in Jevons, Böhm-Bawerk and Wicksell. In a series of brilliant reconstructions in the *Finanztheoretische Untersuchungen* and elsewhere, Wicksell himself indicated the significance of certain aspects of the Classical doctrines in this respect. More recently Mr Edelberg has shown[2] how, if one is willing to give Ricardo the benefit of the doubt in one or two connections, a whole theory of capital and interest on Wicksellian lines can be reconstructed from actual Ricardian material. In any case it cannot be said that important theories of capital and interest played a negligible part in the Classical system. Indeed, if a choice had to be made between the

---

[1] See Stigler, *Production and Distribution Theories* (New York, 1941) pp. 264–5, 373–80. [Note added in 1969.]

[2] 'The Ricardian Theory of Profits', *Economica,* no. 39 (Feb 1933) 51–74.

Classical theories and those modern systems which ignore the Jevonian–Böhm-Bawerkian reconstruction and reject the Classical elements, there is much to be said for the view that the Classical theories would be much less likely to mislead.

But the Classical system as a whole was very vulnerable. It was open to general attack on its theory of value. It was everywhere deficient on points of formulation. And these particular theories of capital and interest were liable to attack, not merely for their obvious deficiencies in this respect, but also for political reasons. As time went on the wage-fund doctrine in particular, instead of being reformulated in those minor respects in which it was defective, became the target of continuous and completely hostile criticism, some of it justified in points of detail, but most of it analytically erroneous and totally beside the point. Nothing could be more superficial, for instance, than the criticisms put forward by writers such as Walker and J. B. Clark of the incontrovertible proposition that wages are paid out of capital. But for political reasons the Classical theories of capital were unpopular and men jumped at any pretext for rejecting them. The result was that, particularly in English circles, much of the economics of the fifty years after 1870 was what Wicksell calls a *kapitallose Wirtschaftstheorie* – an economic theory of *a*capitalistic production. Considerations of capital theory proper, save of a more or less terminological nature, simply disappear from the picture. Professor Taussig's *Wages and Capital* was a gallant attempt to stem the tide – which incidentally carried through most of the modifications necessary to make the Classical theory logically acceptable and completely disposed of the ridiculous myth that it had originated in selfishness and reaction. But it was in vain. When, after the war, Mr Dennis Robertson and Mr J. M. Keynes turned their attention to problems of fluctuation which involved similar considerations, the tradition of a theory of capital had so completely disappeared in English political economy that they had to start completely from the beginning. Nor was the position any better in certain Continental circles. The work of Pareto, valuable as it is in other respects, adds little to knowledge in this connection. It would perhaps be putting it too strongly to say that there is no capital in his equations of economic equilibrium. But it would certainly be correct to say that there is no *time*. Now time is the essence of capital theory.

There was another stream of thought, however, in which the theorems of the Classical economists were by no means altogether abandoned. In spite of his antipathy for Mill and his celebrated denunciation of his 'four fundamental propositions on capital' – 'all wrong', as he said – Jevons had taken over into his capital theory important Classical elements. And in Böhm-Bawerk's 'positive theory of capital' something very like the Classical wage-fund theory, shorn of its obvious defects of formulation, makes its appearance. But Jevons's chapter on capital was only an outline; and, for various reasons, the influence of Böhm-Bawerk was not altogether fortunate. In his critical work, he was undoubtedly unjust to many of his predecessors. This, where it did not create repulsion, created the impression of a much greater lack of continuity than actually existed. And in his positive solution, which in many important respects was substantially correct, the emphasis and arrangement was such as to make understanding of the main elements much more difficult than need have been the case. The sections dealing with the element of time discount are admirably clear and have made a permanent mark on the discussion of the subject elsewhere. But the sections relating to the 'third ground' for the existence of interest – the 'technical superiority of present goods' – are developed in a mode which definitely invites criticism. What, as Wicksell points out, is really the central and fundamentally unassailable core of the Böhm-Bawerkian theory – the discussion of the influence of the varying productivity of productive processes of different lengths on prices, the use of the subsistence fund, and the formation of the rate of interest – only appears as a sort of practical application of these more disputable propositions at the very end of the book.[1] It is clear that many

[1] See *Lectures in Political Economy* (1934) pp. 167–71. See also the quite amazing account of Böhm-Bawerk's own explanation of this inconsistency, namely that the first half of his manuscript was printed before

of Böhm-Bawerk's readers never reach that last section. The result has been that in those parts where the oral tradition of Böhm-Bawerk's seminar was not influential, it came to be thought that the theory of the relation of time discount to interest was Böhm-Bawerk's chief contribution. The propositions relating to the 'third ground' were held to have been disposed of by the criticisms of Professors Fetter and Fisher; and the most valuable element in the solution, therefore – what is really a marginal productivity theory of interest, properly stated in regard to the time element – tended to escape attention.

But not with Wicksell. For Wicksell the productivity side of the question was obviously at once the more important and the more deserving of further elucidation. Steeped as he was in the literature of the Classical system, he had no difficulty in detecting the underlying continuity between Böhm-Bawerk's theory of the subsistence fund and the Classical wage-fund theory, and with his mathematical insight he divined, in spite of all Böhm-Bawerk's disclaimers, the substantial identity between the general marginal productivity analysis and the propositions relating to the varying productivity of different investment periods. He was thus able to present an account of equilibrium of capitalistic production which combined all the best features of these apparently divergent theories, and, by invoking the methods of Walrasian analysis, he was able to present it in a setting much more general than was the case with either Jevons or Böhm-Bawerk. It is true that this theory itself is not complete. It was fully developed in the *Lectures* only for the case of circulating capital. And although later on, in his review of Dr Åkerman's book,[1] Wicksell attempted a solution for the case of capital of varying degrees of durability, it is obvious that this is one of the fields of pure analysis in which most yet remains to be done. But the fundamental ideas of his theory – the

the second was completed, given by Wicksell in his last article, 'Zur Zinstheorie (Böhm-Bawerks Dritter Grund)', printed in vol. III of *Die Wirtschaftstheorie der Gegenwart*, ed. Hans Mayer *et al.* (Vienna, 1928) pp. 199–200. The details of this revelation are such that if one did not know of Wicksell's matchless integrity, one could scarcely give it credence.

[1] [Printed below as Appendix 2 to the *Lectures* under discussion.]

place of the varying productivity of variations in the investment period, the idea of interest as the difference between the marginal productivity of direct and indirect uses of factors of production – these are notions which are not likely to be superseded and which are fundamental as a basis for future work.

V

I come finally to what is probably the best known of Wicksell's contributions – his celebrated theory concerning the relations between money and natural rates of interest and movements in the general level of prices. This is probably Wicksell's most original contribution. The main propositions are certainly not new. As Professor Hayek has shown,[1] there is a very considerable body of passages in the Classical literature in which, in one form or another, they make their appearance. But apart from one isolated passage in Ricardo, which Wicksell says explicitly was only brought to his notice after the publication of his own theory, these passages are not in the most conspicuous or most easily accessible works, and there seems little reason to question that, in so far as any idea implicit in the fundamental notions of economics can be so described, his main idea was original.

Its influence has been far-reaching. It is clear that in Wicksell's own treatment, in certain respects – not unimportant in regard to practical applications – it is not correctly developed. It can be shown that the proposition that the money rate of interest which keeps prices stable is also the rate which clears the market of voluntarily accumulated capital, breaks down when the conditions of capital supply are either progressive or retrogressive.[2] It is clear that it stands in much need of refinement before it can

[1] *Prices and Production* (1931) chap. I, *passim*; 'A Note on the Development of the Doctrine of "Forced Saving"', *Quarterly Journal of Economics*, XLVII (1932) 123–33.

[2] See Hayek, *Monetary Theory and the Trade Cycle* (1933) chap. V, and *Prices and Production*, chap. I; also G. Myrdal, 'Der Gleichgewichtsbegriff als Instrument der geldtheoretischen Analyse', in *Beiträge zur Geldtheorie*, ed. Hayek (Vienna, 1933).

be applied to the interpretation of actual conditions – still more as a guide to practice. The notion of a single rate, either natural or monetary, needs to be replaced by the idea of a *structure* of rates; and the interrelations of these rates, and their relation, not merely to the stream of saving, but also to the risk factor, need much more study. But when all is said by way of qualification, it remains true that the discovery, or rather the rediscovery, of the general relationship involved is one of the greatest single steps forward in monetary economics since the proper elaboration of the quantity theory. It is the key, not only to the more complex problems of fluctuations of monetary value, but also to much that is central in the general theory of capital and the theory of business cycles. Monetary theory and capital theory alike are at an impasse when the theory of money is limited to the simple quantity theory and the theory of capital is divorced from the theory of the money market. The value of money is said to depend on the quantity of money and the velocity of circulation, the rate of interest on the marginal productivity of extensions of the investment period, and the rate of time discount. The relations between the supply of capital and the supply of money, between the money rate of interest and the rates of real accumulation and investment, not to mention the relations between relative prices at various stages of production and the rate of borrowing of the entrepreneurs – all these problems, whose solution is essential to any comprehensive theory of economic change, remain unexplained until this fundamental conjunction has been effected. No doubt in this field it has been left for others to develop the implications of the broad principles which Wicksell laid down, and even now much work still remains to be done. But the main credit of rediscovering these principles and bringing them once more into the centre of discussion must rest permanently with the author of these *Lectures*.

12

New Light on Knut Wicksell[1]

WITH the publication of these two books, the presentation of Knut Wicksell to the English-speaking public is virtually complete. Before the war we had the *Lectures* and *Interest and Prices*, each containing also important supplementary articles. Since then we have had *Value, Capital and Rent*, and the inclusion in the International Economic Association's *Classics in the Theory of Public Finance* of Wicksell's central contribution to the theory of public finance. Now Professor Lindahl has gathered together the most important and hitherto untranslated papers on economic theory and Professor Gårdlund has written what must obviously be regarded as the definitive life. It is to be regretted that more of the *Finanzwissenschaftliche Untersuchungen* is not available. (There is a tiny fragment devoted to the taxation of monopoly in the American Economic Association's *Readings in the Theory of Taxation*.) And some of us would very much like to have an opportunity of more detailed study of Wicksell's views on population theory which played so large a part in shaping his general social philosophy and his public activities. But for the history of economic analysis, what we have is certainly enough to establish him as one of the main figures in the formative period of modern economics. And Professor Gårdlund's *Life* extends the perspective by exhibiting him further in a role much less suspected in non-Scandinavian circles, that of an important social and moral reformer.

Apart from the authoritative editorial appraisal of Wicksell's

[1] A review of *Selected Papers on Economic Theory* by Knut Wicksell, edited with an Introduction by Erik Lindahl (London: George Allen & Unwin, 1968); and *The Life of Knut Wicksell* by Torsten Gårdlund, translated from the Swedish by Nancy Adler, Stockholm Economic Studies, new series, no. 2 (Stockholm: Almqvist & Wicksell, 1958), *Economica* XXVII (May 1960). Reproduced by courtesy of the London School of Economics and Political Science.

general position as an economist, the main value of Professor Lindahl's collection lies not so much in any novelties which it contains as in its provision of background material for and elucidation of positions adopted elsewhere. There are indeed novelties, of which the reassessment of Cournot's theory of duopoly in the review of Bowley's *Mathematical Economics* and the contribution to the theory of tariffs in the last two papers of the collection may be singled out for special mention. But the chief interest lies rather in the papers in which, either by way of comment on the work of contemporaries, such as Pareto or Böhm-Bawerk, or by way of detailed discussion of particular analytical problems, such as the place of marginal productivity in the theory of distribution, the propositions of the final edition of the *Lectures* receive further explanation and illustration. Nevertheless, even taken by themselves, these papers would make the reputation of any economist: they contain the beginnings or the elaboration of some of Wicksell's most characteristic and important contributions, the influence of the rate of interest on prices, the solution of the 'adding-up problem' in the theory of distribution, the restatement of the Böhm-Bawerkian theory of interest in terms of a marginal productivity analysis elaborated with regard to time, and the correction of the Walrasian doctrine of maximum satisfaction. It is a collection of which its publishers, who have contributed so much to the internationalisation of our subject, may well be proud.

When we turn to Professor Gårdlund's *Life* we are likely to have some surprises. The reader of Wicksell's scientific work will have formed the impression of a spirit of exceptional candour and intellectual probity. But he will not have gained any impression of violence of disposition or impetuosity of judgement. It has been known, of course, that he was a strong neo-Malthusian; and the review of Cassel (reprinted in Volume II of the English edition of the *Lectures*) shows a powerful capacity for controversy. But many pure scientists have had very definite views on the population problem; and the gravamen of the critique of Cassel was just that, with his dogmatism, his ignoring of his predecessors and his quite preposterous claims to originality, he had offended so extensively against the code of scientific enquiry. There is nothing here to disturb the impression created by the rest of Wicksell's scientific work, where the calm unfolding of the argument and the studied moderation of the conclusions all go to suggest a spirit at peace with itself and its age.

In fact how different the reality. Professor Gårdlund's *Life* presents a personality much more like one of Ibsen's more apocalyptic characters than the popular idea of the pure scientist – a turbulent social reformer of marked eccentricity of personal behaviour and judgement, the quality and tone of whose scientific work is in sharp contrast with almost all the other circumstances of his life; a figure both nobly courageous and unbelievably naïve, capable of risking his reputation and his livelihood, either for the fine cause of a rational attitude towards the sexual problem, or for a pedantic quirk of conscience which, when his belated appointment to a chair was in question, forbade him to use the traditional forms of address to the monarch in setting forth his application. Perhaps it is wrong to be surprised at all this. Most of the best natural scientists seem to have had the habits and dispositions of artists; and while there have been sedate and non-temperamental economists, they have seldom been very first class. Anyway, it is clear that from now on, those of us who have not known these things before will have to regard Knut Wicksell in a very different light. He was not only an important economist, he was also a leading influence in the general development of northern European radicalism, one of the most significant social movements of modern times.

So far as economic policy was concerned, Wicksell's radicalism developed chiefly in two connections. In the sphere of production, he urged strongly limitation of population, to be brought about not by Malthusian 'moral restraint' but by recourse to deliberate contraceptive methods. In the sphere of distribution, he opposed the regressive tax system of his day, favoured mild progression in income tax and strongly supported the taxation of inheritance. He recommended what we should now call welfare services, particularly education. He also supported the principle of marginal cost pricing for public utilities. Politically he had much sympathy for

H

the Social Democratic Party, but he never became a member; and, while he sympathised in general with working-class movements and participated in many of their manifestations, he inclined to the view that socialism as a prescription for increasing production emphasised the wrong points and ran some danger of diminishing freedom and total satisfaction.

In all this a certain parallelism with John Stuart Mill suggests itself. And this, of course, is no accident. After a profound religious crisis in late adolescence, Wicksell became a convinced Utilitarian and it is probable that he was considerably influenced by Mill's writings. None the less, there is a difference, marked on Wicksell's side by a somewhat greater robustness in action and by a much greater proportion of straws in the hair. On the population problem, both held very strong, indeed, in some respects, perhaps, exaggerated, views. But although in his youth Mill had taken some part in birth-control propaganda, in his maturity he was reticent, not to say mealy-mouthed, on this subject, whereas in the same connection Wicksell continually exposed himself to the full brunt of conservative and religious prejudice. On marriage, both held strong views on the undesirability of permanent ties unrelated to the welfare of children. But whereas Mill satisfied his scruples by a written declaration of no legal force repudiating his rights and then went forward to the normal form of civil marriage with Mrs Taylor, Wicksell utterly refused any existing form of marriage, either religious or civil, and obliged the distinguished woman, Anna Bugge, who had decided to throw in her lot with him, to rest content, despite her own wishes and those of her family, with a contract of his own devising which was in law no marriage at all. Again on freedom of speech both held the strongest views, and expressed them strongly. But it is difficult to imagine Mill capable of the gratuitous silliness of the burlesque account of the Virgin Birth which Wicksell thought it necessary to promulgate as a protest against the blasphemy laws; an 'unforgivable stupidity', to use his wife's words, which was responsible for his – equally unjustifiable – condemnation to a short term of imprisonment at a comparatively advanced age.

Perhaps Wicksell's greatest contribution to economic theory lay in the field of money and prices. Professor Gårdlund's *Life* affords an interesting narrative of his various attempts to translate his theories into prescriptions for practical policy. In general he was a stable-money man; he had no particular use for the gold standard; and during the First World War he was one of the most ardent defenders of the policy whereby the Swedish authorities repudiated the obligation to give notes for gold, holding that this gave a valuable opportunity for preventing further inflation. During the same period he was also a strong advocate of the policy of higher interest rates; and when, this policy not having been carried through, the price level had risen, he went so far as to urge measures which had the aim of reversing this process and restoring the price level of 1914. In this he was certainly ill-advised; the effects of the more moderate deflation which eventually came about are proof enough of that. But as a protest against inflation and the injustices thereof, the passage quoted by Professor Lindahl in which he defends himself against his critics still deserves to be taken seriously, as does also a passage from an earlier article, published in 1898, in which he deals with the contention that a creeping inflation is good for the economy.

> Many people imagine [he writes] that it would be possible to attain still better results if the value of money were, or could be, made not constant but successively variable downwards. . . . They consider that the rise in commodity prices would be a continual incentive to industrial enterprise and thus have a fruitful and stimulating effect on the economic life of the community as a whole. It is not difficult, however, to realise that this is a pure illusion. What one person gains by rising prices another unfortunately loses: but it is a general psychological rule that an unexpected gain, other things being equal, can never compare in importance with an equally large unexpected loss. If, on the other hand, the rise in prices took place with such regularity that it could be foreseen and calculated in advance, why, then, it would of course be taken into account, in all transactions: nothing would be either gained or lost and we should only find ourselves after somewhat more trouble in the same position as if average commodity prices were constant. Were it therefore in our power to arrange these circumstances as we please, it is fairly certain

that all interests would be best served if the standard of value were kept as scrupulously constant as the standard of weights and measures.

Of course, *we* know the answer to all that. Or do we?

It would be very unjust if the great interest of Professor Gårdlund's revelations regarding the details of Wicksell's life were to crowd out recognition of the merits of his book considered as a literary construction. As such it must stand high among the biographies of our profession: and the skill with which its author performs his difficult task deserves great praise. From the outset, with its description of the raw youth, with his religious crisis, his suppressed eroticism, his indolence and his bursts of energy, Wicksell becomes a real person; the middle years, with their intellectual triumphs and their political forays and frustrations, are set forth with clarity and candour against a fascinating background of the Swedish academic and social life of the period; and by the end we are left with a picture, of almost Rembrandtesque intensity, of the old savant with his private humility, his public aggressiveness, his acuteness and his credulity, with the square shoulders of a fighter and the brow of a major prophet, the blasphemer who knew by heart the hymn book and the psalter and the Sermon on the Mount – a late-nineteenth-century 'funny', if you will, who was nevertheless one of the masters of our subject and, despite his occasional *bêtises*, one of the heroes of the never-ending struggle for a more rational social and moral order.

Professor Gårdlund notes 'an undertone of irritation with regard to contemporary English economics' in several of Wicksell's last letters. In the summer of 1925, he wrote to Anna Bugge: 'Yesterday evening and today I have been reading a long article on Marshall by Keynes, quite interesting but so absurdly English, as if no economists existed outside England.' Let us hope we have changed all that. But if the habit of mind complained of should still persist anywhere, Professors Gårdlund and Lindahl have certainly rendered it even less excusable.

13

A Biographical Note on
Edwin Cannan[1]

EDWIN CANNAN, (1861–1935), economist, was born at Funchal, Madeira, 3 February 1861, the younger son of David Alexander Cannan, a native of Kirkcudbrightshire, who held a business post in Australia at the time of the Victoria gold rush, and in Edwin's boyhood resided at Bournemouth. His mother, Jane Dorothea Claude, who died eighteen days after his birth, was the daughter of a Liverpool merchant, of Huguenot descent. He was brother of Charles Cannan.

Cannan was educated at Clifton and Balliol College, Oxford. At Balliol, owing to illness and a consequent voyage round the world, he did not take an honours degree but, in the pass school, took political economy as one of his subjects. In 1885 he won the Lothian essay prize. In the Introduction to his *Economic Outlook* (1912), he gave a characteristic account of the evolution of his studies as an economist. An essay, which was unsuccessfully submitted for the Cobden prize in 1886, was turned partly into his first book, *Elementary Political Economy* (1888), partly into a paper on 'The Bearings of Recent Economics on Individualism, Collectivism, and Communism' (republished in *The Economic Outlook* under the title 'Economics and Socialism') which was read to the Fabian Society in 1889, and contained the germs of much that was most characteristic in his approach to the problems of economic policy. There followed three years' study of the works of earlier economists. This resulted, in 1893, in *A History of the Theories of Production and Distribution in English Political Economy*

---

[1] From the *Dictionary of National Biography, 1931–1940 Supplement* (Oxford University Press, 1949). Reproduced by courtesy of the Clarendon Press, Oxford.

from 1776 to 1848, a work which, in spite of some protest at the sharpness of its strictures on the masters of the past, established his standing in the profession.

On the strength of these writings and perhaps partly because it was believed that his attitude to the main tradition of English political economy was much more unorthodox than in fact it actually was, when the London School of Economics and Political Science was founded in 1895, he was among those who were invited to lecture on economics. Thenceforward, although, by a deliberate choice which sprang from the enjoyment of independent means, his appointment was never on a full-time basis and he resided all his life in Oxford, his teaching at the School was the main preoccupation of his life. He was not created Professor of Political Economy in the University of London until 1907. But throughout this whole period he was the effective head of the Economics Department and played an essential part in building up the main tradition of the School. He retired in 1926 and devoted himself first to the preparation of *A Review of Economic Theory* (1929), which embodies the substance of his great sixty-lecture course on principles of economics at the School, and is as much a running disquisition on past theories and their genesis as an exposition of contemporary doctrine. He then turned to a number of miscellaneous works, some arising from the presidency of the Royal Economic Society to which he was elected in 1932. The universities of Glasgow (1901) and Manchester (1927) conferred honorary degrees upon him. He died at Bournemouth 8 April 1935. He married in 1907 his second cousin, Margaret Mary, eldest daughter of David Cullen, Deputy Surgeon-General, of Cheltenham. The only child of the marriage died in boyhood.

The concern with the history of economic thought, which showed itself in Cannan's first major work, was an abiding interest throughout his whole career. In 1895 he had the supreme good fortune to discover a set of student's notes of Adam Smith's Glasgow lectures which he published with a learned Introduction and Notes the next year (*Lectures on Justice, Police, Revenue and Arms delivered in the University of Glasgow by Adam Smith . . . in*

1763). In 1904 he published, in two volumes, what is acknowledged to be the standard edition of the *Wealth of Nations*. Later there came an edition of the *Bullion Report* (*The Paper Pound of 1797–1821*, 1919).

Cannan was a severe critic of the Classical Economists. Many would say that he was too severe and that, in some instances at least, a better case could be made out for his victims than he was prepared to concede. Nevertheless, he was deeply imbued with the spirit of the Classical outlook – its long views, its wide perspectives, the broad humanity and cosmopolitanism of its approach. The questions which seemed to him to be important were the questions to which the Classical Economists attempted to provide an answer: the question regarding the main causes of the increase of wealth and the conditions determining its distribution. His textbook *Wealth: A Brief Explanation of the Causes of Economic Welfare* (1914) is still probably the best introduction to the study of the economic system from this point of view. He was much less interested in the questions of equilibrium and disequilibrium which have been the main preoccupation of the present generation of economists. He had a strong dislike of the mathematical approach, and an almost passionate conviction that the important economic truths could be expressed, as he tried so hard to express them, in language which would be intelligible to laymen. Coupled with this was a sturdy suspicion of any speculative excursion which did not seem to have a more or less direct concern with practice. While he would have rightly repudiated the suggestion that he was a Classical economist *malgré lui*, for that would have suggested affiliations with the Ricardians with what he thought to be their lack of a sense of history, it is probable that he would not have resented the suggestion of some continuity of outlook, if not of doctrine, with that of the author of the *Wealth of Nations*.

Cannan's work in economics was not confined to the exposition and history of general theory. From a very early stage he took a lively interest in policy; and he played a prominent part in the public discussion of the practical problems of the day. For many years he reviewed current governmental publications for the

Oxford *Economic Review*; and he served a term of office on the Oxford city council. At an early stage, also, his interest in demography led to a prediction, many years ahead of other experts, of 'The Probable Cessation of Growth of Population in England and Wales' (*Economic Journal*, 1895; reprinted in *Economic Scares*, 1933). His profound knowledge of local government and its history received classic expression in his *History of Local Rates in England* (1896; the second edition, published in 1912, contains very important additional matter). His criticisms and disquisitions on various aspects of economic policy during and immediately after the war of 1914–18, reprinted in *An Economist's Protest* (1927), are marked by great practical insight and expository skill. It was in this last connection that he became involved in the great monetary controversies of the day – inflation, stabilisation, the rate of interest, the role of bank credit, and the like; and the vigour of his polemics on some of these topics, especially in regard to the nature of bank credit and the return to the gold standard, is probably responsible for the disproportionate attention which has been given to his attitude towards these questions, to the neglect of his more solid and enduring contributions.

As a teacher Cannan was outstanding. In lectures his delivery was poor. But his sense of the architecture of his subject was superb; and his complete disinterestedness and great learning and good sense, disguised behind a somewhat jaunty informality which endeared him greatly to the young, exercised a profound influence upon all who came into contact with him. In the years following his death, owing partly to his lack of interest in those aspects of pure theory which were the main focus of attention in this country in the inter-war period, and partly to his identification in the public mind with certain practical policies in regard to money which, in their results, proved to be unfortunate, his reputation has tended to be somewhat under a cloud. But his contributions to pure scholarship and to our knowledge of the evolution of incentives and institutions are of lasting value. If it is fair to say that he ignored much that was good in the intellectual developments of the inter-war period, it is equally fair to say that in his own work there is much that is novel and true that has not yet received full recognition.

Cannan was a man of strong personality. A mordant wit and an abrupt manner concealed a character of strong attachments and infinite gentleness and sympathy. He possessed in a marked degree that characteristic British determination to assert his individual rights as a citizen which has done so much for the rule of law in this country; and, although not litigious, if he thought that a principle was involved, he would go to any trouble and expense to defend it. He had little feeling for the arts, save for the modes of the sweet, wholesome English prose that he himself handled with such distinction. But he had a great interest in the day-to-day history of the face of England and he was a leading authority on roads which he studied for many years, first as an ardent cyclist, and then as a driver of a 'baby' Austin which he learned to drive at the age of sixty-six.

14

Montagu Norman: A 'Monarch' in the City[1]

IN 1873 Walter Bagehot, the great editor of *The Economist*, wrote a book entitled *Lombard Street* about the organisation of the London money market. One of the chapters dealt with the government of the Bank of England; and a considerable part of it was devoted to the question whether the Governor should, or should not, be appointed for more than two years – which was then the customary period of office. Bagehot decided against; and one of the grounds for this decision was the belief that 'a permanent Governor of the Bank of England would be one of the greatest men in England. He would be a little "monarch" in the City; he would be far greater than the Lord Mayor.'

The book I am discussing[2] is about a man who fulfilled this prediction. Montagu Collet, Lord Norman, was the first Governor to hold office for a long term of years. He was first elected in 1920 and he finally retired in 1944. There can be no doubt that he was a 'monarch' – and not a little one at that – in the City and that he was 'far greater than the Lord Mayor'. He was indeed one of the most influential figures of his age.

I must confess straight away that Montagu Norman was never one of my heroes. I met him only once and, although he was very courteous, I did not warm to him on that occasion – probably my fault. I was not in such disagreement with the things he was trying to do as were many of my colleagues. But his mode of doing them, his almost exhibitionist secrecy and the tone of no explanations no apologies, of his very occasional public utterances did not appeal

[1] A broadcast Third Programme talk reprinted from *The Listener*, 6 June 1957. Reproduced by courtesy of *The Listener*.
[2] Sir Henry Clay, *Lord Norman* (London: Macmillan, 1957).

to me: it seemed to me then, and it still seems to me, to have done much harm to causes which I think important. It is only right that I should reveal this degree of bias. I hope it will not lead to unjust judgements.

Let me begin by saying a word or two about the book itself and its significance. There can be no question that it is very important. Its author, Sir Henry Clay, was intimately associated with Lord Norman and he had free use of all relevant documents. The result is indispensable reading for anyone interested in the history of the inter-war period and the practice of central banking. There is the history of the return to gold in 1925 from Lord Norman's point of view. There is the banking end of the political crisis of 1931 – with the telegram from America which caused all the bother. There is an incomparable account of the relationships between the main central banks during the whole of this troubled period. It is perhaps true that, owing to Sir Henry's death ere he had given it a final polish, the style is sometimes a bit dull and heavy; revision by another hand could not add the sparkle. But the intrinsic interest of the material atones for all that: and the last chapter, a personal sketch of the Governor by an anonymous colleague, is a subtle and distinguished piece of writing.

Now for some estimate of the man and his achievements as they emerge from this narrative. First, let it be said, against all ill-natured criticism, that he was a great public servant and a devoted and inspiring leader. The man who could evoke such a tribute as is paid him by Mr Cobbold, the present Governor, in the Foreword to this book, was clearly no ordinary character. Obviously he exercised an almost magnetic power over those who came in contact with him. 'All in all,' says the author of the last chapter, 'he was a man of such stamp and stature that any country may deem itself fortunate if it is served by more than one in the course of a single generation.' This is high praise. But even his severest critic must admit that Lord Norman gave his life to the Bank and to the public of which he conceived the Bank to be the servant. It is in this connection, I suppose, that his achievement was most enduring and least open to question. The Bank of England has always stood high among national banks by reason of its financial strength and its high standards of financial morality. But when Norman came to the governorship it was still a somewhat old-fashioned, semi-private institution, run to an extraordinary extent by part-timers. When he left it, it was a fully developed public office with a permanent staff of superb expert quality and a sense of vocation fully comparable to the highest traditions of the administrative grade of the British Civil Service, perhaps the finest set of public servants in the world. All this was peculiarly Norman's creation.

A further quality for which, surely, history will give him great credit was his internationalism, his sense of human solidarity. In an age when Keynes could say that never in the lifetime of men then living had the universal element in the soul of man burnt so dimly, Norman was a good citizen of the world. He appreciated the momentous importance of repairing the shattering impact of war. He spent himself in the effort to foster financial co-operation between nations. Some may say that he was prepared to sacrifice too much for the international connection. I certainly would not. He made his mistakes. I suspect that he was much too willing to attribute to Dr Schacht the same whole-hearted devotion to decent values as he had – there is a certain reticence in the narrative about all this.[1] But when we have the whole story of the struggle through these years to restore stability to a world in violent disequilibrium, I am clear that a high place will have to be given to his tireless efforts.

Now for the other side of the picture. All great men commit errors; and some have sufficient good fortune to be spared the consequences. Not so Norman: it was his misfortune to be associated with the momentous error of policy which, in 1925, put us back on the gold standard at a rate which was inappropriate; and whether he was conscious of it or not, he paid for it through

[1] When this review was first published, one who was well qualified to know wrote to me to say that it did less than justice to some of Dr Schacht's non-publicised actions during that period. I have left my sentence as it stood. But I think it is only right to say that it may be unfair. [Note added in 1969.]

years of anxiety and financial embarrassment. I say he was associated with this error. Clearly the *formal* responsibility was not his: that lay with the Chancellor of the Exchequer, Mr Churchill; and there were others who as expert advisers were very deeply involved. But he was Governor of the Bank of England, clothed with immense prestige, and, as such, he must bear a major share of the *substantial* responsibility for a decision which gave rise to so many troubles. If he had advised against it, the thing would never have happened.

On this point I find Sir Henry Clay's apologia unconvincing. It is true that there was a good deal of bad luck involved. If the French had not undervalued the franc, if there had not been an American boom, if the strike in the coalmines had not lasted so long, and so on and so forth, then perhaps things might have been different. But the fact remains that all these things would have been easier to cope with had the initial overvaluation of sterling not taken place. And the lamentable thing is that it ought not to have taken place. A hundred years before, after the Napoleonic War, a similar policy had led to similar difficulties. The generation of experts, of whom Norman was the leader, had forgotten, if indeed they had ever learned, all the lessons of the lingering misery of 1815–23. Even Ricardo, the foremost advocate of that earlier restoration of the old parity, had urged that, if the depreciation in terms of gold was more than 5 per cent, devaluation was the preferable alternative. After the 1914–18 war the pound was depreciated by far more than that. But no responsible advocate of sound money took devaluation seriously. How much difficulty would have been avoided, how much unemployment and loss of product might have been spared, if those who advised us had banished from their minds the nonsense about making the pound look the dollar in the face and stabilised early at a lower level. The whole history of the world would have been different.

I regard this episode as the main technical error of Norman's career. It is, however, I suspect, typical of something which seems to inform many aspects of his conduct and which in the end perhaps did as much damage as any single misjudgement – I mean his excessive reliance on hunch and intuition, the lack of recourse to systematic thought in his approach to the problems with which he was confronted, and his unwillingness to explain. This comes out most vividly perhaps in the account of his stewardship which he gave to the Macmillan Committee, especially in his interchanges with Keynes and McKenna. I well remember the impression this made on me when first I read the report. I was very orthodox at the time – considerably more orthodox, I now think, than I ought to have been. But the spectacle of Norman's patent unwillingness to formulate coherent answers to questions on the most fundamental aspects of policy filled me with dismay. I did not know what impression it made on the enemy; but I knew that it frightened me.

Why this attitude? An admirer of Norman, Mr I. J. Pitman, writing recently in *The Times*, has endeavoured to explain it in terms of a settled philosophy. There was a clash, he argues, between two opposing conceptions. Keynes and McKenna were seeking scientific rules in an area where science is inappropriate, whereas Norman, wiser in his generation, had the approach of the artist, realising that, where bank credit was concerned, 'it was people and what people thought . . . which alone mattered – in other words, that it was art which could never become science'. He recalls a conversation during the war in which Lord Norman talked to him on these lines.

If this was so, then I can only say that the Governor was the victim of a tragic oversimplification. Of course the idea that banking, especially central banking, can all be reduced to a set of scientific rules is palpably absurd. Of course economists who attempt to apply general principles to particular instances without knowledge of the relevant circumstances often say foolish things – very irritating to practical men. But equally it is a mistake to suppose that the conduct of monetary policy in the modern world can afford to dispense with systematic reason and analysis. Art and intuition may have been a sufficient guide in the comparatively peaceful days of the period before 1914 – though they did not leave us without our ups and downs. But today it is not so.

A man cannot fly a jet aircraft without instruments just because he is good with a horse; and a central banker, however superb his hunches, cannot manage a modern credit system without all the aid an admittedly defective economic science can give him. Art and science are both necessary.

I imagine that Mr Pitman's recollection of his talk with the Governor is correct. But I suspect that the ultimate explanation of the Governor's attitude, as he depicts it, is to be found not so much in philosophy as in psychology. Both Sir Henry Clay and the author of the last chapter in the book admit Norman's inability to explain himself; and if, as Mr Pitman contends, he held systematic analysis to be unnecessary, I cannot help feeling that this was the rationalisation of a weakness, a compensation for something missing – the last infirmity of a noble mind, if you will. Unconsciously he elevated what was in fact a deficiency into a principle of action, the justification of a mystique – the appalling danger of being explicit about anything more than single particulars.

Whether this is so or not, I am sure that Norman's conduct of public relations had results which were quite deplorable. Confronted with the almost aggressive parade of reticence and disguise, ignorant people suspected all sorts of sinister implications which did not exist at all. What is more, the perfectly good reasons which often underlay particular decisions were overlooked and the case for sound policies was allowed to go by default. Take, for instance, Norman's dread of the paralysing influence on his control of the market of a large floating debt – which like a Wagnerian *leitmotiv* appears again and again through this narrative. How much easier would it be for his successors today, how much better informed would outside opinion have been, even among professional economists, had this been ventilated more frequently, and with more detailed explanations, in public. But it was not to be. The result was that, whatever its reputation in the circle of Treasury officials and the Governors of other central banks, the Bank tended to lose the confidence of that outer circle of men of goodwill without whose support in the long run the conduct of policy becomes more and more difficult. It is always easy to find very convincing arguments for reticence on any particular occasion; but, cumulatively, the effect is bad; and in emergencies you are without the intelligent backing which otherwise you might have enjoyed. Whether nationalisation was inevitable or not is a question to which no one can give a definite answer. But I am fairly clear that any support which the Bank might have had in resisting such a change was hopelessly weakened by Norman's conduct of public relations. The change which he most dreaded – the dragging of central banking into politics – was, in part at any rate, facilitated by his own policy.

In this connection I should like to draw attention to what to me is a significant contrast. There is another Norman in the line of Bank directors, Montagu's grandfather – George Warde of that name – a powerful influence in his time, one of the leading men behind the Bank Act of 1844 and an acknowledged authority on banking. He, too, was a highly-strung man: according to Clapham, his health rendered his election to the Chair inexpedient. But in regard to public relations there could not be a more striking contrast between his behaviour and that of his grandson. If there were matters of policy about which public opinion was undecided, then George Warde, like the illustrious Horsley Palmer, the greatest of Montagu Norman's nineteenth-century predecessors, was all for arguing it out in public in a quiet and dignified manner. The literature of monetary theory was enriched by more than one pamphlet from his pen; and his occasional contributions in the shape of letters and papers were numerous. If the Bank was under criticism and he thought the Bank was right, he defended it. If improvement was desirable he submitted his thought to his colleagues and to the public. A sense of admiration and affection comes over one as one reads these productions – so reasonable, so moderate, so free from any dramatisation of the issues. This is the way in which the debate was conducted a hundred years ago, when the great tradition of the City was at its height, and one cannot but feel a sense of loss in the tight-lipped silence which has superseded it.

It may still be argued, however – and I am sure that it is still felt

by some for whom I have very real respect – that in the circumstances of our own day this sort of thing has become impossible.
To all such I would say: 'Look west, my friends.' There, across
the Atlantic, under the auspices of the Federal Reserve Board,
the tradition of our own classic days has continued. The leaders
and the able technicians of that institution take the public into
their confidence. They discuss policy – needless to say, in suitably
circumspect terms. They discuss technique. They have led the
way in the publication and the systematic analysis of bank statistics.
An important branch of knowledge has developed under their
fostering care, to which the equally able technicians on our own
side have contributed not a jot – at any rate in public.[1] I know that
the American way of life is different from ours and that the
American constitution permits habits which might well be thought
inappropriate to ours. But I cannot believe that all this difference
has been necessary. Is it really true that the contrast between the
splendid monthly bulletin of the Federal Reserve Board and the
meagre annual reports of the Bank of England is part of the
necessary order of nature? I must say that when I think first of
the position of immense moral strength which has been built up
by the Federal Reserve Board in relation to public opinion in the
United States and then of the often misinformed criticism with
which the conduct of our own central bank is surrounded, I
cannot feel that, in this respect, the Norman discipline has been
particularly successful.

Therefore, I hope that the authorities at the Bank of England,
who are responsible for this book and who are rightly proud of the
Norman tradition, will remember that the tradition has more than
one element, and that while they cherish and revere the memory
of Montagu for his zeal in the public service and his power in
the command of men, they may also keep in mind the example
of George Warde, with his lucidity and patient candour, and

[1] It is to be hoped that any reader of this reprint will notice the date.
Much has changed since then and today I should regard the publications
and pronouncements of the Bank as immune from the strictures passed
therein, and indeed, as contributing much to public enlightenment. [Note
added in 1969.]

remember that, in a democratic age, the preservation of values and the creation of an informed public opinion demand, not only intuition and devotion in action, but also systematic reasoning and the frank explanation of policy as it evolves. Not so easy in these days of nationalised banking with the Chancellor in the background. But I fancy there is still some elbow room for those who really wish to take it.

15

Harrod on Keynes[1]

I

THE publication, less than five years after the death of its distinguished subject, of Mr Harrod's *Life of Lord Keynes* is something of a literary event. Lord Keynes was so many-sided a figure, the issues with which he was concerned were so controversial, that it would be a miracle if any biography, written at this date, should be regarded as immune from criticism; and the somewhat personal nature of Mr Harrod's narrative, together with the vigour with which he argues disputed questions, make it likely that what he has written will not be so regarded. Nevertheless, he has placed both us and the future very greatly in his debt. He has gathered together a vast body of information, indispensable for judgement on Lord Keynes's achievement, but likely to have disappeared had the writing of a biography been deferred; and he has made of it a book which, whether it commands agreement or not, it is exceedingly difficult to stop reading. My own judgement is that it will long continue to be read.

II

Lord Keynes was not one whose genius was unappreciated during his lifetime. What Dr Johnson said of Burke was true of him; it was impossible to spend a casual five minutes in his company without realising that you were in the presence of a most unusual man. Both in his conversation, with its lightning swiftness and its kaleidoscopic variety, and in his prose style, with its infinite

[1] A review of *The Life of John Maynard Keynes*, by R. F. Harrod (London: Macmillan, 1951); reprinted from *The Times*, 26 Jan. 1951. Reproduced by courtesy of the Times Publishing Co. Ltd.

resources of vigour and exquisite cadence, he had command of a certain magic which made all that he said or wrote the centre of attention. From the publication of *The Economic Consequences of the Peace* in 1919 to his death in 1946, throughout the English-speaking world he dominated the intellectual scene; and his influence left a profound mark on public policy. The future historian of social thought may well call this period the period of John Maynard Keynes. Yet it is not at all easy to find any simple formula to describe wherein this ascendancy consisted.

That Keynes was a great economist is not open to serious question. At all stages of his thought, whether you agree with him or not, there is a quality which can only be described in these terms. The combination of practical grasp and theoretical insight, which is to be found in everything he wrote, is something which has not appeared more than four or five times in the history of economics.

But the exact nature of his achievement is not so easy to summarise. Much of his most striking work was concerned with particular applications, where the uniqueness of his contribution consists, not so much in new theory, as in the revelation of how existing theory can be applied; and the status of the *General Theory*, where his concern was with the widest type of generalisation and where his claims to far-reaching innovation were emphatic, is still a matter of some dispute. It must be admitted, I think, that a case, which is not intellectually negligible, can be made for the view that his claims in this respect were overstated; that some of what he thought to be novel was in fact in line with developments of the past, and some of what was truly novel was one-sided in its emphasis.

Yet to leave it at that would be unjust. Economics, as Keynes once said, is not so much a body of settled doctrine as a mode of approach; and whatever may be the verdict of posterity on the detailed propositions of the *General Theory* or the adequacy of its scope, it is safe to say that it has made an imprint on our mode of approach which is lasting. It is one of the few books of which it can be said that no one who has read it without prejudice can feel that his own thinking can ever be the same again. It is not true, as has sometimes been assumed, that before its appearance there was no discussion of aggregate output, employment, and income; but it is true that no significant discussion since then has been immune from its positive influence.

Keynes was, of course, much more than an economist. Both in his day-to-day preoccupations and in his remoter objectives, his main concern was not with mere technique but rather with the ultimate underlying human issues: justice, order, improvement, the clear arena for the intellect and the creative imagination. This was one of the secrets of his power. In his hands economic analysis was so obviously not a dismal science constricting the human horizon, but rather a necessary discipline of thought designed eventually to liberate the spirit – no danger of the ultimate values being ignored by him who realised them so conspicuously in his own life and style. Thus his various writings have a double significance: they are at once contributions to the solution of the particular questions with which they are concerned and, at the same time, a running commentary on the deeper problems with which our society is confronted.

III

If it is difficult to find a concise formula for Keynes's intrinsic qualities, it is still more difficult at this stage to make any correct estimate of the total effect of his influence. It should go without saying that the presence in our midst of a being of this kind was itself an enrichment of the general atmosphere: the spiritual flatness of our pygmy age now that he has gone is sufficient testimony to that. But the influence of genius of this degree of force is seldom only in one direction; and the influence of Keynes, if I am not mistaken, was no exception in this respect. He contributed much of illumination and inspiration; but he sometimes contributed to confusion. He shook age-long error and prejudice, but he also sometimes shook essential foundations. There was indeed something of the final mystery of ancient mythology about the nature of his genius – destroyer, preserver, creator, irreducible elements in the picture. And although in any assessment of his conscious aims and in the memories of his friends it is the preserver and creator which must be uppermost, a level view, if that be possible, cannot overlook directions and occasions when the influence of the destroyer was evident.

Take, for instance, his attacks on the Treaty of Versailles, which first brought him to the notice of the general public. *The Economic Consequences of the Peace* is one of the most magnificent pleas for humanity and justice of this or any other age. Yet there can be little doubt that the form of his reaction against the follies of part of the settlement did some harm as well as much good. It led to an oversimplification of the German problem – to which, having regard to his considerable distaste for many things German, he was always curiously insensitive. And this, in turn, led to an inability to do justice to important elements in the French case, which, through his immense influence on public opinion, contributed something to fateful misunderstandings. I confess that, in my judgement, there are elements in his later work whose influence has been similarly double-sided.

Mr Harrod devotes much space to the last period of Keynes's work as adviser to the Chancellor. In this I think he is right, although considerations of public interest at some points still preclude a complete picture. Although, to the future, it is for his thought and his general influence that Keynes will be important, in the perspective of his own career this phase has a special significance. It was at this stage that he was no longer in opposition; no doubt now which elements were chiefly operative, the destroyer quiescent, the preserver and creator fully extended. If our financial affairs were conducted with more enlightenment than usual, if we were more successful in avoiding inflation than any historical precedent could have suggested to be possible, it is to his influence that this must be largely attributed.

Nor was this influence confined to domestic policy: of the broad outlines of our external economic policy, the Lend-Lease arrangements during the war, the loan settlement which averted collapse when it was over, the structure of economic institutions which an idealistic vision of the future endeavoured to erect, he was clearly the chief architect. He was not always a good *negotiator*; it was part of the tragedy of his end that he was apt to wear himself out on small matters where his impetuous spirit was ill at ease and where lesser men could have done at least as well. But as an *envoy* he was supreme. Not even Mr Churchill could state more magnificently the case for this country than Keynes at his eloquent best.

V

It is yet too early to do justice to these high themes. Indeed, for those who knew Keynes well it is virtually impossible to do so. To them, and perhaps especially to those who saw him in the last stages, battling against bodily weakness and eventually dying for the cause as certainly as any soldier on the field of battle, judgement of the public figure and the public achievement is too much mixed up with associations of the man himself: behind the brilliance and the vision, the authority and the paradox, the occasional arrogance and the dissolving persuasiveness, the private Keynes whom Mr Harrod so well delineates – the cheerful companion, the loving son, the devoted husband, a man keenly sensitive to beauty of all kinds and the small enduring joys of life, a man who, in a wider circle than most, was not only greatly admired but also greatly loved.

16

Robertson's *Lectures on Economic Principles*[1]

WHEN it first became known that Sir Dennis Robertson was editing for publication the three-term course in economic principles which he had given at Cambridge since the war, some may have thought – as did the present writer – that this was a pity and that the reproduction of lectures, however distinguished, was inferior to their transformation into a full-blown treatise. But, now that publication is complete, it is clear – as we ought to have known – that Sir Dennis knew best. For, with characteristic stylistic insight, he has perceived that by preserving the lecture form he avoids the necessity of all sorts of technical apparatus of little intrinsic interest, while permitting himself the liberty of asides, inappropriate in a severer framework, which lend much greater piquancy to the treatment than would be possible in a treatise.

As a result he has produced a work which certainly kills two birds with one stone. It is an excellent introduction for beginners – not children, of course, but beginners of reasonably mature years, capable of treating economics as a serious subject. And at the same time it is a work which, like most of the best works on general principles, will yield its highest value only to those who are well conversant with the subject and are in a position to appreciate the nuances and periphrases with which the distinguished author makes subtle allusion to, or avoidance of, special theorems or difficulties. All of which must give it a special place among works of its kind. It is only necessary to compare any small sequence of

[1] A review of *Lectures on Economic Principles*, by Sir Dennis H. Robertson, 3 vols (London: Staples Press, 1960), *Economica*, XXVII (Feb 1960). Reproduced by courtesy of the London School of Economics and Political Science.

paragraphs with a sequence of similar length in the more popular textbooks of the day to realise that here is a texture and weight of quite a different order. It has the quality of conversation that you feel *must* be written down.

For reasons which are not entirely apparent, it appears in three very slender volumes. Presumably there were some good reasons for this. But it may well militate against its use as a textbook; and it is, therefore, very much to be hoped that in future editions it will appear between two covers only – it would still run to only just less than 500 pages. What is much less easy to understand is why a reputable firm like Staples should issue these volumes with spines which are not uniform. Vol. I has a simple asterisk to denote its place in the series and the Staples shield or arms at the bottom; Vol. II, 'Vol. II' instead of two asterisks, plus the shield or arms; Vol. III, 'Vol. III' and no shield or arms. Has ever so important a work in economics been so casually treated? The only consolation I can think of is that, in years to come, this blemish may give this edition some slight extra value for the more devout of the race of collectors. 'Robertson, D. H., *Lectures on Economic Principles*, first edition, three volumes, in prime condition *with the non-uniform spines*' – thus we may conceive the antiquarian booksellers' catalogues of the year 2060.

The contents are divided according to the volumes. Vol. I deals with preliminary notions and the theory of price – demand and utility, factor combination, costs, competition and monopoly, joint supply and price discrimination, etc.; Vol. II with distribution in the sense of the pricing of the factors of production – demand and productivity, rent, capital and interest, profits and the demand for and supply of labour; Vol. III with money and fluctuation – monetary equilibrium, banking, stagnation theory, money and interest, the trade cycle and trade cycle policy. Throughout all this the treatment is enlivened by illustration from contemporary events and side glances at problems of contemporary policy.

It will be seen from what has just been said that these lectures stand deeply rooted in the Marshallian tradition of arrangement, and a very brief glance at the substance will show that this influence is not limited to arrangement. Even in Vol. III, which is largely built on Sir Dennis's own contribution, there can be detected some continuity with the mood, if not the detailed technique, of *Money, Credit and Commerce*, still more with the earlier and more virile evidence before the Gold and Silver Commission and the Committee on Indian Currency. I do not know what Marshall, whose sense of humour often seems to me to have been somewhere in the neighbourhood of absolute zero, would have thought of some of Sir Dennis's more playful witticisms, particularly of the drawing depicting a forlorn and self-abasing 'Rent' standing forever debarred from 'entering into' a magnificent Graeco-Roman edifice labelled 'Cost of Production'. But I suspect that, on a calm survey of his intellectual progeny, he would have found more of his own instinct for reality and conception of the role of theory, and a more faithful use of his own particular methods, in Sir Dennis than in any other.

It would be a great mistake, however, to regard these lectures as merely a translation of, or variations upon, Marshallian themes. It is true that the main drift of the argument in Vols. I and II tends on the whole to Marshallian conclusions. Measurable utility, consumer surplus, the time element in the determination of normal values, marginal productivity and the importance of the supply side in long-run distribution theory – these are indeed all there. But the exposition is intensely personal and is enlivened through-out by critical sallies and incorporation of recent improvements. Sir Dennis is very much in touch with a world-wide profession; and although, outside those spheres of Vol. III which are especially his own, he tends to conservatism in his choice of techniques, he is well aware of other usages; and where they lead to results bear-ing on the main corpus of principles as he conceives them, he contrives, either by way of critical rejection or acceptance and assimilation, to keep his readers in touch. The exposition of in-terest theory in Vol. II with its borrowings from Lerner, Ramsey and Champernowne is an especially felicitous example of this process of judicious modernisation.

As for Vol. III, of course it is predominantly original. Much of it is based upon earlier work by its author. But nowhere has he provided so complete a synthesis. And now that it can be surveyed in this form, it is possible to see more clearly than ever before his achievement in this sphere. I mentioned *Money, Credit and Commerce* to draw attention to background and continuity. But it is hardly an exaggeration to say that the difference between that work and these lectures represents a substantial part of the progress of thought since Marshall in the subjects with which they deal. Doubtless not all: there have been, and there are, other important participants and other important contributions. Nor can it be said that all the progress is as yet consolidated: this part of the lectures is much more occupied with controversy than the rest. We do not agree about all these matters yet; and very important issues of policy are involved. Yet I submit that no one, reading this part of Sir Dennis's book, could seriously argue that we were not now far nearer to a proper understanding than we were thirty years ago. And no one with even a speck of justice in his make-up could deny to Sir Dennis a very appreciable share of the credit.

It would be inappropriate in a short notice of a work like this even to begin critical comment on matters of detail: that can wait for different contexts in which specific references are appropriate. But it is perhaps not out of place to enquire concerning the general impression. How does the Marshallian tradition, as embodied and developed in this work, commend itself at the present day as a mode of approach and a method of analysis? Many of the developments of the last seventy years have occurred by way of criticising Marshall and his intellectual habits; so many of us have been brought up, as it were, on running Marshall-critiques. How does it seem when restated and developed from Sir Dennis's point of view? How does it survive the acid of contemporary doubt?

In my judgement, well. Let me hasten to say that by this I do not wish to express complete agreement with all the positions adopted: I have broken friendly lances with Sir Dennis in the past and I hope and expect to do so in the future. Nor do I wish to seem unaware of the various strictures that could be passed on grounds of insufficient rigour. It is quite true that this kind of approach is, so to speak, *quasi-literary* in manner. It does not set out its analysis in the form of strict mathematical deductions. It makes no attempt at exhaustive definitions and classifications. It would be wrong to say that it proceeds by instinct; for that would imply a kind of a-scientific mystique. But it would not be unfair to say that, in contrast to the more rigorous and abstract systems, it proceeds by way of common-sense appraisal of relevance, of a selection of simplifying assumptions to keep the argument down to earth and of a determination throughout to judge each section of analysis, not only by its internal consistency but also in relation to a general perspective. It is a bit of an art as well as a science. But, for all that, and also in contrast to many more abstract systems, it does deliver the goods. For if we are honest with ourselves, we have to admit that when we condescend to talk about the real world, then, however pure and high-falutin our analytical fancy, in a great many cases at least, we have to adopt something like these simplifications. And if we are considering the matter as teachers rather than pure research workers, I am pretty clear that a training which begins from this kind of basis is much more likely eventually to produce what we should call an economist than one which begins with all sorts of bits and pieces of severer techniques which, whatever be their promise for the future, have not as yet found their pedagogic bearings. I am clear, too, that it will be much more of a general liberal education. A man will learn more of the real world from this kind of theory than from any number of more formalistic exercises; and he will learn, too, habits of thought which will help the establishment of a proper perspective if he considers the world either in order to run it or to change it.

Select Index of Proper Names

pp. 186–8; lacunae in his theory of economic policy, pp. 186–8; his influence on Wicksteed, pp. 191–2; affiliation of his capital theory with classical elements, p. 219

JOHNSON, W. E.   His *Pure Theory of Utility Curves* cited, pp. 28–9

KAHN, R. F.   Relevance of his theory of the multiplier to the transfer problem, p. 37
KEYNES, JOHN MAYNARD.   On the transfer problem, pp. 36–7; the Keynesian revolution, pp. 37–40; his bad memory for anything in which he was not intensely interested, p. 38; his analysis of the *General Theory* essentially an example of the Marshallian statical method applied to the macro-economic sphere, pp. 44–5; his false picture of Bentham on the functions of the state alluded to, p. 76; named as representative of the main classical position on the functions of the state, p. 76; his classification of Malthus as a pre-Keynesian queried, pp. 90–1; his explanations of economic fluctuation devoid of connection with classical capital theory, p. 218; his eminence as an economist and a public figure, pp. 243–5; complexity of the nature of his influence, pp. 245–7; his insensitivity to the nature of the German problem, p. 246; his public services during World War II, pp. 246–7
KIRCHMANN, HANS.   His *Studien zur Grenzproduktivitätstheorie des Kapitalzinses* cited, p. 211
KNIGHT, F. H.   His conception of opportunity costs, p. 18; his 'Relation of Utility Theory to Economic Method in the Work of William Stanley Jevons and Others' cited, p. 170; his 'Some Fallacies in the Interpretation of Social Cost' cited, p. 201; his 'Suggestion for Simplifying the Statement of the General Theory of Price' cited, p. 202

LARDNER, D.   States formula for profit maximisation in terms of marginal revenue equal to marginal cost, p. 30
LASKI, HAROLD.   High degree of improbability of his story, quoted by Stilinger, of what Bain told Morley about Harriet Taylor, p. 113
LAUDERDALE, EARL OF.   His under-consumption theory denied by Ricardo, p. 37
LAVINGTON, F.   Cited as an inheritor of the Marshallian theory of money and the capital market, p. 38
LECLAIRE.   His experiments in co-partnership praised by Mill, p. 145
LESLIE, CLIFF.   His *Land Systems* reviewed by J. S. Mill, pp. 153–4; his strictures on excessive reliance on the deductive element in classical economics, p. 171
LINDAHL, E.   His development of the Wicksellian theory of money and credit cited, p. 38; his *Die Gerechtigkeit der Besteuerung* cited, p. 216; his *Selected Papers on Economic Theory by Knut Wicksell* reviewed, pp. 223–4
LLOYD, W. F.   A pioneer of the marginal utility theory of value, p. 16
LONGFIELD, M.   His discussion of Irish absenteeism and its recognition of the influence of demand in international trade, p. 34

McCLEARY, G. F.   On Malthus and diminishing returns, p. 61
McCULLOCH, J. R.   Schumpeter's allegation that there were no conspicuous Ricardians save him, James Mill and De Quincey, p. 58; his *Discourse on Political Economy* reviewed by Mill, attacked by Malthus, p. 119

I